THE IRRITABLE MALE SYNDROME

Managing the four key causes of depression and aggression

Jed Diamond

RODALE

This edition first published in the UK in 2005 by
Rodale International Ltd
7–10 Chandos Street
London W1G 9AD
www.rodale.co.uk

Printed and bound in the UK by CPI Bath using acid-free paper from
sustainable sources.

1 3 5 7 9 8 6 4 2

A CIP record for this book is available from the British Library
ISBN 1-4050-7745-X

This paperback edition distributed to the book trade by Pan Macmillan Ltd

Notice
This book is intended as a reference volume only, not as a medical manual. The
information given here is designed to help you make informed decisions about your
health. It is not intended as a substitute for any treatment that you may have been
prescribed by your doctor. If you suspect that you have a medical problem, we urge
you to seek competent medical help.

Mention of specific companies, organizations or authorities in this book does not
imply endorsement by the publisher, nor does mention of specific companies,
organizations or authorities in the book imply that they endorse the book.
Addresses, websites and telephone numbers given in this book were accurate at the
time the book went to press.

RODALE

LIVE YOUR WHOLE LIFE™

CONTENTS

ACKNOWLEDGMENTS

For my children, Dane, Evan, Jemal, Angela, and Aaron, and my grandchildren, Shelby, Jacob, Cody, Teanna, Sierra, Deon, Derrick, Hailey, Drayke, and Christian. You are the hope of the future.

My wife, Carlin, is really the coauthor of this book. A great deal of what I know about the Irritable Male Syndrome I learned from the person who was living with someone who was suffering from it.

The guys in my men's groups have helped heal my wounds and have put up with my continuing requests of "Tell me what it's been like for you."

Nancy Ellis-Bell is the agent every writer longs to have. She is passionate about books, truly cares about her authors, knows the publishing business from top to bottom, and is a master of her craft.

The people at Rodale Inc. have helped bring an idea to reality. I want to particularly thank executive editor Jeremy Katz; Kathryn C. LeSage, whose creative editing has made this book much more complete and readable than it would have been otherwise; Cathy Gruhn, whose publicity and promotion team have helped get the word out about the book; and many others who have worked behind the scenes to put this book in your hands.

My many colleagues have been wonderfully supportive over the years. There are way too many to mention, but you know who you are. Some of you have been particularly supportive of this book, including Reid Baer, Dan Bollinger, Jean Bonhomme, Jimmy Boyd, Jim Bracewell, Malcolm Carruthers, Jane Chin, Gordon Clay, Sam V. Cochran, Will Courtenay, Mitch DeArmon, Vickie DeArmon, Warren Farrell, Mary Furlong, Larrian Gillespie, Tom Golden, Frank Gomez, Michael Gurian, Ron Henry, Bert Hoff, Steve Imparl, Courtney Johnson, Stephen Johnson, Siegfried Kasper, Bill Kauth, Joe Kort, Sid Kramer, Howard LaGarde, John Lee, Pat Love, John McManamy, the Men's Health Network, Siegfried Meryn, Hari Meyers, Fredric E. Rabinowitz, Damian Sebouhian, Rich Tosi, and Clement Williams.

Finally, I want to thank the thousands of men and women who have opened their lives to me. May their courage inspire others as it has inspired me.

WHAT WE'RE LEARNING FROM THE FEEDBACK OF 10,000 MEN

When I began the research for this book, I had some ideas about the Irritable Male Syndrome (IMS) based on my experiences working with male clients and their partners, and on the thousands of e-mails I had received from people who had read my previous books. I knew that there was a relationship between IMS and the hormonal changes that males experience while going through puberty and at midlife, when going through andropause (male menopause). I also believed that there was a relationship between irritability, aggression, and depression in men.

What I *didn't* have was data from a large number of men. When I finalized my agreement with Rodale to publish *The Irritable Male Syndrome,* my editor allowed me to put the two questionnaires I had developed for the book on the *Men's Health* magazine Web site. The response was overwhelming. Nearly 6,000 men filled out the Irritable Male Syndrome Questionnaire, and nearly 3,500 filled out the Male Depression Questionnaire. The men ranged in age from 10 to 75.

In order to analyze the voluminous data pool, I hired Courtney Johnson, who is an expert in psychological testing with Ph.D.'s in statistics and psychology from Duke University. The information was quite interesting and gives us the first look into the world of men experiencing the Irritable Male Syndrome. The men were asked a series of questions and had four options for answers: almost never, once in a while, often, or almost always. The following highlights stood out:

- **Stress is a significant issue for men.**
Only 8 percent said they are almost never stressed.
Forty-six percent said they are often or almost always stressed.

- **Sex is a major concern.**
Forty percent of the men said they are almost never sexually satisfied.

- **Depression and irritability are related.**
Twenty-one percent said they are depressed often or almost always.

Only 9 percent said they are almost never irritable; 40 percent are irritable often or almost always.

• **Emotions related to anger are significant.**

Only 7 percent of the men said they are almost never annoyed; 50 percent are annoyed often or almost always.

Eight percent of the men said they are almost never impatient, while 57 percent said they are impatient often or almost always.

Nine percent said they are almost never tired, while 54 percent said they are tired often or almost always.

Ten percent said they are almost never frustrated, while 45 percent are frustrated often or almost always.

Eleven percent said they are almost never dissatisfied, while 45 percent said they are dissatisfied often or almost always.

Twelve percent said they are almost never sarcastic, while 54 percent said they are sarcastic often or almost always.

Seventeen percent said they are almost never exhausted, while 43 percent said they are exhausted often or almost always.

Forty-six percent said they are bored often or almost always.

• **Emotions related to depression are significant.**

Only 7 percent said they almost never have a desire to *get away from it all*, but 62 percent said they often or almost always desire to get away.

Only 11 percent said they almost never have a strong fear of failure. More than half—55 percent—said they often or almost always have a strong fear of failure.

Twelve percent said they almost never feel burned out, compared with 44 percent who said they feel burned out often or almost always.

Twelve percent said they almost never feel empty, while 48 percent said they feel empty often or almost always.

Only 13 percent said they almost never veg out in front of the TV or engage in mindless activity, while 51 percent said they veg out often or most of the time.

Fourteen percent said they almost never feel gloomy, negative, or hopeless, but 51 percent said they often or almost always feel gloomy, negative, or hopeless.

Another 14 percent said they almost never engage in fantasies of sex through flirtations, pornography, or emotional intrigue, but 50 percent said they do so often or almost always.

Forty-six percent said they often or almost always feel sorry for themselves or feel pathetic.

Fifty-one percent said they often or almost always have sleep problems.

Likewise, 51 percent said they are self-critical and focus on failures often or almost always.

ARE YOU EXPERIENCING
THE IRRITABLE MALE SYNDROME?

I developed a questionnaire with 50 questions to help determine whether someone is suffering from IMS. The full quiz and scoring process are in chapter 2. In analyzing the results of the test, Dr. Johnson and I found that there are 14 questions that significantly predict whether a man is suffering from IMS.

Do you find you are more:

1. Grumpy?
2. Angry?
3. Gloomy?
4. Impatient?
5. Tense?
6. Hostile?
7. Lonely?
8. Stressed at home?
9. Annoyed?
10. Touchy?
11. Stressed at work?
12. Overworked?
13. Unloved?
14. Jealous?

If you answer yes to six or more of these, you may be suffering from IMS. I suggest you take the more complete test in chapter 2.

ARE YOU EXPERIENCING MALE DEPRESSION?

Many studies show depression affects women about twice as often as men. This is surprising since suicide rates are 3 to 15 times higher in men. My own research, and that of a number of scholars in the field of men's health, indicates that men suffer depression much more than previously thought. I believe we have been missing many depressed men because we haven't been asking the right questions.

I developed one other questionnaire with 50 questions to help determine if someone is suffering from male depression. The full questionnaire and scoring process are in chapter 4. In analyzing the results of the test, we found that there are 15 questions that significantly predict whether a man is suffering from depression.

Recall how you have felt over the past 2 weeks and think about the following statements.

1. Things are stacked against me and others disappoint me.
2. I have felt gloomy, negative, or hopeless.
3. I feel sorry for myself or sometimes feel "pathetic."
4. I am irritable, restless, and frustrated.
5. I know I feel hostile even though I don't always let it show.
6. My feelings are blunted and I feel numb.
7. I am becoming more withdrawn from relationships
   with my family and friends.
8. I need to show I am right and have the last word.
9. I feel empty.
10. I maintain strong boundaries and push others away.
11. I feel I have little of value to give to others.
12. I have difficulty concentrating.
13. I feel suspicious and guarded.
14. I am very self-critical and often focus on failures
    as a provider and/or protector.
15. I have very little emotional energy.

If five or more of the statements describe your recent state of mind, you may be suffering from depression. I suggest you take the more complete test in chapter 4.

HOW TO USE THIS BOOK

This book is divided into three sections. The first describes the Irritable Male Syndrome, how we can recognize it, and the devastation it can cause. The second part deepens our understanding of IMS and examines the underlying causes. The final part of this book offers help for the men and women who are affected by the Irritable Male Syndrome.

Since this is a new field of clinical study, I have tried to document what we know with source notes that begin on page 267. While seeking to explain what we know about the Irritable Male Syndrome with clinical rigor, I have also made every attempt to write in a way that will engage readers at every level of knowledge.

Ultimately, this book is written to help people who suffer and to prevent future pain and suffering. I would very much like to hear about your experiences and how the book has been helpful to you. You can reach me by email at **jed@menalive.com** and **jed@theirritablemalesyndrome.com**.

You can also check both of my Web sites for the most up-to-date information on the Irritable Male Syndrome. Visit **www.menalive.com** and **www. theirritablemalesyndrome.com**. The latter site includes a complete bibliography and listing of resources where you can get help.

PART 1

THE PROBLEM

*"When women are depressed, they either eat or go shopping.
Men invade another country."*
—comedian Elayne Boosler

CHAPTER 1

THE IRRITABLE MALE SYNDROME
What Is It, and Is It Real?

Q: What do you call a man who is always tired, miserable, and irritable?
A: Normal.

Q: How can you tell if a man has Irritable Male Syndrome?
A: You ask him to pass the salt, and he yells, "Take, take, take—that's all you ever do!"[1]

These little corkers, which appeared in the *Daily Mirror,* illustrate some important aspects of what many men, and those who must live with them, are experiencing these days. First, it seems that stress has become a normal part of modern life and more men are taking out their frustrations on those who are closest to them. Second, men's irritability, blame, and anger seem excessive and more explosive. Ask a guy an innocent question, and he jumps down your throat. What's going on here?

For some men, this kind of irritability has come on slowly over a period of months and years. For others, it seems like someone has flipped a switch and Mr. Nice has turned into Mr. Mean. "God, it's like he's hormonal," one woman told me. When I told her she wasn't too far from the truth, she snapped back, "I knew it."

Since I began my study of this subject, I have received thousands of letters from men and women describing their experiences. What follows are typical of what women and men have told me.

A WOMAN'S VIEW

A letter I received recently, from a woman named Barbara, is a typical example of what women experience with men suffering from the Irritable Male Syndrome:

> *For about a year now (it could be even longer—it's hard to know exactly), I have gradually felt my husband of 22 years pulling away from me and our family. He has gradually become more sullen, angry, and moody. His general life energy is down, and his sex drive has really dropped off.*
>
> *Recently, he has begun venting, to anyone who will listen, about how horrible we all are. He is particularly hard on our 19-year-old son, Mark. It's so surprising because our son has always been superindustrious and competent. My husband has always shared my view that Mark is one of the hardest working kids we know. But all of a sudden, that has all changed. Mark still works from 6:30 A.M. until 4:30 P.M. every day, but now his dad accuses him of being unmotivated, lazy, and anything else he can think to say that is negative.*
>
> *If the kids aren't living up to his standards, it is my fault. When they're good, it is because he has been such a positive influence in their lives. If there's a problem, it must be because of the way I've raised them. I know that sounds bizarre, but that's how he thinks.*
>
> *He blames me for everything these days. If his socks or underwear are missing, I must have put them somewhere or done something with them to piss him off. I'm not kidding— that's what he tells me. The thing that bothers me the most is how unaffectionate he has become. I don't even get the hugs and affection like I did in the past. And when he does touch me, I feel grabbed rather than caressed. My husband used to be the most positive, upbeat, funny person I knew. Now, it's like living with an angry brick!*

A MAN'S VIEW

Although men are generally not as aware of the problem or willing to admit that they suffer from the Irritable Male Syndrome, one man who filled out the questionnaire on the *Men's Health* magazine Web site was quite aware. He even responded to my request for more in-depth feedback about his experience. Rick is a 52-year-old married man with children ages 22 and 26. His responses are typical of many men who have spoken out.

> *I think my irritability is related to the time of life I am in and to the stresses that seem to be mounting both at work and at home. I'm an electrical engineer, and I work for a large company in the Midwest. There has been a great deal of "consolidation" over the past few years, and many people have been let go or forced into early retirement. Even though I have been here a long time and I don't think I am vulnerable to losing my job, I still worry.*
>
> *There is always so much to do, and there never seems to be enough time to do it all. I have trouble staying on top of it all. I don't have much physical or mental energy these days. All of this is affecting my sleep. My wife keeps asking me what's wrong. I don't know what to tell her. I usually answer that nothing is wrong. When she persists, I often snap at her.*
>
> *Although I love my wife, I feel we have grown apart over the years. We used to be very close, but now we often seem like opposites—and that creates its own kind of stress. I can feel unappreciated, unheard, uncared about. She expresses the same feelings. Even though we are aware of it, we don't seem to be able to do anything about it. It's very discouraging and depressing.*
>
> *For me, depression and irritability are closely linked. I don't really lash out that often. I mostly hold the feelings in. I don't want to fight, but sometimes things erupt, and I blow up at her. I can tell she's hurt. I feel guilty, and that makes me angrier. It seems to be a vicious cycle. She says I am often sarcastic and cutting. I don't think I am, but maybe she's right.*
>
> *When we're out having fun, I can go from being happy-go-lucky to crabby in the blink of an eye. Something small will happen. I take it personally and become irrationally angry. For instance, I'll be at a bar with some friends, and if the waitress is slow in getting to the table, it infuriates me. Sometimes I'll say*

something hurtful, like "It's about time you got around to doing
your job." Other times, I'll just leave and go home, fuming all
the way.

I know I lack a sense of general well-being much of the time.
I have come to doubt my ability to be a reliable, dependable,
likable person. My confidence in myself is low. When I feel
hateful or annoyed with everyone, I just want to isolate myself.
That way, I don't have to deal with them, and I won't do things
I'll regret later. As a result, I have become estranged from my
wife and children. Even at work, which used to be a place
where I felt comfortable and had a lot of friends, I feel cut off
and isolated.

This depression/irritability "syndrome" affects everything in
my life. I feel that I have achieved very little of what, as a young
man, I had hoped to achieve. I long to be much more confident
and competent, much more relaxed, much more self-sufficient,
and much more successful.

A MULTIDIMENSIONAL PROBLEM IN LIFE

IMS is a multidimensional problem that affects, and is affected by, hormonal, physical, psychological, emotional, interpersonal, economic, social,
sexual, and spiritual changes. One of the reasons it is so difficult to understand and deal with is its complexity. In our 21st-century world of high
technology and specialization, we tend to see every problem in either-or
terms. It's either physical *or* psychological; biological *or* social; personal *or*
interpersonal. The result is that we go to one specialist to treat our hearts,
a different one to take care of our psyches, and still a third to deal with
physical pain. No one deals with the whole person, much less the person
in the context of his family, community, and social environment. We are
learning about the very nature of life, how our genes lay the foundation for
who and what we are. But we seem to be losing the larger picture of what
it means to be a healthy human being.

Who do we go to see about the increasing stress in our lives? Where do
we learn about andropause (male menopause) and the changes in men as
we age? How do we find out about the hormonal tides that affect males at
all ages? What do we do when our problems are larger than can be under-

stood by looking at our own lives? We are social beings and can't be understood apart from our partners, our children, our parents, our friends, our communities, the world we live in, and our view of the spiritual world that lies beyond.

WHAT IS IMS?

In trying to describe something that is new, it is difficult to come up with a short, accurate, and useful definition. In some sense, this whole book is my attempt to define what I mean by the Irritable Male Syndrome. What follows is my current definition. I expect it will change through time as we gather more information and conduct further research.

> Irritable Male Syndrome: A state of hypersensitivity, anxiety, frustration, and anger that occurs in males and is associated with biochemical changes, hormonal fluctuations, stress, and loss of male identity.

Let me share with you what went into this particular definition. Working with males who are experiencing the Irritable Male Syndrome (and those who live with them), I have found that there are four core symptoms that underlie many others.

The first is **hypersensitivity.** The women who live with these men say things like:

- "I feel like I have to walk on eggshells when I'm around him."
- "I never know when I'm going to say something that will set him off."
- "He's like a time bomb ready to explode, but I never know when he'll go off."
- "Nothing I do pleases him."
- "When I try to do nice things, he pushes me away."
- "He'll change in an eye-blink. One minute, he's warm and friendly. The next, he's cold and mean."

The men don't often recognize their own hypersensitivity. Rather, their perception is that they are fine but everyone else is going out of their way to be irritating. The guys say things like:

- "Stop bothering me."
- "You know I don't like that. Why do you keep doing it?"
- "Leave me alone."

- "No, nothing's wrong. I'm fine. Stop asking me questions."
- "The kids always ___." Fill in the blank: It's always negative.
- "The kids never ___." Fill in the blank with any one of the "right" things that the kids don't do.
- "Why don't you ever ___?" Fill in the blank: "want sex," "do what I want to do," "do something with your life," "think before you open your mouth," "do things the right way."
- "You damn ___." Fill in the blank: "fool," "nag," "bitch." As IMS progresses, the words get more hurtful.

Or they don't say anything. Instead they increasingly withdraw into a numbing silence.

One concept I have found helpful is the notion that many of us are "emotionally sunburned," but those around us don't know it. Think of a man who is extremely sunburned and gets a loving hug from his partner. He cries out in anger and pain. He assumes that she knows he's sunburned and that since she's "grabbed" him she must be trying to hurt him. She has no idea he is sunburned and can't understand why he reacts angrily to her loving touch. You can see how this can lead a couple down a road of escalating confusion.

The second core IMS emotion is **anxiety.**

Anxiety is a state of apprehension, uncertainty, and fear resulting from the anticipation of a realistic or fantasized threat. As you will see as you delve more deeply into the book, IMS men live in constant worry and fear. There are many real threats that they deal with in their lives: job insecurities, sexual changes, relationship problems. There are also many uncertainties that lead men to ruminate and fantasize about future problems.

These kinds of worries usually take the form of what-ifs: What if I lose my job? What if I can't find a job? What if she leaves me? What if I can't find someone to love me? What if I have to go to war? What if something happens to my wife or children? What if my parents die? What if I get sick and can't take care of things? The list goes on and on.

The third core emotion is **frustration.**

Princeton University's WordNet offers two definitions that can help us understand this aspect of IMS.

1. The feeling that accompanies an experience of being thwarted in attaining your goals. Synonym is *defeat.*

2. A feeling of annoyance at being hindered or criticized.

WordNet also offers an enlightening example to illustrate the use of the word: "Her constant complaints were the main source of his frustration."[2]

IMS men feel blocked in attaining what they want and need in life. They often don't even know what they need. When they do know, they often feel there's no way they can get it. They feel defeated in the things they try to do to improve their lives. The men feel frustrated in their relationships with family and friends and on the job. The world is changing, and they don't know where, how, or if they fit in.

Author Susan Faludi captures this frustration in her book *Stiffed: The Betrayal of the American Man.* It's expressed in the question that is at the center of her study of American males: "If, as men are so often told, they are the dominant sex, why do so many of them feel dominated, done in by the world?"[3] This feeling, often hidden and unrecognized, is a key element of IMS everywhere.

The fourth core emotion is **anger.**

Anger can be simply defined as a strong feeling of displeasure or hostility. Yet it is a complex emotion. Outwardly expressed, it can lead to aggression and violence. When it is turned inward, it can lead to depression and suicide. Anger can be direct and obvious, or it can be subtle and covert. Anger can be loud or quiet. It can be expressed as hateful words or hurtful actions, or in stony silence.

For many men, anger is the only emotion they have learned to express. Growing up male, we are taught to avoid anything that is seen as the least bit feminine. We are taught that men "do" while women "feel." As a result, men are taught to keep all emotions under wrap. We cannot show we are hurt, afraid, worried, or panicked. The only feeling that is sometimes allowed men is anger. When men begin going through IMS, anger is often their primary emotion.

Whereas anger, frustration, and anxiety can occur quickly and end quickly, the first IMS emotion, hypersensitivity, can last a long period of time and can trigger the other three feelings over and over again. It can have a major impact on men's whole lives. "When we're in a mood, it biases and restricts how we think," says Paul Ekman, Ph.D., a psychology professor and the director of the Human Interaction Laboratory at the University of California, San Francisco, School of Medicine.[4]

In describing this kind of negative mood, Dr. Ekman, one of the world's experts on emotional expression, continues: "It makes us vulnerable in ways that we are normally not. So the negative moods create a lot of problems for us, because they change how we think. If I wake up in an irritable mood, I'm looking for a chance to be angry. Things that ordinarily would not frustrate me, do. The danger of a mood is not only that it biases thinking but that it increases emotions. When I'm in an irritable mood, my anger comes stronger and faster, lasts longer, and is harder to control than usual. It's a terrible state . . . one I would be glad never to have."[5]

As we explore IMS in more depth, be aware that we are talking about a problem that isn't easily categorized or circumscribed. It is slippery and elusive. It can wreak havoc in the lives of men and those who love them, and it can remain hidden from scrutiny. I know—IMS nearly destroyed my family and me.

UP CLOSE AND PERSONAL

One of the reasons I wrote *The Irritable Male Syndrome* was to help the many men and women who suffer from a problem they don't understand. As a therapist, I'm sad to see so many midlife couples split up at the very time they could be enjoying each other the most. I'm often frustrated to see the tension that builds between young men and their families—tensions that can tear a family apart and can lead to alcohol or drug abuse, aggression, or violence. It angers me to see so many of our young men—good, caring guys—end up involved with the criminal justice system.

The other reason I wrote this book is a lot more personal and close to home. After many years of a wonderful marriage, something seemed to be eating at the very roots of the joy and commitment between my wife and me. Carlin and I had both been married before and had merged our families when we got together. She had three sons, and I had a son and a daughter. We raised her youngest son and my daughter together. There were difficulties, stresses, and strains, but we worked through them pretty well. We each felt we had found the love of our life, the person with whom we would spend the rest of our days. We felt that we had learned a lot about ourselves, that we had healed a good deal of our past wounds, and that we knew how to create a healthy marriage and family.

The change was nearly imperceptible at first. Looking back, it seems to have begun close to the time our last child left home. We were together, without the day-to-day responsibilities of parenting. My psychotherapy practice was growing, and we had the extra money to enjoy a few more luxuries and some trips together. Carlin seemed to blossom. After coming back from a personal retreat, she started a school—The Diamond Wise School for Sacred Living and Joyful Action. It quickly drew the kind of students she was looking for: adults who wanted to explore new aspects of their lives and create a balance between the spiritual and the practical, the inner and the outer worlds. I joined the school as well and liked putting my professional role aside to become a student again. It was a new experience but one that felt right, to have Carlin teaching me the things that she knew best.

Though the changes all seemed to be positive, they created major shifts in our lives. I was glad Carlin was becoming increasingly successful in her work, but I began to feel slightly uneasy. The thoughts rarely broke through the surface, but just underneath I wondered whether she would surpass me in success. (She had just written her first book, and everyone, including me, thought it was exceptional.) My conscious mind was delighted at her success, but my less conscious self was feeling threatened and competitive.

I'd often dreamed of a time when she would move out into the world more directly and take on more of the financial responsibility for our family. I saw myself as taking more time to rest and relax, with more time for non-work-related activities. I thought I might like to learn to play the guitar, sing, or dance. I'd always wanted to learn metal sculpture. But somehow it wasn't happening. Rather than cutting back on work, I was doing even more. I told myself it was so we'd have more money to do the things we both wanted to do. The truth was, I had spent so much of my life on the run, winning races, reaching for success, that I didn't know how to slow down or change gears.

Although I talked a lot about taking more time for ourselves, we didn't do it. I was frustrated with myself and uneasy about my future, but I couldn't see that. Instead, my gaze turned outward. Something wasn't right, and through my distorted lens it looked like the problem was Carlin. I started to become more critical, impatient, and dissatisfied. At the beginning I kept the feelings bottled up inside. Things were mostly good, I told myself. If there were some problems, I was sure they would clear up and go away by themselves.

I am an excellent counselor and therapist. If I had seen someone like this Jed character in my practice, I would have told him he was heading for a fall. I can usually tell when someone is under a great deal of stress, and I can often predict that if he doesn't take action to reduce the stress, there is going to be some kind of breakdown in his body, his mind, or both. But this Jed Diamond guy was not a client, and I couldn't be an objective, concerned therapist. I was too close to see clearly.

I recently found some notes I wrote at the time when Carlin and I were having our difficulties. Looking back, it's amazing how "off" I was. I still wonder how Carlin was able to put up with me. "I try to tell her how I feel, but when I do, she says I'm blaming her for my problems. She tells me it's hard for her to be loving when I'm so angry all the time. Goddamn it, what does she expect? She's always nitpicking at one thing or another. It's like I can't ever do anything right. Nothing I do pleases her. She's always criticizing me for one little thing after another. If I don't pick up this or put away that, she's on my case. Isn't there anything she likes about me?

"She tells me I'm being angry. Yeah, I guess I'm angry. Who wouldn't be, with what I am forced to put up with. When I try to talk to her about it, she turns silent or walks away. She acts like she's afraid of me. Is she nuts? I've never hit her. I've never even threatened her. Hey, I know people who are really angry. I work every day with guys who beat their wives. That isn't me. Why can't she see that I love her? All I want is to be close to her again."

Things stayed stuck and got worse. Carlin kept trying to get me to see someone for help. But I was sure that would have been a total waste of time and money. The problem wasn't me, it was her. And even if I did have a problem, I didn't need a therapist to tell me about it. And even if I did need a therapist, there wasn't anyone around who was really that good. And if there were someone good, I didn't want people seeing me in a therapist's office. How would that look for my business? What would people think about a therapist who couldn't handle his own problems?

We all have our excuses, guys, don't we? What are yours? I found out the only difference between you and me is that I may have more sophisticated excuses.

I finally decided to see a doctor some weeks later. I had to make it clear that I wasn't going because Carlin wanted me to go. I was going because I wanted to see how things were with me. Inside, of course, I was convinced that the doctor would tell me I was fine and that I would be able to come back and tell Carlin, "See, even the doctor says I'm fine. So if there's a problem, it must be you."

Fortunately for me, for her, and for our marriage, the doctor said I did have problems and suggested medications, therapy, and marriage counseling. I thanked him and said I'd think about it. As I was going out the door, he hit the spot. He told me that one of the main symptoms of this kind of problem is that men don't think they have a problem.

I waited 2 weeks and made an appointment with another doctor. This doctor was more sympathetic and did a more complete evaluation. I was convinced she would see that if there was a problem, it was minor and nothing I needed to be concerned about. Instead, she validated what the first doctor had told me, nearly word for word. I had finally run out of excuses. I began getting help.

In addition to starting medications, therapy, and couples counseling, I began reading everything I could find on depression, attention deficit disorder, anger, aggression, worry, and irritability. One of the most insightful things I read was written by Kay Redfield Jamison, Ph.D., a psychiatry professor at Johns Hopkins University School of Medicine in Baltimore and former director of the UCLA Affective Disorders Clinic. In her exceptionally fine book *An Unquiet Mind,* she talked openly about her own struggles with mental illness and her road to recovery. Hers were the first words that captured what I had been experiencing over the previous 5 years.

> *You're irritable and paranoid and humorless and lifeless and critical and demanding, and no reassurance is ever enough. You're frightened, and you're frightening, and "you're not at all like yourself but will be soon," but you know you won't.*[6]

CARLIN'S VIEW

Shortly after I began therapy, the doctor asked Carlin to write down her concerns and what things had looked like through her eyes. This is what she had to say.

> *The thing that is most troubling about Jed are his rapid mood changes. He's angry, accusing, argumentative, and blaming one moment, and the next moment he is buying me flowers and cards, and leaving me loving notes. He'll change in an hour from looking daggers at me to being all smiles and enthusiasm.*
>
> *He gets frustrated, red in the face, insisting that we have to*

talk, then cuts me off when he judges I have said something offensive to him. I become frozen inside, feeling that no matter what I do or say, it will be "wrong" for him. The intensity and the coldness in his eyes scare me at these times. I usually shut down, and it takes a lot of time for me to return to an open feeling toward him. My openness, trust, and joy in being together have suffered greatly.

He never seems satisfied with how things are in the present. If we do something nice together, he can't relax and enjoy it. He jumps ahead and wants to know when we can do it again. He's never satisfied, always restless. No matter what we have he always wants "more."

His forehead is often wrinkled with worry. He seems to analyze everything, looking for problems. When I ask him what he is thinking about, he always says, "Nothing special." It's so frustrating trying to get through to him that I have stopped trying. His intensity is way out of proportion to the situation. Little things become exaggerated. If I'm 10 minutes late coming home, he looks at me like I've committed a federal crime.

He's extremely observant at times. His eyes follow me around the room, and he'll often follow me or suddenly appear beside me when I'm not expecting it. He invades my privacy without apology but has an intense need for privacy himself. He'll read things I have on my desk, and he acts surprised if I become upset. At other times, he ignores me and acts like I'm not even around. We can go for long periods without talking to each other, and when we do talk, it is superficial. Then out of the blue he will want to get close. Sometimes he just seems to want sex. Other times it's like he's a little boy afraid to be away from his mother.

He's become hypersensitive. He needs earplugs to sleep, claiming the slightest sounds bother him and keep him awake. He can't tolerate having a light on if he wants to sleep, so I can't even read a book at night. If I touch him, most of the time he draws away as though he's been burned. Just about anything can trigger a fight.

I've grown tired of arguing with him. Nothing seems to ever

*get resolved. It seems he thrives on the intensity of the argu-
ments. If I try to talk reasonably, he becomes defensive. If I try
to match his intensity, things escalate until we stand screaming
at each other. He comes out of these bouts and wants to make
up and get close. For me, it's just tiring. I am desperately tired
of being blamed for his pain. I think I can still revive my feelings for him, but right now I feel I have to protect myself from
what I am judging as his emotional abuse.*

*I have lost a lot of feeling for Jed. I have talked to him many
times about how I can only open up and close down so many
times. I feel like a clam. I tentatively open up to see if things are
safe. But no sooner do I get my shell partly open than I get
blasted again. I'm reluctant to risk getting hurt again. It's
become safer to stay closed. I am fairly content at this time to
find my joy and play with my friends, my work, and other creative activities.*

*I haven't the slightest interest in an affair. I do have a great
desire to have a supportive, easy, and loving relationship with
Jed and to enjoy life with him. One of the things that attracted
me to him in the beginning was his "up" energy and what I saw
as his joy for life. It's been difficult living with him through
these times. I'm glad he's finally been willing to reach out for
help. I am hopeful that he will find something in his investiga-
tion that will break through for him and for us.*

WHAT I'VE LEARNED
ABOUT THE IRRITABLE MALE SYNDROME

Here's what I have discovered about IMS:

- Though it can start out mild, it can become extremely serious.
- The people living with an IMS male often receive the brunt of his acting out.
- The symptoms are similar to those of andropause (male menopause), but IMS is not limited to middle-aged men.
- The symptoms are also related to male-type depression, often expressed through irritability rather than sadness.

• Though it is most noticeable in men going through major transitions such as adolescence or midlife, it can occur at any age.

• At first, the man himself may be quite unaware that anything is wrong.

• As the problem progresses, he may recognize that something is wrong but blame the problem on something or someone else.

• The earlier it is recognized and addressed, the easier it is to treat.

• Getting through to a man suffering from IMS can seem impossible at times. As Barbara said earlier, "It's like living with an angry brick."

• Whether the problem is caught at earlier or later stages, there is always hope for men with IMS.

• We need to recognize that this is a new disorder. There is much we do not know. I'm learning along with my clients. Scientific studies are just beginning to take place.

• As a therapist who has worked with men and couples for many years, and as a man who is dealing with IMS in his own life, I know we can't wait until all the information is available before we share what we do know with people who are suffering.

In the spirit of explorers, let's move ahead. It is my hope that we can begin to get some clarity on understanding the Irritable Male Syndrome and how to best treat it.

IMS, ADOLESCENCE, AND ANDROPAUSE

Anyone who has watched a boy become a young man has seen the symptoms of the Irritable Male Syndrome. One day he is a sweet, caring child. Overnight, it seems, he turns into a monster. He becomes irritable and angry, sullen and withdrawn. He can spend hours alone in his room, lost in music or the latest video game. When he interacts with us at all, he can bite off our heads at the slightest provocation—or over nothing at all. Nothing we do is ever right; nothing seems to comfort his restless spirit.

On rare occasions, we get a glimpse of the person we once knew. We see him underneath the bravado and blame. But most of the time, it's like living with a raging stranger. His anger may be controlled, but we can see it burning just under the surface, ready to explode at any minute.

This time of life may be difficult, but it is comprehensible. We understand he is going through a profound change. Though we can't see them, we know that hormones, especially testosterone, are pulsing through his veins. We can feel the tides surge and recede and crash on the shores of his body. We are aware that there are physical changes we *can* see. He gets hair where he used to be smooth and soft. His voice deepens. He eats as if food were about to be outlawed. His body fills out and his muscles take on the quality of a man's. His growth spurts seem to occur overnight.

There are also psychological and sexual changes. His sense of self is changing as fast as his body. When he was 10 or 11, he seemed to know who he was, where he fit in the world. There was a sense of comfort and security. By the time he was 12 or 13, that had begun to change; and by the time he was 14 or 15, whatever sense of self-esteem and self-knowing he may have had had turned upside down.

Though he may have had a mild interest in sex a few years ago, he is now obsessed with it. He'll do his best to hide it from you, but you know he is masturbating at every opportunity. His penis appears to have a mind of its own and seems perpetually stuck on the "hard" setting, much to the embarrassment of the young man and those from whom he must try to hide his state of arousal.

Emotionally, he is on a roller coaster. One minute, he is on top of the world. The next, he has plunged into the depths of despair. He can turn from nice to mean in the blink of an eye. Mostly he is on edge, agitated, tense, and unable to relax. He can also zone out and withdraw into his own private world. Alcohol, drugs, and music are often used to accompany or drive his ups and downs.

Interpersonally, it is like relating to a hurricane. We are buffeted by the winds of his changes. We want to help. We want to make this transition easier for him. We may remember our own teenage years and understand some of his difficulties. But it is rarely clear what we can do. He pulls us in and pushes us out again. We perpetually feel confused and battered.

The only things that make life tolerable are the occasions when we are in the eye of the hurricane. We revel in the times when things are peaceful. We might have a wonderful meal together, a family gathering, a holiday outing. But things don't stay calm for long, and soon we are back again in the midst of the storm.

We all know this stage of life. If we are males, we may remember it from years ago—though the memories are uncomfortable and we may try to forget. If we are females, we may remember brothers or boys in our classes and our own adolescent changes. As adults, we may have sons who went through this stage or may still be going through it.

Adolescence and young adulthood have always been a difficult time of life. They seem even more difficult now than when I was growing up. Though everyone gets through this stage of life, some have more difficulty than others. "They long for love, acceptance, and approval from their parents and peers," say Dan Kindlon and Michael Thompson, authors of *Raising Cain: Protecting the Emotional Life of Boys.* "They struggle for self-respect. They act impulsively, moved by emotions they cannot name or do not understand."[7]

Given the experiences of all young men growing up, we may wonder if all of them are experiencing Irritable Male Syndrome. Is this just a normal characteristic of growing up? Or is there something different about what some of these young males experience?

Just when a man thinks all the trauma and pain are in the past, he is thrown into them again. His adolescence is behind him, but now he is moving into midlife. Male menopause, also known by the more scientifically accepted term *andropause,* occurs in all men, generally between the ages of 40 and 55. In some men, it can occur as early as 35 or as late as 65. Some clinicians and researchers define andropause simply in terms of a decline in the male hormone testosterone (hypogonadism) below a certain functional level. By that criteria, not all men go through andropause, and for those who do, the treatment is simply to supplement testosterone to restore the hormone to more youthful levels.

In my experience, andropause is like adolescence: All males go through it, though some have more symptoms than others. It is hormonally driven, but it is more complex than simply a shift in hormone levels. Physical, psychological, social, and sexual changes also occur. If we slightly expand Kindlon and Thompson's quotation about adolescent boys, it could apply to many midlife men: We long for love, acceptance, and approval from our partners and peers. We struggle for self-respect. We act impulsively, moved by emotions we cannot name or do not understand.

Does that sound like anyone you know? If you're a teenager or midlife man, does it sound like you?

It seems to me that male adolescence, andropause, and the Irritable Male Syndrome are obviously related. But exactly *how* are they related? Are they all the same thing? Is one a subtype of another? Based on my own research and clinical experience, it seems to me that Irritable Male Syndrome is the more inclusive term. I believe that all adolescents will suffer, to a greater or lesser degree, from IMS. I also believe that all men going through andropause will likely have to deal with IMS. As we will see later in this chapter when we examine the research of Gerald A. Lincoln, Ph.D., who coined the term *Irritable Male Syndrome,* IMS is characteristic of all men— and quite possibly, all male mammals.

THE BIRTH OF A NEW CONCEPT

In the course of my career as a therapist, I have sometimes been aware of dealing with a disorder long before there was a name for it. I have also found that it can often take a long time for a disorder to become recognized by mainstream sources.

One of my surprising findings in working with men going through andropause was how significant hormonal changes were in the lives of these men. Though midlife men were reluctant to recognize how much of their lives were influenced by hormonal shifts, women immediately "got it." "I knew there was something 'hormonal' about his behavior," many women told me in talking about their partners. "Now a lot of his behavior makes sense."

Another thing that became evident was how similar midlife male changes were to the changes that young men go through between 15 and 25 as they make the transition from childhood to adulthood. Both groups of males experienced significant hormonal changes. Both groups went through marked emotional ups and downs. Both were sorting out and dealing with developing new identities. And both were dealing with significant sexual changes.

I saw the great stress these men were under, much of it beyond and outside their awareness. They expressed their stress in different ways. Some drank; others became depressed. Some became aggressive; others withdrew and hid. Some had heart attacks; others had nervous breakdowns.

I found that men going through andropause expressed a constellation of feelings and behaviors that seemed to display different aspects and intensities of "irritability." These included hypersensitivity, impatience, anger, blame, defensiveness, arguing, sullenness, silence, and withdrawal. Further, these men went from being nice and considerate to being mean and destructive seemingly overnight. They could also go back and forth between acting loving and hateful time and time again.

Finally, I received letters from hundreds of women and men who said they saw their partners or themselves in the stories in my books *Male Menopause* and *Surviving Male Menopause*. But I found something interesting and unexpected. I received letters from men outside of the normal andropause age range of 40 to 55. Some men were in their thirties, saying they had many of the same symptoms and wondering if male menopause could be starting earlier for them. I heard from men in their sixties and seventies who told me they were well past their midlife passages but were experiencing many of the symptoms I mentioned. I also heard from mothers of teenage boys and young men, who told me, "My husband and my son seem to be going through the same thing. I recognize them both in the pages of your books."

In my practice as a therapist, I looked back and saw that I had been treating males at all ages, particularly males in adolescence and midlife, for a problem that seemed to have a lot of common features. I kept seeing these males, treating them and their families as they came to me for help, without being quite sure what to call the problem. As the picture became clearer, I began to see a pattern of sudden irritability, anger, and blame that I came to call the Jekyll and Hyde Syndrome.

DR. GERALD A. LINCOLN
AND THE ORIGINS OF THE NAME *IMS*

In early 2002, a colleague sent me a copy of an article by Gerald A. Lincoln, Ph.D., of the human reproductive sciences unit at the Centre for Reproductive Biology in Edinburgh, Scotland. Dr. Lincoln had recently published the results of his studies on animals in the journal *Reproduction, Fertility, and Development*. In the paper, titled "The Irritable Male Syndrome," he described what he had observed in male animals following the withdrawal of testosterone, saying that the "irritability-anxiety-depression syndromes associated with withdrawal of sex steroid hormones are well-recognized in the female." They are, he noted, connected with changes associated with the ovarian cycle and include premenstrual syndrome, postnatal depression, and menopause. "The occurrence of a potentially similar behavioural syndrome in males following withdrawal of testosterone (T) has received less attention. A clear behavioural response to T withdrawal is predicted, however, because T has well-defined psychotropic effects in relation to sexuality, aggression, performance, cognition and emotion."[8]

Dr. Lincoln defines IMS as "a behavioural state of nervousness, irritability, lethargy, and depression that occurs in adult male mammals following withdrawal of testosterone." In the endnote to his paper, he lists a number of synonyms for the word *irritable,* including *ill-tempered, edgy,* and *hypersensitive.* Antonyms include *cheerful* and *complacent.* We might ask, then, why not call this syndrome the Testosterone Withdrawal Syndrome, the Ill-Tempered Male Syndrome, the Edgy Male Syndrome, or the Hypersensitive Male Syndrome?

I think the Irritable Male Syndrome is a good term for a number of reasons. First, though Dr. Lincoln's work focuses on testosterone withdrawal, I believe that IMS is related to hormone fluctuations in general (increases as well as decreases) as well as to stress, loss of male self-esteem and identity, and biochemical changes. I will also offer evidence to show that all four of these causes are interrelated. For instance, stress can cause a lowering of testosterone levels and a decrease in self-esteem. Likewise, lower testosterone levels can contribute to stress.

Second, in my research for my books *Male Menopause* and *Surviving Male Menopause,* irritability was the symptom that men and women listed most commonly to describe males going through the transition periods of "middlescence" and "adolescence."

Third, I believe irritability is the symptom that is generally seen the earliest. Since we want to deal with the problem as soon as possible, it is good to be on alert for those symptoms that occur early.

Fourth, I believe that irritability links together a number of other, more serious, symptoms.

Finally, Irritable Male Syndrome, or IMS, has a parallel to PMS in women. As you'll see, there are significant similarities in the kinds of mood changes that men and women go through when they experience shifts in hormone levels.

WHAT'S IN A NAME?
IRRITABLE, MALE, SYNDROME

When most people see the words *irritable* and *syndrome* in close proximity, they think of some medical problem like irritable bowel syndrome. Let's take a deeper look at exactly what is encapsulated by the term *Irritable Male Syndrome*. Beginning with dictionary definitions is often a good way to start. *Webster's Revised Unabridged Dictionary* offers this definition:

> **Irritable:** Very susceptible of anger or passion; easily inflamed or exasper-
> ated; as, an *irritable* temper. "Vicious, old, and irritable."—Tennyson.[9]

There is another meaning that adds to our knowledge: "Susceptible of irritation; unduly sensitive to irritants or stimuli."[10] We'll see that this undue sensitivity is a key aspect of the irritability.

The "male" part of Irritable Male Syndrome is pretty straightforward. The *American Heritage Dictionary of the English Language* offers this tri-part definition of *male*:

1. Of, relating to, or designating the sex that has organs to produce spermatozoa for fertilizing ova.
2. Characteristic of or appropriate to this sex; masculine.
3. Consisting of members of this sex.[11]

The *American Heritage Dictionary* offers this definition of *syndrome*:

1. A group of symptoms that collectively indicate or characterize a disease, psychological disorder, or other abnormal condition.
2. (a) A complex of symptoms indicating the existence of an undesirable condition or quality.
   (b) A distinctive or characteristic pattern of behavior: the syndrome of conspicuous consumption in wealthy suburbs.[12]

These definitions point to a number of important distinctions. Syndromes are not necessarily medical abnormalities that fall under the purview of the medical establishment and hence need to be treated with some kind of drug or other therapy. In fact, syndromes aren't necessarily diseases at all. They can indicate particular patterns of behavior. As we will see, IMS is too complex to fall within a single professional discipline or to respond to a limited treatment approach.

IS IMS A REAL OR MADE-UP SYNDROME?

When I wrote the book *Male Menopause* in 1997, I was prepared for some people to find the idea of men going through menopause (or viropause, the male climacteric, or androgen deficiency in the aging male, as it is also called) absurd. One woman told me she would believe there is such a thing as male menopause when men can have babies. Some research-oriented professionals told me there was no scientific evidence to support the concept. One said, "Menopause, andropause, viropause, or bullshit, it's all the same. It doesn't exist." Some who are sensitive to the "medicalization" of normal life processes told me this was just an attempt by the pharmaceutical industry to create a new disease that people should buy drugs to treat.

Later, as the book sold well and found an audience, and as male menopause continued to be researched and discussed in the United States and around the world, a more rational debate began to take place. The prestigious *British Medical Journal* published a series of articles by respected physicians in the field who looked at the pros and cons of male menopause.[13] At the Second World Congress on the Aging Male, held in Geneva, Switzerland, there was a general consensus among the 1,000 delegates that male menopause exists and should be treated. In February 2002, I gave a presentation on my own research on male menopause at the Third World Congress on the Aging Male in Berlin, Germany.

There seem to be three stages in deciding whether a problem is real and should be treated. The first is that the concept is ridiculed and laughed at. In the second stage, the idea is taken seriously and debated by professionals working in the field. In the third stage, either the concept is found useful and is adopted or it is found wanting and it disappears. Of course, a similar process goes on within the general public. Sometimes, the public is ahead of the professionals in deciding if a problem is real. At other times, the professional health community leads the way.

There was a time when we laughed at and ridiculed women who said they had emotional changes associated with hormonal fluctuations. Most people now accept that PMS is real and can be treated. Columnist Liz Langley, writing for the *Orlando Weekly*, feels this same understanding will soon be extended to men. "Just as men have had to concede that there's a real, scientific reason for our moody silences and sharp behavior, and it's PMS, not RBS (raving bitch syndrome), we might be able to take comfort in the fact that they have to confront this crap, too. It might just be IMS rather than IBS (insensitive butt-hole syndrome) that makes them as dumbfounding as they can be."[14]

Since the Irritable Male Syndrome is a new concept, I expect that many people will ridicule the idea and dismiss it. At this stage, it is too soon to see whether IMS will eventually be widely recognized. While the debate goes on, I will continue to offer what knowledge I can. I will continue to help people who feel they or their loved ones are suffering from IMS, and I will continue to be receptive to new information as time goes on. For now, let's take a look at whether you or someone close to you has IMS.

CHAPTER 2

FINDING THE FACTS, HEARING THE TRUTH

"Am I Suffering from IMS?"/
"Am I Living with an IMS Male?"

I learned a lot about who was suffering from the Irritable Male Syndrome from letters I received from men and women. Here are two that are typical. A 32-year-old man wrote:

> Over the past 3 years especially, I have noticed that my relationship with my wife has begun to deteriorate. In the past, there were open displays of affection and frequent verbal affirmations. Now, I seem to be irritable all the time. My attitude seems to be "Don't come near me; don't talk to me; I had a hard day; I want the entire world to piss off." She now rarely tries to hug me, never initiates sex, and talks to me probably about half as much as she used to. It's got to the point where I find out what's going on in her life from my mother or sisters. We're both miserable.

A 57-year-old woman sent a terse letter about the man she lives with.

> Last January, a man came home from work with my husband's face but did not act at all like him. I have known this man for 30 years, been married to him for 22 of them, and have never met this guy before. Mean, nasty, and cruel are just a few words to describe him.

Since you're reading this book, you are aware that something is wrong. If you're a woman, you may feel that the man in your life has changed for the worse. You are probably confused about what is going on. You may blame yourself and wonder what you are doing wrong. You may blame him for turning against you. You have tried your best to do and say the things that would make everything all right, but nothing seems to help. You try to be responsive to his needs, but he is so unclear and changeable that it's nearly impossible to give him what he wants. You feel damned if you do and damned if you don't.

You may feel as if you are losing the person you most love and care about. Your sex life is probably not good. There is often tension in your lovemaking, and even when there is passion and excitement, something is missing. What you miss even more than the enjoyment and comfort of lovemaking is the feeling of safety and intimacy you once felt. The gentle touches and warm smiles are distant memories. Where he used to feel warm and cuddly, he now seems cold and prickly. You may feel you are on an emotional roller coaster, whipped up and down and side to side. There are times you'd just like to get out and walk away, but you remember how things used to be and long for what you hope can still be in the future. You probably feel hurt and you likely feel lonely. You long to get back the man you loved and used to know.

If you're a man, you may be aware that life is more stressful than it should be. At times, you may feel that the hassles of life are more than you can take. You think you should be able to handle things, but you sometimes think how nice it would be to get away from it all. You can't understand why all your efforts to make things better seem to have the opposite effect. You're tired of feeling that nothing you do is right.

It seems that the people you most rely on are no longer on your side. People at work seem more adversarial than supportive. Old friends may have dropped away or are no longer as close. Your children treat you differently, and you may have lost connection and contact. Your wife or partner seems to withdraw from you sexually. Where she used to feel warm and cuddly, she now seems cold and prickly. She seems to nitpick at the smallest things you do or forget to do. It's increasingly difficult to relax around her. You feel guarded and protective but also lonely and misunderstood. You, too, long to have the kind of relationship where you can relax and enjoy the ease of intimacy you seem to have lost.

Both men and women come to feel lonely, unloved, and uncared for. Because they don't understand what is going on, they have a tendency to blame themselves or their partners. When I see a man and woman in counseling, each wonders why the other is acting with such disregard for the person they say they love. They both wonder why the world they live in has become a place of annoyance and anger rather than comfort and joy.

She may blame herself or him. He, more often, has a tendency to blame her. Inside, however, he may be extremely self-critical and down on himself. Both are caught in a downward spiral of unhappiness, pain, and confusion. As time goes on, these destructive patterns can become more and more entrenched.

Though IMS is most noticeable in midlife men who are in relationships (usually because their partners receive the brunt of their irritability and recognize that something is wrong), it can be present in males of any age and any relationship status. We see it in boys who are experiencing the first hormonal fluctuations of adolescence. Mitch DeArmon, director of the Leadership Works Mentoring Program, told me about Alex, a 14-year-old boy who turned a great deal of his irritability and anger inward. Looking at Alex in his chair, Mitch told me, it was hard to match that passive 14-year-old hunk with the graffiti writer and vandal who sneaked out of the house at midnight. Mitch recalled the boy's demeanor:

> At first, he didn't want to be there at all. It was clear from his attitude, his clothing, and his demeanor that he was reluctant to be anywhere. He slouched down in his seat, merging with the chair. His hat rode low over his forehead, and the hair emitting from it was trained flat against his head. His responses were quiet murmurs that always required an adult to ask each question again.
>
> But I wasn't too concerned. One of the things I know about adolescent boys is that looking like they are not listening is an art form. Irritability was the mask he used to hide his pain.

Once the common turmoil of adolescence has passed, we continue to see IMS in young men who are attempting to make their marks on the world and attract sexual partners. We see it even in older men who are losing jobs, losing contact with children through divorce, and losing their positions and power in the world. We see it in our elder males, who often feel useless and unneeded. In other words, we see it in our husbands and partners, our fathers and sons, ourselves.

THE MEDICAL COMMUNITY WAKES UP,
AND THE MEN RESPOND

The medical community is notoriously slow in recognizing new problems. A few pioneering practitioners, however, are beginning to understand IMS. "IMS is incredibly common—up to 30 percent of men experience it," says Christopher Steidle, M.D., clinical associate professor of urology at the Indiana University School of Medicine in Indianapolis. "This is a male version of PMS, or premenstrual syndrome."

Larrian Gillespie, M.D., an expert in treating men and women going through hormonal changes, agrees. "Under the circumstances of stress and particular dietary changes, men exhibit symptoms of Irritable Male Syndrome, much like women do with PMS."[1]

Nearly 10,000 men filled out two questionnaires about male irritability and depression that I posted on the *Men's Health* magazine Web site. A number wrote to me personally, talking openly about the ways irritability had affected their lives and the lives of those closest to them. Here is a response from one man that is typical of many.

Paul Riches is a 32-year-old married man. He scored 103 on the Irritable Male Syndrome Questionnaire, which put him in the extremely irritable category. He works as a logistics consultant in the wireless telecom industry. Like many men I spoke to in the course of gathering information for my research, Paul said he came from a family where irritability and anger were a problem.

> *My father was a classic type A personality who sacrificed all of his personal pleasures to provide a good life for his family. Unfortunately, what we really needed was a strong, positive male role model, and instead we wound up with a monster who would arrive home in the evening and snap everyone's heads off verbally if they did or said anything to upset him.*
>
> *Occasionally, we would get together for a family vacation, and it would be "Europe in 14 Days at Mach 3." We would wake up in the RV at 6:00 in the morning to find that we were driving into Paris, and my dad had been behind the wheel since around 4:00 A.M. It wasn't about being a family, it was about needing that sense of accomplishment. God forbid anyone*

should want to actually stop and look around, because Dad had
no compunctions about tearing a strip off you if you didn't do
exactly what he had planned.

Unfortunately, many of our fathers' characteristics get passed along to us, as Paul sadly acknowledges.

I believe I have truly turned into my father's son. I have noticed
that my relationship with my wife has deteriorated significantly.
Where we used to share affection openly and often, I find I am
more and more hypersensitive, irritable, and angry. I bite her
head off at the least little thing, and I don't even know why I'm
doing it.

As far as relationships with others, here's a quick example:
One of my professors in college nicknamed me Mr. Grumpy,
and that name has stuck with me. My reputation often precedes
me. I often come across as cheery and helpful, then it's as though
a dark cloud comes over me and something will set me off.

Although I hate to admit it, my work life has suffered
because of my irritability. The last company that I contracted
my services to merged with a larger firm, and I was told I would
have a new position. However, when it got time for the
changeover, I was told the position was no longer available. I
chatted casually with several people and got the impression that
it was not my work that was the issue. Because of my shortness
with co-workers and my irritability, I received the reputation of
being "difficult to work with."

When I asked Paul what he would say to other men in his situation, he pulled no punches in sharing what he had learned the hard way.

Deal with it as soon as possible, not down the road after you've
done significant damage to your marriage, your friendships, and
your reputation. Do whatever it takes to get a handle on it, no
matter what. The short-term pain of dealing with it outweighs
the long-term damage it will cause. Look at your wife, look at
your kids, look at your career. Now imagine it's all gone
because of some stupid male pride. "Well, my dad was a tough

*old guy, and I'm going to be just like him." That was my dad,
and that attitude almost killed him and destroyed his family.
Wake up, guys, before it's too late.*

IMS IS ULTIMATELY ABOUT VIOLENCE

When I began studying IMS in myself, my clients, and the thousands of people who called and wrote to me, I was struck by the level of violence that was occurring. Although most cases of IMS didn't lead to the most extreme forms of violence—murder or suicide—there was a great deal of verbal and sometimes physical abuse directed at others. I was also struck by the degree of hostility that was turned inward.

In addition to acting out our anger on others, we IMS males often take out our frustrations on ourselves. We might scream and yell at our wives, then later beat ourselves up in our own minds. Many of us become depressed and dysfunctional. We also develop all the manifestations of too much stress and strain in our lives, such as overeating, alcohol problems, diabetes, and heart disease.

The World Health Organization defines violence as "the intentional use of physical force or power, threatened or actual, against oneself, another person, or against a group or community, that either results in or has a high likelihood of resulting in injury, death, psychological harm, maldevelopment, or deprivation."[2]

Besides death and injury, this definition also includes the myriad and often less obvious consequences of violent behavior, such as psychological harm, deprivation, and problems in relationships. It also covers a wide range of acts, going beyond physical acts of overt violence to include threats, intimidation, and withdrawal of love and support. It encompasses interpersonal violence as well as suicidal behavior and armed conflict.

To understand the complexity of IMS, we need a framework that allows us to see the common features of and linkages between different types of violence. This will allow us to develop a holistic approach to prevention and treatment. In 2002, the World Health Organization published a report, *World Report on Violence and Health*, that offers a useful framework for understanding IMS and violence.[3]

The report divides violence into three broad categories: self-directed violence, interpersonal violence, and collective violence.

Self-directed violence includes suicidal behavior as well as ways we abuse ourselves through destructive habits and behavior.

Interpersonal violence focuses both on the family and the community. In the family, we can look at violence directed at our partners, children, or elders. In the community, we focus on violence expressed toward both those we know (anger toward those we date or work with, for instance) and those we do not know (such as the violence of road rage or rape).

Collective violence is the use of violence by people who identify themselves as members of a group against another group or set of individuals in order to achieve political, economic, or social objectives. It can take a variety of forms: armed conflicts within or between states; genocide, repression, and other human rights abuses; terrorism; and organized violent crime. The typology also captures the nature of violent acts, which can be physical, psychological, sexual, or expressed through deprivation or neglect.

What may begin with a small degree of irritability may lead to anger, aggression, and murder. It can also lead to great sadness, depression, and suicide. I think of irritability as the tip of the iceberg that, if not understood and treated, can lead to increasingly serious problems.

In this chapter, we will look at the symptoms of IMS in its earlier stages. In later chapters, we will explore the more serious aspects.

US AND THEM:
WHY ARE MEN SO ANGRY AT WOMEN?

Although men experiencing IMS can take out anger and frustration on anyone, they are most often directed at women. Why do we direct our dissatisfactions, discontent, and aggression toward the ones we are supposed to love the most? Why do we seem to do the most hurtful things imaginable and then apologize and swear they will never happen again, knowing as we make the promise that we are unlikely to keep it? Why do we continue to inflict pain even when we know we are doing so and we try to stop?

There seems to be some truth for both sexes in the old saying "We can't live with them and we can't live without them." Though there are certainly many women who can do hurtful and hateful things to men, there seems to be something unique about the degree to which men take out their frustrations on women. There also seems to be something special about the fear that so many men have of being without women in their lives.

In his book *Misogyny: The Male Malady*, anthropology professor David D. Gilmore explores cultures from Western Europe to the Middle East, from the jungles of South America to the remote uplands of New Guinea, from preliterate tribal peoples to modern Americans. He looks at ancient and modern cultures and all those in between. He finds that in all places and in all times, there has been a tendency for men to fear and hate women. He discovers that "men love and hate women simultaneously and in equal measure, that most men need women desperately, and that most men reject this driving need as both unworthy and dangerous."[4]

Obviously, this isn't the case with *all* men. Though this ambivalence is played out in all societies, individual men differ in the degree to which it affects them. For some of us, the fear and rage are extreme. Others control it well, and it seeps out only at times of change and stress. The fear and hatred can be expressed in thoughts and actions as well as through art, writing, poetry, and fantasy. We can see it in the works of many famous writers, including Swift, Schopenhauer, Nietzsche, Strindberg, Tolstoy, Pound, D. H. Lawrence, and Norman Mailer.[5]

After offering hundreds of pages of quite interesting and compelling evidence to lend credence to his thesis, Gilmore concludes that this "love/hate" dynamic is rooted in men's unique dependency on women. He points out that in most cultures, a man depends upon his mother and later his wife for everything from food preparation and domestic care to emotional support and nurturing.

Gilmore also reminds us that every man is dependent on a woman to mate with him, carry a child within her body, give birth to the baby, and feed and care for the child until it is able to live on its own. Men depend on their wives, he tells us, for procreation and continuity. "To bear the sons who will assure them a measure of immortality, protect them in war, care for them in their dotage, validate their masculinity, and assist them in their god-given task of continuing their line."[6]

Men love women for what they can give us, but we are also frightened at the degree of our dependency. "So man must cling helplessly to woman as a shipwrecked sailor to a lifeboat in choppy seas," says Gilmore. "He desperately needs her as his salvation from all want and from oblivion; his dependency is total and desperate. But, and here's the rub, man must also separate from woman to achieve anything at all. He must overcome his desire to regress to infantile symbiosis with her if he is to be accountable as a man."[7]

So men depend on women for the continuation of our existence, but we must separate ourselves to maintain our sense of masculinity. This double bind creates a feeling familiar to many of us: "I want to be close, but when I'm close, I want to be free."

This bind is inherent in the reality of being male. It is so much a part of us that, as with the air we breathe, we are not even aware of its existence. However, at times of change, such as adolescence, midlife, or when we are overstressed or depressed, our anger begins to emerge. It starts as irritability and can grow outward into anger, aggression, and violence, or inward into sadness, depression, and suicide.

"And of course," says Gilmore, "this powerful double-sided fixation creates a concomitant fear: the fear of abandonment, loss, withdrawal, disillusionment, and failure in life's most precious endeavors. Fraught with images of defeat, despair, and death, the fear of abandonment leads to regressive depression, panic, guilt, self-doubt, and ultimately to the rage of the thrall. The impotent rage leads to aggression; and aggression, in turn, needs a scapegoat."[8]

Though IMS may have a special connection to male vulnerability toward women, it can affect all of our relationships. There is often a fragility in the male psyche that our irritability and anger attempt to hide. We are uncomfortable in situations where others may seem more powerful than we are. That's why, outside of our relationships with our intimate partners, we often see IMS express itself in work environments where we must deal with supervisors, in sibling relationships where one is older or stronger, and with our parents, who always trigger our remembrances of being children.

All this, of course, goes on outside our awareness. These universal, epic battles are fought in the darkest parts of our psyches. All we "know" is that our partners seem to be cold and withholding. They and the rest of the people around us refuse to give us what we need. They seem to go out of their way to irritate us. If we're irritable—and it's a big if at the beginning—we're sure the cause lies somewhere outside ourselves. To think otherwise would bring up fears too difficult to confront.

So, if you've read this far and this section has been upsetting, or if you question its validity, or if you think it's all true and you're so disheartened you want to give up, don't despair. Take a deep breath. Remember that it has taken a lot of time to get to the place where you decided to read this book. There is plenty of time to work through to a more positive future.

You only need to take one step at a time. From here, we will take another look at how we can recognize the Irritable Male Syndrome.

THE IMS QUESTIONNAIRE

The Irritable Male Syndrome manifests itself through a number of feelings. The following questionnaire will help you recognize where it is present in yourself or in someone you care about and its degree of seriousness. Everyone is irritable from time to time. Life is inherently stressful, and there are inevitably things that bother us. What we want to know, though, is how irritable we are. Is our irritability excessive? Has it become entrenched? Does it seem to be getting worse? Is it causing problems in relationships with family, friends, or community?

We don't have a precise instrument to measure IMS. Like so much in the psychological sciences, IMS can be understood only by asking questions and helping you reflect on what the answers mean in your life.

A man's score on this questionnaire should be a guide, not an absolute indicator that there is or is not a problem. Please don't use this to "prove" that you don't have a problem. Even if your score does not suggest that you have IMS, behavior that is causing stress in your family should be taken seriously. On the other hand, a wife or other family member should not use a man's "high" score to "prove" that he has a problem. Though a high score is usually indicative of the Irritable Male Syndrome, trying to force that awareness on a man is likely to make him more defensive.

IRRITABLE MALE SYNDROME QUESTIONNAIRE

I ask men completing the questionnaire to look as deeply and honestly as they can at feelings and actions that may be difficult to acknowledge. We often feel a great deal of guilt and shame about what we are doing. We may be very aware of how much pain we cause to those we love and at the same time be unable to change how we express (or do not express) ourselves. Remember, the purpose of this book is to understand what you experience and give you the tools to change.

For the women who fill out the questionnaire, I ask you also to be honest about what you experience. Some of you may have a tendency to deny how violent things have become. For instance, it may be difficult to acknowledge how angry, aggressive, unloving, and mean your man may be.

Others of you may have difficulty recognizing and accepting how much pain your man is experiencing. You may have trouble seeing how stressed, worried, troubled, and depressed he is.

For those emotions felt rarely or not at all, score 0; those felt sometimes, score 1; those felt frequently, score 2; and those felt most of the time, score 3. Your total score can range from 0 to 150.

Reflect on how often you (or the person you are rating) felt the following emotions or needs during the past month:

	Not at All	Sometimes	Frequently	Most of the Time
1. Angry				
2. Impatient				
3. Blaming				
4. Dissatisfied				
5. Moody				
6. Fearful				
7. Discontented				
8. Hypersensitive				
9. Exhausted				
10. Grumpy				
11. Easily upset				
12. Bored				
13. Aggressive				
14. Unloved				
15. Unappreciated				
16. Tense				
17. Touchy				
18. Tired				
19. Unloving				
20. Lonely				
21. Hostile				
22. Overwhelmed				
23. Destructive				
24. Demanding				
25. Depressed				
26. Frustrated				
27. Withdrawn				
28. Mean				

(continued)

	Not at All	Sometimes	Frequently	Most of the Time
29. Sad				
30. Scared				
31. Numb				
32. Explosive				
33. Defensive				
34. Denial of problems				
35. Critical				
36. Troubled				
37. Desire to overeat				
38. Desire to drink or use drugs				
39. Need to withdraw behind TV, newspapers, or computer				
40. Desire for increased time at work				
41. Need to sleep more or trouble with sleep				
42. Impulsive				
43. Worried				
44. Less intimate				
45. A pull to argue and fight				
46. Sarcastic				
47. Jealous				
48. Stressed				
49. Uncompassionate				
50. Uncommunicative				

I developed the following results based on my clinical experience and on responses from the 9,453 people who took the Irritable Male Syndrome and Male Depression Questionnaires on the *Men's Health* Web site.

0 to 25: No or few signs of IMS.

26 to 49: Some indications of IMS. May need help or watchful waiting to see if things improve or get worse.

50 to 75: IMS is likely, and it is advisable to seek help.

76 or more: IMS is definitely present, and getting help is most important.

Note: As men, we are generally less in touch with our feelings and not as comfortable acknowledging the feelings we do know about. As a result, our scores on this questionnaire will usually be lower than our true irritability levels. It's often helpful to have someone who knows us well fill out the questionnaire as well as give feedback on how they see us.

A woman filling this out may find it difficult to know what the man is feeling. Some of the answers may be more obvious than others. If he suddenly begins pounding his fists on the front of the refrigerator (I used to do that a lot—the fridge was solid enough to let me know I was hitting something but had enough give that I didn't break my hands) while yelling loudly about how stupid you are, you have a pretty good idea that he is angry and explosive. On the other hand, it may not be as easy to know whether he is sad, scared, numb, or depressed.

Don't get hung up on the score. Some men are naturally more irritable than others. Some families can tolerate, and even thrive, in situations where anger, moodiness, and explosiveness are common. For others, even a low degree of irritability may be too much. Use this questionnaire as a guide to help you explore what is true in your own life and what is good for your family and those you love and who love you.

Men and women, I ask you to be compassionate with yourselves and those who care about you. No matter how bad things have become, there is hope for the future. My wife and I came through this most difficult time and our relationship is stronger than it ever was. I have worked with thousands of others for whom the same is true.

The first step toward change is acknowledging, without blame or shame, how things really are. No one likes living with an irritable male, least of all the male himself. I hope that by the end of this chapter, or by the end of the book, you will be able to say, "Yes, that's me. I may not like what I see, but I'm sick and tired of feeling this bad and causing others so much pain." Or you may say, "Yes, that's him. He's not crazy or bad, but I'm not going to put up with things as they are. I'm ready for a change."

HEARING FROM THOSE EXPERIENCING IMS

Looking at your score on the questionnaire and exploring your answers with someone you care about can be helpful in determining whether you are experiencing IMS or living with an IMS male. Another powerful tool is to listen to the stories of others. A glimpse into the lives of other men and women can be a mirror that allows you to see into your own life. You may recognize someone close to you in these stories. You may recognize the person who looks back at you each morning when you shave.

THE STORY OF DONNA AND GEORGE ROLLINS

This is a couple who came to me because IMS was causing problems in their lives. Here's how Donna experienced the problems:

Five years ago, my husband turned 50. Since then, our lives have been turned upside down. I feel I have been wandering in the wilderness trying to understand what is going on. We've had our ups and downs during the 24 years we have been married, but I'd say, on the whole, we've been happy.

George owns his own retail business, and I've been a part-time bookkeeper while the kids are growing up. We have all the things we've been striving for. We have a nice house, drive new cars, and have good friends. Our 22-year-old son is away at college, and our daughter is getting ready to go next year.

Just when I thought we could really enjoy our time together, my husband has totally changed. At first, little things bothered him. If I didn't have dinner prepared at the exact time I promised, he'd snap at me. When I got in a slight car accident, he nearly went ballistic. He accused me of not knowing how to drive.

Work has always been stressful. Owning your own business means you have to be "on" all the time. We always worried about whether the business would make it, then wondered if it would survive. Now that it's successful, he seems even more uptight and indecisive. One minute, he says he wants to sell it and retire. The next, he tells me the thing to do is to expand. It's been driving me nuts.

I guess I could take all that, but now he's been taking things out on me. The irritability now is nearly constant. It seems that nothing makes him happy. Frequently, he is on the verge of rage. He's never hit me, but the way he looks at me is frightening. He gets a certain look in his eye that makes me shiver. What's so confusing is that he used to be patient and laid-back. For most of our marriage, he was the gentlest and kindest man you'd ever want to meet. Now he's become so angry and hurtful I hardly know him.

When I ask him what's wrong, he either ignores me or snaps at me. When I reach out to touch him, he pulls away like my touch is poisonous. "I feel like all the passion has drained out of me," he says. A year ago, he started counseling. A lot of issues from his childhood began to surface. I thought this would help him get rid of some of the anger and bring us closer together. But now he's decided to move out.

He tells me, "I love you, but I'm not in love with you." That cuts me to the bone. How can the man who so recently told me he was more in love with me than when we got married all of a sudden decide that he is no longer in love? It's like waking up one morning and finding out your husband has decided he's your brother now, not your lover.

It's been the worst nightmare of my life. I'm beginning to see that he is experiencing a great deal of anxiety and depression. At times, he is angry and blaming. At other times, he acts almost like a zombie. He seems so cold and heartless, and I wonder where his humanity has gone.

It's not knowing what I can count on that drives me nuts. I ask him if he wants a divorce, and he says no. I ask him if there's anything I can do to make things better, and he says no. I ask if he'll go to counseling, and he says no. Everything he says is negative and there's no room for dialogue. It's like talking to a post.

Now he's having a serious flirtation with a woman he has met. He tells me it's not sexual; she's just someone he can talk to about what's going on with him. I want to tear out my hair. "Why can't you talk to me?" I scream in my head. I love this man. I don't want our relationship to end. I know he's going through something, and I want to help him heal.

At this point, I have no confidence that my husband will move through this and get to the other side without destroying our marriage. He seems stuck in the transition, and I fear that when he finally moves through it, he will choose to walk away from the

*marriage because he doesn't want the commitment, the responsi-
bility, and the restrictions. I wonder how this will affect our children. Whatever happens to us, I want him to have a relationship
with them. Still, I can't help feeling resentment that they will continue to have a place in his life, while I will be excluded.*

POINTS OF UNDERSTANDING

- Although IMS can occur at any age, it is quite common at midlife.
- It can often feel like everything you thought you knew about a rela-
tionship is in question.
- IMS often strikes those who are the most successful. "Having it all"
can be a curse as well as a blessing.
- The first symptoms can be quite mild and difficult to distinguish from
the kind of irritability that is a normal part of life.
- Later, the irritability becomes more prevalent and/or more blaming
and angry.
- IMS at midlife often is related to unresolved issues from childhood.
Abuse that may have been hidden or covered up through the years begins
to emerge.
- A man feels that the life force is draining out of him and that he must
escape if he is to survive.
- Though he may still love his partner, he now feels that something vital
is missing. He often expresses this by saying "I love you, but I'm not in love
with you."
- He may feel a need to move out, find his own place, and find himself.
He is vulnerable to flirtations or affairs. As I say in my book of the same
title, he is "looking for love in all the wrong places."
- It takes a very courageous and insightful man to recognize that IMS is
contributing to whatever problems he is experiencing. Learning about it
and working through these issues may be the most difficult and important
thing he does in his life.

THE STORY OF HENRY AND BARBARA ROBINSON

One of the men who had the courage to see the truth is Henry Robinson.
Henry is a 38-year-old man who is married, with 10-year-old twin boys.
He said he recognized himself when reading my book *Male Menopause*.

Here are his insights:

To tell you the truth, I never would have read your book or even thought that I had a problem. It was my wife who bought the book. She didn't say anything to me or suggest I read it. Often, when I'd come home late from work, I'd see her reading it and underlining things with a pen. One night when she was out with a group of her women friends, I started glancing through the book, curious about what she had marked. I couldn't believe it. Nearly every page had things marked. When I read them, it was like having a mirror held up to my own life.

For the first time, I began to understand something about what was going on with me. I began to understand why I felt so stressed, how the stress was affecting me physically and emotionally, and why I was getting so angry at the people I love the most. One of the main reasons I refused to consider my wife's concern that my anger was causing problems in our life was that I felt ashamed. In the world where I live, men don't have emotional problems—and if they do, they work them out themselves. When I read other men's stories, I realized that I wasn't the only one who had these problems.

As far back as I can remember, I was always good at what I did. I was a whiz in school. I liked to learn, and I was good in sports—a great combination. Everything seemed wonderful until I was about 10. My dad lost his job and began drinking. Or it could have been the other way around. I was too young to know. I do remember the fights that began to occur. There was never any physical violence, but there was a lot of screaming, things were broken, and my dad punched his fist through the wall on a number of occasions. I was terrified and tried to comfort my younger sisters.

I found that I could hide from the pain of my home life by spending more time reading books and playing basketball. Things went on like this until I graduated from high school, when my parents finally separated. My dad eventually went into treatment and found out he is manic-depressive and has an alcohol problem. He still goes to meetings and takes medications to this day.

In college, my interest in biology deepened, and I decided to go into medicine. I liked people and was always interested in what made them tick. It wasn't until I was actually in medical school that I realized I was searching for answers to what had happened to my father. I was also trying to understand my own dark moods.

Once I became a doctor, I saw people in my practice every day, tried to fix what ailed them, and listened to their problems. I always felt overwhelmed. There was never enough time to really help people. I got tired of seeing the same people with the same problems. Every one of my patients seemed to be suffering from stress-related diseases. The best I could do was patch them up and send them out until the next time.

When I came home, I just wanted to tune out. Barbara wanted to talk and tell me about her day. She wanted to talk about us and what was going on with us. I didn't want to hear it. I can see now that I was afraid to slow down enough to see how bad things were becoming. I'm an action kind of guy, and if I can't see a solution, I don't even want to acknowledge that there's a problem.

POINTS OF UNDERSTANDING

• IMS is often related to increasing stress in a man's life.

• Women usually recognize IMS before their husbands do.

• Men often feel ashamed of their feelings and think we should work out our problems by ourselves.

• IMS in adulthood can be related to what we didn't get as a child (for instance, enough contact with our mothers or sufficient connections with our fathers) as well as what we did get (such as exposure to excessive anger or violence, or alcohol or mental health problems in our parents).

• Many of us hide our pain by getting immersed in our work. When that doesn't work, we may try other things, such as eating or drinking more.

• IMS is not a disease but rather a signal that there is something out of balance in our lives.

THE STORY OF JOSH, AGE 15

I first met Josh when he was referred to me by his high school for getting in a fight with another kid. His teachers were concerned because it was so uncharacteristic of Josh, whom they described as "a quiet but likable kid who is very intelligent, gets his work done, and doesn't cause problems."

When I asked him what had happened, he shrugged. When I pressed for details, he said the other kid had called him a name that he didn't appreciate. At first, he didn't want to say what the name was. Finally, he let out "faggot" in a low, quiet voice. As we talked more, he said he didn't have a problem with people who were gay. But, he added, "that's not me, and I don't like people saying it is."

He assured me the fight had been "no big deal" and wouldn't happen again. Something in the tone of his voice, a touch of sadness, made me want to see him again. I told him he was probably right, it had been no big deal, but I wanted to talk to him a few more times just to be sure. To say he was unenthusiastic would be a grand understatement. Still, he didn't put up any major opposition.

Over a period of three or four sessions, I found that Josh's father had left when he was 5 years old. "He had some kind of mental problem I think, but I don't remember him, and I haven't seen him since he left. My mom doesn't talk about him." On the surface, Josh seemed to have accepted his father's departure. He did his best to cover his feelings. As we talked together over a period of months, he began to express a range of emotions. At first, he was angry that his father had left. Later, he talked about the sadness and hurt he felt. Below the sadness and hurt was a great deal of fear. "I worry that I might go crazy like he did," Josh confided one day. He seemed relieved to talk about things that had been bottled up for a long time.

Although he got along in school and had a few friends, he lived most of his life inside a world of fantasy. He played video and computer games whenever he could, imagining himself to be an invincible hero who killed the bad guys and ended up with the beautiful girls. Although he was a good-looking young man, he was shy and rarely talked to girls at all.

The one time he had asked a girl to go out with him and some friends, she had rejected him. "She shot me down," he said. When I asked him how he felt about that, he shrugged his shoulders. He looked totally crestfallen. Recalling a similar experience from my own youth, I asked if he felt like he had been kicked in the groin and needed some respect. He got tears in his eyes as he looked up. "Yeah, I do want respect, but it's more like I was thrown on the garbage heap."

More tears came as he continued. "That's how I feel most of the time, like a piece of garbage." His voice got more intense and increasingly strident. His eyes were dark and intense behind the tears.

"I don't fit in anywhere. I feel like I'm from another planet. I hate my mother, I really do. She's so fucking nice and encouraging." He mimicked a singsong voice: "'Things will turn out okay, Josh. You're really a great kid. You'll find a girlfriend. I know you will.'

"I don't want her goddamned happy talk. Life sucks and I don't see anything that makes me think it will get any better. Most of the kids use dope. The others smash each other on the football field or in some other violent sport. We're always getting ready for our next war or killing some poor people because our government wants to protect our 'foreign interests.' What am I doing here? Where am I going? What's my future going to be like? Do I even have a future?"

Josh finally ran out of steam. It was clear he had been holding in a lot for a long time. I put my hand on his shoulder. He flinched at first but didn't pull away. "I'm glad you trusted me enough to let me into your world," I told him. "I don't know that I have a lot of good answers, but I can sure tell you that you aren't alone anymore."

Points of Understanding

• What may seem like "boys just being boys" can be boys just being boys or it can mask more serious issues.

• We need to listen carefully to what boys tell us about what is going on with them. They most often communicate first through action and only later, if at all, in words.

• Trying to cheer him up or tell him he is really a good kid does not help as much as asking how he is feeling and what he needs. Sometimes we have to guess. Even when we guess incorrectly, if he believes that we sincerely want to understand, he may tell us how it really is with him.

It's often difficult to distinguish IMS in young males from normal teenage angst. We need to be careful that we don't label normal behavior as problematic. On the other hand, we also need to guard against the tendency to deny problems because "that's just the way boys are." I think of IMS as occurring on a continuum. On one end are those kids who are really doing okay and just need support getting through adolescence and becoming adults. On the other end are the ones who are in trouble and in danger of developing serious problems.

One of the reasons I developed the Irritable Male Syndrome Questionnaire was to help distinguish those who may need help from those who are doing relatively fine and just need support. A high score on the questionnaire is one indicator of more serious problems. I also look for a number of other indicators that are often present in kids like Josh.

1. How isolated does the person feel?
2. Is he beginning to feel hopeless about his future?
3. Has he experienced significant losses, such as divorcing parents or rejection by a friend?
4. Does he keep his feelings bottled up until they become explosive?

"Although our boys urgently want to talk about who they really are, they fear that they will be teased, bullied, humiliated, beaten up, and even murdered if they give voice to their truest feelings," says William S. Pollack, Ph.D., author of *Real Boys' Voices*. "Thus, our nation is home to millions of boys who feel they are navigating life alone—who on an emotional level *are* alone—and who are cast out to sea in separate lifeboats and feel they are drowning in isolation, depression, loneliness, and despair."[9]

THE STORY OF KIM AND BILL ROGERS

This personal tale told to me by a woman named Kim Rogers illustrates the way in which a significant loss can trigger the start of the Irritable Male Syndrome.

My husband, Bill, just turned 57. A year ago, his high-profile job was phased out. He had expected to be named department head, so he came home stunned. At the time, he seemed to adjust okay and quickly found a consulting job in a related field. However, things haven't been the same since.

The twinkle in his eye is gone, and he seems to have lost self-confidence. Our sex life has gone downhill. He couldn't get an erection one time, and since then he seems to be avoiding sex altogether. He's begun to drink more than I think is good for him, but he denies that there has been any change. He has always been athletic and taken good care of himself, but now he has become obsessive. He insists on running at least 5 miles a day, 7 days a week. If something comes up that disrupts his schedule, he becomes infuriated. He's taking all kinds of supplements—so many that they are overflowing our cabinets.

He joined a 24-hour gym and sometimes he doesn't come home until all hours. I've wondered whether he is seeing another woman. He tells me he is at the gym, and I guess I believe him. If I try to talk to him about how he's feeling or what's going on, he bites my head off. He'll yell at me one minute then want to have sex the next. What's going on? His behavior is becoming more bizarre. I love my husband, but I would never have believed he'd act this way toward me. I keep trying to play the "brave and understanding" spouse, but I feel like I'm seeing a man with a double personality. The strain on me is tremendous!

He won't admit that there's a problem, but he'll glare at me like everything I do is wrong. He's told me he is unhappy and wants his freedom. When I get mad and say, "Well, leave if that's what you want to do," he just huffs and stalks off into the other room.

He tells me he's felt cheated his whole life but won't tell me what he feels he's lost. It seems he has everything he's ever wanted. I certainly don't deny him anything. But nothing I can do seems to make him happy. He's so emotionally raw right now. I don't know who I will experience when I get home, Dr. Jekyll or Mr. Hyde.

Points of Understanding
  • A job change can precipitate IMS. The impact of losing a position may be stronger than we think.
  • Self-confidence and self-esteem are often tied to our position in the

world of work. When those shift, the very ground of our beings are shaken.

• Sex and self-esteem cycle together. When self-esteem goes south, so does sex drive; and when sexuality is off, self-esteem drops.

• Use of alcohol, nicotine, drugs, or other forms of escape may increase. We often deny that this is occurring or that it's a problem.

• We may become obsessive about our health—what we put in our bodies and physical exercise. It's as though we are trying to outrun our fears rather than deal with them.

• Mood swings are confusing and maddening. We may be hateful one minute and push you away. The next minute, we want to feel your loving embrace. We can act like angry teenagers who are trying to "prove" you don't really love us. We act as nasty as we can, seeing if we can drive you away while hoping you love us enough to stay.

• A partner being "brave and understanding" can border on being a doormat to an IMS male's bad temper. Sometimes he needs the kind of "hard love" that says, "I love you and I'm not going away. But you have to knock off this horrible behavior. It's hurting me, and it's destroying our relationship."

• We practice the approach-avoidance dance. We threaten to leave, but we want to stay. We want to be free, but we're afraid we may be throwing away the best thing we've ever had. Again, think teenagers. They want to be on their own but don't want to cut their ties to home base.

• Men, particularly the ones who've been pretty good husbands and fathers, often feel they've sacrificed themselves for others. (We sure don't have a corner on that market. How many women feel the same way?) We think to ourselves, "When will it be my time? When do I get to cut loose and have fun?"

AN IMS SUCCESS STORY:
JILL AND ROBERT JEFFERSON

I've found that many people become discouraged when they come to recognize that they or someone they love is experiencing IMS. They can feel that their lives are so disrupted and that there is so much distance in their relationships that things can never be repaired. So although I will be talking about healing the Irritable Male Syndrome later in the book, particularly in part 3, I want to end this chapter with a success story.

You will hear a lot of success stories. This one is particularly heartening.

When I first met Jill, a woman in her late forties, she had no hope that her husband would recover from his IMS. Even if there were a chance he would heal, she was sure their relationship would not survive. Here is the story of two people who had the courage to confront their worst fears and see things through to the end.

I believe my husband is experiencing the Irritable Male Syndrome. Our life has been wonderful—at least I thought it was. Then everything turned upside down. My husband attended a training program away from home for 5 weeks last June and July. Things have not been the same since. I knew there was something wrong when I met him at the airport. He was very moody but said nothing was wrong and wouldn't talk about it. When we made love, he found it difficult to obtain and keep an erection. I told him, "It's okay. It's not a big deal. Don't worry." He rolled away from me and seemed to be angry. When I reached out to touch him, he got out of bed and went into his study and worked.

I tried to be understanding. I love my husband deeply and wanted us to work through whatever was wrong. I kept asking him what was wrong. He just got irritated and pulled away when I tried to touch him. We did had sex a few times. I say sex because it was not lovemaking. It must be in the middle of the night, in the dark. He would nudge me and push at me to notice he had an erection, but he would not reach out to me. There wasn't any tenderness. I would end up feeling more lonely and distant afterward than I did before.

I finally got him to talk to me about what was troubling him. He said that the week before he was to return home from the training program, he realized he didn't want to come home, that he was unhappy with his work and his life. He said he still loved me but wanted to be on his own. He said he had tried to be a good husband and father but now he wanted to be free. "I have a job lined up overseas, and I'm going to take it."

He said he'd been thinking about this for quite a while. He had already made all these plans on his own. He told me he knew I wouldn't go along with what he had to do and would want a divorce, so he might as well just get on with it.

After my initial shock, I could reach out and touch him. "So what are we talking about here?" I wanted to know. "How long will you be gone? When will you come back? What do I do with our new house while you're away?"

"That's the problem," he told me. "I don't know the answers to any of those questions. I can't even guarantee that I'll want to come back. I know I can't ask you to wait for something that may not happen, but I don't want to lose you."

I couldn't believe what I was hearing. I wanted to run out of the house screaming. I felt like my head was going to explode. "Let's see if I have this right," I thought to myself. "You want to go off and live in Europe. You don't know when you're coming back. You don't know if you're coming back. You want me to take care of everything while you're gone. And you want me to wait for you in case you decide to come back. You must be insane. I would have to be out of my mind to even consider such an arrangement. You were probably right. Getting divorced is the only answer."

That's what I was thinking. But somehow what came out of my mouth was "I love you. If that's what you need to do, I'll try to work it out. I don't know if I can handle what you are suggesting, but I don't want our marriage to end, and I'm willing to give it a fighting chance."

I didn't know if I was being the biggest fool in the world or the craziest. That didn't stop me from helping him make arrangements. Within 2 weeks, he was gone.

He said he'd call when he got settled into his new job, which he did. Then it was a long time before I heard from him again. I was worried and lonely. When he finally did call, he said he was very busy working 12-hour days and I shouldn't worry. He told me he was okay but didn't ask much about me. He wanted to know how our daughter, Cara, was. I told him she and her husband were doing fine, but she missed him, too, and didn't really understand what was going on.

I decided to use this time to do something for myself. I've always been interested in learning Italian, so I'm taking classes at the college. I've also decided to go back and study maths. I was always intimidated by numbers, but I decided if I was going to have to take care of all the bills and household activities, I better learn how to deal with money better. Besides, I feel I have something to prove to myself. I want to know I can take care of myself. I'm not going to just sit here pining away for Robert. If he's going in search of himself, I might as well use the time to learn about me.

The first months were the most difficult. When we'd talk, there was so much tension. It seemed like we were avoiding talking about us and our future. (I wondered if we even had a future.) He never talked about coming home for a visit or my going over there.

Gradually, things began to shift. One time, as we were hanging up, he said he loved me. I got a big smile on my face, and my heart opened wide. He began asking about what I was doing and began taking a real interest in my school program. He even seemed proud of the progress I was making, and he encouraged me to continue.

During one of our talks, he said he wanted to come home for a visit. Waiting for him to come was agony. Finally being together was wonderful. Things were different, but a lot of the irritability and fear were gone. He seemed happy in a way I hadn't seen him in years. We romped around the house like two little kids. I've known this man for nearly 30 years, but it was like discovering each other for the first time.

One visit led to another and, pretty soon, we were talking about our future life together. He's still overseas, but now I feel like we've connected again. I feel like we're a couple again. He sounds so happy when we talk. He says he is learning new things about his work and about himself.

He says when he comes back he might like to go back to school. He's always wanted to do metal sculpture and explore his artistic side. I never would have believed that my macho, military husband would ever say he wanted to go back to school and learn from someone else.

Robert is finding joy he had lost. He seems so happy now. Although in the past he was always loving, he wasn't a great listener. Now, he really wants to know what's going on with me. I can tell he wants to know me. We're getting to know each other again.

The irritability and anger have just about gone away. We joke a lot more and we're more playful with each other. He seems to have found what he needed to find. Looking back now, I can see that he needed to make a major change in his life, but he didn't know what it was, how to talk about it, or how to bring it about. A lot of his irritability, anger, and blame came out of his need to shift away from his old life to a new life.

What makes me feel the best, what makes me smile and giggle, is that I've got my best friend back. We tease each other and laugh a lot. We talk like we never have before. We're falling in love all over again. He seems to be truly happy with himself now, not at all worried about aging or about the future. I'm overjoyed.

Who would have ever believed that irritability and anger would be the impetus for a life change that was necessary for both of us? Who would have ever believed that his leaving would bring us closer together? Who would have believed that his despair would change to excitement and hope for the future?

I'm so glad I didn't jump ship when things got bad. As we approach 50, we're like little kids who are excited about everything in life. We're planning to travel together and thinking of living in Europe. Why not? I know we'd both love it. It really doesn't matter where we live as long as we're together.

Points of Understanding

• IMS is often a message from our inner world that something isn't right, that some change needs to be made.

• We often fail to recognize our inner callings, instead becoming irritable and angry with those around us.

• We can have an almost irrational need to break away and be free: "I don't understand it; I just have to leave."

• We often see our partners as the ones who are holding us back. In truth, it is our own fears that hold us back.

• If we can talk about our own truths, no matter how confused they are, there is the possibility of a change that we and our partners can live with.

• When we stop blaming others, we find out we are on the same side. We want to be close and also free.

• With courage and trust, we can allow each other the freedom we need to change and grow.

Robert and Jill's case is a particularly extreme one. Most men do not want as drastic a change as the one that Robert requested, and most women don't have the flexibility to do what Jill did. While supporting her husband's move to Europe was a very difficult decision, Jill eventually felt good about it. Had she "just gone along" without finding anything in the situation that benefited her, it wouldn't have worked.

What we can learn from Robert and Jill is that, in the end, IMS may turn out to be the best thing that ever happened to us. It may force us to make changes that need to be made.

In the next chapter, I'll explore how IMS that remains unrecognized and untreated can lead to anger and violence.

CHAPTER 3

"ACTING OUT" IMS
Irritability, Anger, and Violence

The Strange Case of Dr. Jekyll and Mr. Hyde, written by Robert Louis Stevenson in 1886, has become a mainstay of stage and screen throughout the world. It speaks to something in the human psyche, particularly in the male mind.

The story is about Dr. Henry Jekyll, a physician pursuing a lifelong quest to separate the two natures of man and get at the essence of good and evil. Refused help by his peers and superiors, he begins experiments on himself. He meets with success—and shocking results. His own evil nature surfaces as a separate identity: Edward Hyde. Hyde begins murdering the members of the Board of Governors, who previously refused assistance to Jekyll's cause. Throughout the story, Jekyll fights in vain to keep his darker half under control.

I have increasingly met with women who feel their mates have undergone some kind of transformation, from loving to mean, from sensitive to uncaring, from involved to absent. One of these was Sharon, a 38-year-old woman who came to see me because she was at her wit's end and didn't know what to do. Her husband, Barry, is a 42-year-old lawyer whom she describes as "very successful, good-looking, and very physically fit."

> *I have been trying to tell my husband that he has changed into a Jekyll/Hyde personality overnight, but he won't believe me, and he blames all his frustration on me. He pursued me in college, and we got married after graduation. We have been married 19 years, with 18½ of those being wonderful and blissful. He even said just 7 months ago, "You still turn me on after all these years" and "You don't need to wear makeup—you're*

beautiful just the way you are." We have two great kids, a 15-year-old daughter and a 10-year-old son. Barry has been the ideal husband and father for all these years—until now.

Most of this seems to have started after he visited a close friend in Minnesota. Barry came back a day early, freaked out because his friend Warren seemed so depressed. He told me Warren and Susan haven't made love in 9 months. He asked me if I was still attracted to him. I told him of course I was, that he didn't have anything to worry about.

I thought that would settle things, but over the next few weeks, things got worse. He went from being one of the most gentle and kind men I know to being aggressive and hostile. He'd alternate between yelling and screaming at me and withdrawing into silence. At first, he wouldn't tell me what was wrong. Finally, we had a heated discussion that lasted well into the night and early morning. Through the hours that we talked, he told me he "wanted his space." "I'm not sure if I want to continue to be a married family man. . . . I can't decide if I should stay or leave. . . . I've always been someone's son, husband, father. Now I want to put myself first."

How can someone who has been such a dedicated husband and father make such a strong statement that he is not sure he wants to continue to be a family man? He doesn't have the other symptoms [of IMS], like tiredness and weight gain; but he has a hard time kissing me and being touched. When I try to kiss him, he turns his head away. It's devastating.

POINTS OF UNDERSTANDING

• Men experiencing IMS can change, seemingly overnight, from peaceful to agitated, from loving to mean, from contented to discontented.

• Although not always the case, there may be some triggering event, such as a crisis with a close friend or relative.

• Often, a man describes his roles as a son, a father, a husband, a friend. He may feel trapped and start to believe that he has lost touch with his sense of self, his own sense of identity. "When will it be time for me?" he may want to scream.

• In his fear and confusion, he may feel he has to pull away, destroy the old in order to move on to something new.

• As Robert and Jill demonstrated in the previous chapter, however, with the right kind of support and understanding, many men can find themselves without breaking up a successful relationship and loving family.

THE WARNING SIGNS
OF A RELATIONSHIP HEADED FOR A BREAKUP

We all know of relationships in which the couple is forever fighting and unhappy. The heat is too high. Rather than warming, it burns. We also know couples who have given up on having a good relationship and have settled for one where they are physically together but emotionally distant. The cold is not refreshing; it freezes the flow of love and good cheer.

Fortunately, there is someone who has actually studied what works and what doesn't work in relationships. For the past 30 years, psychologist John M. Gottman, Ph.D., author of *Why Marriages Succeed or Fail . . . And How You Can Make Yours Last*, has studied thousands of couples. As a result, he can predict with 94 percent accuracy which couples will stay married and which will divorce. For instance, he found that couples who argue a lot are not more likely to divorce than couples who avoid fights. Conflict, even heated conflict, can be compatible with a healthy marriage.

So what are the warning signs of a marriage that is in trouble?

Dr. Gottman calls them "the four horsemen of the apocalypse." I call them the red alerts of impending IMS damage. The presence of these signs in a marriage is not necessarily, by itself, an indication that the husband has IMS. But most marriages affected by IMS do have these problems. When you see any of these four signs occurring on a regular basis, the relationship is in danger if not treated immediately.

From the least to the most destructive, they are:

1. Criticism
2. Contempt
3. Defensiveness
4. Stonewalling[1]

CRITICISM: THE FIRST RED ALERT

We all have complaints about things our partners do. Complaints are specific. "Listen, dear, I'm angry that you forgot to pick up my coat at the dry cleaner." Criticism, on the other hand, involves attacking someone's personality or character. It is general and, often, blaming. "Can't you ever remember anything? Do I always have to remind you of everything? What's the matter with you?"

It's not a long jump from complaints, which are healthy, to criticisms, which are destructive. What's important is that we recognize the criticism and acknowledge it. "Look, I know I blew up at you and said some things I didn't really mean. I was just angry because I needed that coat for an important meeting tomorrow."

Problems occur when criticisms go unacknowledged. What happens is that we don't feel heard or cared for, so the next time something occurs, we become critical even more quickly. We might say to ourselves, "Damn, she forgot again. She really doesn't care about me. Maybe she's trying to undermine my success at work. She never was supportive of me." A negative cycle gets activated, and criticism often goes back and forth between partners. When we hear continuous "criticism," we know the first red-alert signal of serious IMS is upon us.

CONTEMPT: THE SECOND RED ALERT

What separates contempt from criticism is that, in the former, the tone of voice and language are insulting and psychologically abusive. If you've ever been on the receiving end of contempt, you know that it can hurt more than being hit.

Many of us were raised in families in which our parents abused us with words. One man I worked with in therapy recalled times when, as a little boy, he had done something wrong. He was directed to wait in the toilet until he was told to come out. "That was frightening and humiliating enough," he recalled. "But what happened when I came out was even worse." He broke down in tears and began shaking as he recalled the event. "When I came out, nothing was ever said . . . but my little suitcase was sitting by the door." I asked him what that had meant to him. "It meant I was a useless piece of shit and I'd probably be put out on the street at any time," he said.

Contempt can come in words, or it can be expressed with no words at all, through actions or body language. We are aware of its presence when there are *insults, name-calling, hostile humor,* and *mockery.* The person on the receiving end is often cut to the bone. The person who is delivering the contempt often mocks with hostile justifications. "What's the matter with you? You know I'm only joking." "Hey, lighten up, you take everything too seriously." When contempt enters the picture, we know the second red alert is flashing.

DEFENSIVENESS: THE THIRD RED ALERT

Although Dr. Gottman calls defensiveness the third horseman, I have found that it can often slip into second place. When we are criticized, it is easy to become defensive. When we are ridiculed or held in contempt, we can become even more defensive. Once defensiveness takes hold in a relationship, it is very difficult to hear each other, to resolve problems, or to rekindle the loving feelings that once were present.

When we are caught in defensiveness, we feel that our partners are going out of their way to "get us." It seems that they deliberately misread situations or lie about what really happened. "You agreed to pick up the food for dinner," she tells him with anger and resentment in her voice.

"I did not," he maintains. "I never agreed to do that."

"What?" she replies, her voice rising in disbelief. "Are you crazy? You know you said you'd do it."

"Don't tell me what I know," he yells back. "You're irrational. I can't even talk to you." He stomps out of the room, and she is left feeling furious, hurt, and resentful.

"The fact that defensiveness is an understandable reaction to feeling besieged is one reason it is so destructive," says Dr. Gottman. "The 'victim' doesn't see anything wrong with being defensive."[2] But defensiveness never leads to agreement or better communication; it always tends to escalate the conflict. He often feels that she is out to get him. She often feels she can't rely on him because "he never tells the truth."

One of the first indicators that we are slipping into defensiveness is when we find we are *denying responsibility* before we have even fully heard the other person's concern. No matter what she is concerned about, he insists, vehemently, that he didn't do it.

We all occasionally deny responsibility for things, particularly when we feel guilty or foolish. However, when it becomes a regular occurrence, serious defensiveness has set in.

Sometimes, we will accept responsibility but *make excuses* for the way we have behaved. Here, while we agree that we did it, we claim that it wasn't our fault because some external circumstance beyond our control forced us to act the way we did. Do you know the comedian's defensive quip? It was "The devil made me do it." We come home late and don't call. When our wives get upset, we become indignant. "I couldn't call because I was in a meeting," we say. "You don't expect me to leave in the middle just to tell you I'm alive?"

When we notice that defensiveness has become the rule, rather than the exception, we know the third red alert is trying to get our attention.

STONEWALLING: THE FOURTH RED ALERT

Though all four red alerts are important to watch for, stonewalling may be the most relevant for understanding Irritable Male Syndrome. I still remember my client who concluded that she was living with "an angry brick." She described a relationship that had been good for 12 years of marriage before deteriorating over a period of 8 years. "We used to fight a lot," she said. "I hated the fights, but at least I knew there was some life in our relationship. Now, we never fight and we rarely talk."

When I talked to her husband, he was totally discouraged. "What's the use?" he said. "Nothing I say is going to make any difference. She doesn't give a damn about me or what I want. All she cares about is getting her way. I've given up trying."

By the time a couple has got to this stage, all four lights are flashing. The relationship boat is in danger of sinking, but rather than panic, there is a feeling of resignation. "I just don't have the energy to fight anymore," people will tell me. There can also be a sense of almost magical optimism. "I'm finished trying. Maybe things will just get better on their own." They rarely do.

When I talk to stonewallers, they often claim that they are really trying to keep things under control. They say they are trying to be the rational ones who prevent more fights from happening. They imply that their partners are out of control and too emotional, and that they themselves are just being neutral and balanced. "I just want to get through the day without getting into it again," one man told me. "She gets so distraught. I'm just trying to cool things out."

What stonewallers don't realize is that their lack of emotional expression is not at all neutral. It speaks loudly in its own way, making things worse in the relationship. Often, the more stony and silent he becomes, the more frustrated and angry she becomes. Pierre Mornell, M.D., captured this destructive interaction in the title of his book *Passive Men, Wild Women*. From the outside, it is obvious that the stonewaller is angry and judgmental. All of his feelings are just being held tightly inside.

WHY MOST STONEWALLERS ARE MEN

Although women can be the ones who hold back their emotions, more often it is men. Dr. Gottman estimates that about 85 percent of stonewallers are men. "The reason, I believe, may be biological," he says. People often think that women get overwhelmed by their emotions while men handle things more calmly. That may be just what we see on the surface. "Men tend to be more physiologically overwhelmed than women by marital tension," says Dr. Gottman. "For example, during confrontations, a man's pulse rate is more likely to rise, along with his blood pressure. Therefore, men may feel a greater, perhaps instinctive, need to flee from intense conflict with their spouse in order to protect their health."[3]

Women often get angry at men who won't express their emotions, who won't deal with the conflict in relationships. Many assume that if a man isn't dealing with things, it's because he doesn't care. The contrary may be true. He may care a great deal—so much that he becomes overwhelmed by the emotions that the conflict arouses in him.

Dr. Gottman calls this physiological reaction to emotional upset *flooding*. "First, the male's autonomic nervous system, which controls much of the body's stress response, may be more sensitive and take far longer to recover from emotional upset than does the average female's," says Dr. Gottman. "Second, men may be more reactive because even when they withdraw from an argument, they are more likely to repeat negative thoughts that keep them riled up."[4]

By the time a man gets to the stonewalling stage, things often feel hopeless, both to him and his partner. I want to tell you that they are not. The bad news is that a lot of damage has already been done. The good news is that the pain has usually been caused because neither the man nor the woman understood what was going on. Over the months and years, without trying to, they have made the problem worse. Now that they have an understanding of what is going on, they can—if they have the desire and courage—make things better.

VIOLENCE AGAINST INTIMATE PARTNERS

They are an interesting group of men. They range in age from 25 to 40. They come from all over the area, and they are engaged in a variety of jobs. Most are married, with children. The weather has been nice, so we have been meeting around picnic tables behind the old fire station. People walking by might conclude that this is a group of firefighters or perhaps dads planning a sports day schedule for the coming year.

In fact, the men have all been arrested on domestic violence charges and are part of a year-long program I direct that is set up to teach the men better ways of dealing with their anger. When you talk with these men, you wouldn't suspect that anger is a problem in their lives. They are generally soft-spoken. They care about their families and say they wouldn't do anything to hurt them. Nevertheless, they were each involved in blowups that were serious enough to draw the attention of the police.

Mark is a 27-year-old man who has been married for 4 years. He and his wife have a 3-year-old son. He is good-looking and full of energy, and he talks easily. When asked what brought him to the program, he—like most of the men—describes the incident as though it were quite minor:

> We'd been partying pretty good, and Cary kept bugging me about my drinking. I told her I was fine. Later in the evening, she started in again. She also said I was flirting with her girlfriend at the party. "You're imagining things," I told her. She kept on nagging me in a loud whisper that I was afraid someone would hear.
>
> I've learned to go along with what she says when she's like this. "Yes, uh-huh, sure, I will, whatever you say, dear. You're right. I won't drink any more tonight. I love you." I nod and smile. Her words go in one ear and out the other.
>
> I had a few more drinks. What the hell. I work hard and deserve to have fun on the weekends.
>
> The first thing that got me really pissed off was that she wanted to drive us home. At first, I wouldn't give her the keys.

It's my car, and I don't want her to mess it up. I wasn't drunk. I've driven home safely a hundred times like this. She kept bugging me, and I finally tossed her the keys. Later, when the police came, she said I threw them at her, but she's lying.

As soon as we got in the door, she checked our son and then started ragging me again. "You're always doing this, you're never doing that . . . ," on and on.

I just wanted to go to sleep, so I started for the bedroom. She said something that pushed me over the edge. I turned around and told her to shut up. She made a smart remark, and we got into it. A neighbor heard us yelling and called the police. That's about it.

When I pressed Mark about what he meant when he said, "We got into it," he was pretty vague at first. "I just blew up." When pinned down, he acknowledged, "I pushed her." What else, I wanted to know.

"She started hitting me and I just held on to her arms to defend myself. I pushed her away to keep her from hitting me more, and she fell into the wall. Really, it was no big deal. By the time the police got there, things settled down and would have been fine if they'd have just left us alone."

Points of Understanding

• Those involved in domestic violence are not out of the ordinary. They are, in many ways, just like us.

• Domestic violence is universal. According to the World Health Organization's *World Report on Violence and Health*, "violence against intimate partners occurs in all countries, all cultures, and at every level of society without exception."[5]

• Around the world, events that trigger male violence in abusive relationships are remarkably consistent. According to the *World Report on Violence and Health*, they include the woman disobeying or arguing with the man, her questioning him about money or girlfriends, the man believing the woman does not have food ready on time or is not caring adequately for the children or the home, and the woman refusing to have sex. Another trigger is when the man suspects the woman of infidelity.[6]

• Anywhere from 30 to 80 percent of domestic disputes occur when one or both parties are intoxicated. There is clearly a relationship between alcohol use and domestic violence, though the exact nature of that relationship is not clear. One study conducted by William Fals-Stewart, Ph.D., a clinical psychologist at the Research Institute on Addictions at the University of Buffalo in New York, concluded that men who drink alcohol and also have a predisposition for physical violence toward their female partners are more likely to be violent on the days they drink alcohol.[7] Dr. Fals-Stewart found that the odds of any male-to-female physical aggression are 8 times higher on days when the men drink alcohol than on days with no alcohol consumption, with the chances of severe male-to-female physical aggression more than 11 times higher on drinking days. Moreover, compared to days of alcohol abstinence, the odds of male-to-female violence on days of heavy drinking (six or more drinks in 24 hours) by the male partners are more than 18 times higher—and the odds of severe violence are more than 19 times higher. "We found that the timing of violent episodes was more likely to occur during or shortly after the drinking episodes," says Dr. Fals-Stewart.

• Men tend to minimize the extent or the effect of violent behavior. They usually are quite ashamed of their behavior, although that is not always obvious. They want to deny that it happened.

• Violence is not limited to adults, of course. Young couples also deal with violence in their relationships. According to the National Center for Injury Prevention and Control, "violent behavior that takes place in a context of dating or courtship is not a rare event." As examples, the center offers the following statistics:[8] A review of research found that prevalence rates of nonsexual, courtship violence range from 9 percent to 65 percent, depending on whether threats and emotional or verbal aggression were included in the definition. A study of 13–14-year-old male and female students indicated that 25 percent had been victims of nonsexual dating violence and 8 percent had been victims of sexual dating violence. Summarizing many studies worldwide, the average prevalence rate for nonsexual dating violence is 22 percent among male and female high school students and 32 percent among college students. Females are somewhat more likely than males to report being victims of violence.

• The currently popular "feminist" approach to domestic violence, which posits women as the victims and men as the aggressors, may be misguided—and may actually be making the problem worse. "Women are not merely passive prisoners of violent intimate dynamics," says Linda G.

Mills, a professor of law and social work at New York University in New York City and herself a feminist scholar. "Like men, women are frequently aggressive in intimate settings."[9] More than 20 years ago, *Prone to Violence* by Erin Pizzey and a landmark study by Murray Straus, Richard Gelles, and Susan Steinmetz documented the truth that women and men commit violence against their spouses with roughly equal frequency and at all levels of severity. Yet nearly all of us still believe that domestic violence almost always involves men as the aggressors and women as the victims. Our social perception that women are "good" and men are "bad" often blinds us to the reality. Also, men are much less likely to report abuse. Being abused by a woman is seen to be "unmanly."

As I mentioned earlier, for many years I have led a group for men arrested for domestic violence. In 2002, for the first time, I was asked by the court system to start a group for women who had been arrested for violent acts against their intimate partners. Both groups use a similar process to help participants take responsibility for their actions and find better ways of dealing with anger and conflict.

I have found similar issues in both groups. Violent men and women often feel powerless and use intimidation and anger as a way to control their partners. Violent men and women often have low self-esteem. Both groups are insecure about their positions in their relationships, fearful that their partners may leave them, and quite jealous of their partners' activities. In both groups, alcohol is often a problem and the violent person is usually intoxicated when arguments become violent. Both groups see themselves as victimized by forces outside themselves, such as their partners, the opposite gender ("Women/men are just that way"), or society in general. They often feel hopeless about their abilities to be successful in life.

Part of the reason I have been successful in leading such groups is that I have walked in their shoes—on both sides of the street.

MY OWN STORY OF ANGER AND VIOLENCE

I remember having rages when I was growing up. They would come on at times when I was frustrated or angry, and they seemed to take possession of my senses. I was an only child. I was also shy and didn't have a lot of friends. I did have a dog I loved dearly. He was white with a big brown spot that covered his rump. I called him Spotty. When I was maybe 6 years old, we'd roam the hills behind our house, chasing squirrels and gophers. We were inseparable. Where one of us was, you'd find the other. We'd play together, and I'd laugh and roll around on the grass with him.

There was a darker side to our interactions. At times, in his exuberance, Spotty would hit his head against my chin or nip at my leg. It was at those times that I would often fly into a rage. I would grab Spotty by the throat and squeeze. He'd struggle and choke. I would look down, see what I was doing, and immediately stop. It felt like I was awakening from a trance. I knew it was me who had choked my closest friend, and at the same time I didn't know it was me. I felt terribly guilty and ashamed. I would apologize to Spotty, hold and stroke him, and promise that it would never happen again. He couldn't tell anyone what was happening, and I was too ashamed to let anyone know. The rages continued.

My father had been gone since I was 6, and my mother did various jobs in order to support us. One of her jobs was watching other people's children. One of the kids she watched was a little girl who was 4 or 5 years younger than I. Occasionally, when my mom was busy, she'd ask me to keep an eye on the girl. I dreaded those times because that little girl terrorized me—even though I was much bigger than her and nearly twice her age.

Whenever we were alone, she would pinch me so hard I'd nearly cry. At other times, she would punch or kick me. She would laugh at my tears. I didn't know what to do. I had been taught never to hit a girl, never to hit anyone smaller than me, and to resolve all disputes with words. I was immobilized. She would hurt me, and I would take it, holding my feelings inside and praying that my mother would come back soon. Even by then, I had learned that big boys don't cry, that if you run away from trouble, you are a coward, and that no one likes a telltale. I got through those times by acting like I was made of stone.

As I got older, I would generally keep my feelings buried as deeply as I could. I spent very little time around other kids. School being what it was, kids being what they were, and me being short and slightly built, I was picked on often. Usually, I would joke and talk my way out of danger. I walked away from those situations I couldn't talk my way out of. But if I felt cornered and the taunting, teasing, or attacks didn't stop, I came unglued. I would launch myself like a madman. The other kid would usually end up bleeding.

When I grew up, I was always attracted to feisty, fiery women. An excitement and passion would spark when I was with such a woman. But the same thrills that made our relationship interesting also created a lot of conflict. In one relationship, the last big fight could easily have killed one of us and put the other one on trial for murder. We had been in one of our long-running arguments, and I kept trying to stop things before they got worse. "Let's give it a rest. I'm tired of fighting," I screamed.

She wouldn't let it go. She wanted to keep talking. "You always want to avoid getting down to what's really going on," she screamed back.

I prided myself on never having hit a woman—and this woman had pushed me to my limit on more than one occasion. One of the things that kept us from going over the edge was an agreement that if either of us felt like we were going to become violent, we could call a timeout and go into separate rooms for a cooling-off period. I knew I badly needed to cool down. I could feel the heat coming into my face, the volcanic activity beginning to shake my insides. I called a timeout, walked into my room, and shut the door. The violent panic began to recede.

I wasn't in the room 3 seconds when the door flew open. My wife was standing in the doorway, yelling. "You're always running away, you coward. Why don't you stay and work things out?"

I was instantly on high alert. I could feel the adrenaline rushing through my body. I tried to breathe slowly and talk calmly. "Get out of here. We have an agreement about taking our own space. Leave now; we can talk about this later." I felt the panic rising inside me.

She turned to leave, then wheeled on her feet and came back at me. She came right up in my face and started to poke me in the chest with her index finger. Once, twice, three times she poked me. I lost all sense of control. The red rage took me over. I grabbed her by the hair, pushed her up against the wall, and brought back my fist. I knew that when I hit her I wouldn't stop, I couldn't stop. I didn't care. Nothing mattered but making the rage and terror I felt inside go away. My fist came forward, and it truly was as if in slow motion. I could see the hair and blood and bone. At that moment, I had another sight. It was of my fist going through the wall and coming out the other side of the house.

When I hit the stud in the wall, my fist stopped cold. I could hear bones break. I felt I was about to pass out. We were on our way to the emergency room before the red rage drained out of me and the pain enveloped me. I felt very grateful that I hadn't killed my wife, happy I was going to the hospital instead of to prison, and determined to rid myself of violence in my life.

As you remember from chapter 1, I am still working on these issues. As the saying goes, "You've come a long way, baby." It's good to feel that I have passed the time when frustrations and stresses will lead to violence.

It isn't easy to think about these painful memories or share them in this book. But I have found that the more we share our stories, the more connected we all become and the more we heal.

POINTS OF UNDERSTANDING

• Violence is often passive-aggressive. We are wounded by others, we keep our pain inside, and then it creeps out in anger or explodes in rage.

• Our adult anger is related to trauma we experienced as a child. In all my years as a therapist, I have never seen a violent person who had not experienced some form of violence earlier in life.

• Trauma is in the mind of the person experiencing it. What may seem like a minor event (my father leaving when I was 6, the loss of my mother's attention when she had to leave the home to find work, the little girl pinching and hitting me) can have lasting results.

• Irritability, anger, and rage can poison all relationships, particularly the ones with people closest to us. (They are the ones most likely to trigger past hurts.)

• Even if we hold in our anger, if we become good men, caring men, nurturing men, we expend a tremendous amount of energy guarding against the eruption of that anger. We become like the little boy holding back the waters by putting his fingers in the dike. Even before we run out of fingers, we find we don't have a lot of energy for anything else.

• Whether our anger is being held in check or coming out in irritability, impatience, or grumpiness, we find it increasingly difficult to get in touch with and express our love.

• The cycle of violence can be broken, but we need to catch it as early as possible if we are to prevent damage to our most intimate relationships.

There continues to be a great deal of controversy about the extent of domestic violence, who does more of the abusing, and who suffers the most damage. No one disagrees, however, with the reality that there are some men who abuse women, some women who abuse men, and some men and women who abuse each other. All agree that violence is on the increase and that we need to understand it if we are going to prevent it.

IRRITABILITY AND ANGER
BETWEEN FATHERS AND DAUGHTERS

"It's Will," Sheila told me. "He's acting very strange. He's very moody. He can be quiet and easygoing one minute, then fly off the handle the next. What really bothers me the most is how he treats our daughter."

Sheila went on to tell me that she and Will have three children, two boys and a girl. Both she and her husband had had previous relationships in which they'd married young, got divorced, and vowed they'd never make that mistake again. Though they have been together for 20 years and consider themselves a committed couple, they never formally married.

They live "off the grid" on solar power and have raised their children in a small community, surrounded by nature. She says they have had a great life together. "I really couldn't have asked for a better guy," she says. "He has been a hard worker and has always been kind and considerate. One of the things I've always liked most about him is that he's a great father. He has been totally involved in the kids' school and their extracurricular activities. All three of the kids have been into sports. Our oldest son, Kevin, is also a fine musician. Donald is a computer whiz, and our daughter, Daphne, is a champion volleyball player at her school and has been dancing since she was 5."

"It sounds like a wonderful family," I said. "So what's been going on between father and daughter?"

"I don't know exactly," Sheila said. "They used to be really close, but now they don't get along at all. Will has become critical of Daphne. He wants her to tell him everything she's doing, but it's like he's looking at her with a magnifying glass, looking for flaws.

"He gets totally upset with her around dating. He thinks she's getting involved with boys too soon. She's 14 and not really dating yet. The kids go out in a group. She has told me about a boy she likes a lot, but she says she really doesn't have time to get too serious. Will, on the other hand, is sure that she's having sex, that she's going to get pregnant and drop out of school. He's told me—only half kidding, I think—that she can start dating when she's 25 and have sex after he's dead."

When I spoke to Daphne, she was angry and indignant about her father's behavior. "It's like he's always watching me. I feel like he's just waiting for me to make a mistake or mess up. He used to be so easygoing and fun to be around, but now I dread coming in the door. I never know what mood he's going to be in."

"I can see you're really upset about what's happening between you and your dad," I said. "It sounds like you've been pretty close through the years, and the way he's been acting toward you is causing some real pain."

"I don't know what's the matter with me," Daphne went on. The tears were beginning to flow now. "I must be doing something wrong, but I don't know what it is. I know he loves me, but I don't think he trusts me or respects me."

Will finally came in to see me. It wasn't easy to get him there. He kept saying that he was happy to come in and discuss how things were going in the family. Then he kept missing his appointments. There was always some excuse. One time, he had to work late at the clothing store that he owns. Another time, he said he overslept.

When he finally came in, I suggested that it wasn't easy coming to discuss family issues. I told him I was very appreciative that he had taken the time to come in. At first, he seemed genuinely surprised that his wife and daughter thought something was wrong. He initially said that things were fine and that his wife and daughter were just being oversensitive. Finally, he did say that he was concerned about Daphne. "Kids are growing up way too fast these days. The first thing you know, they're in trouble."

"What kind of trouble are you concerned Daphne's going to get herself into?" I asked.

"I don't know, just trouble," he said.

It was clear that he was avoiding the obvious. "Are you concerned that Daphne's going to get involved sexually?" I asked.

"No. . . . I mean, yes. . . . Well, maybe," Will stammered. "She's a good-looking kid. I can see how the boys look at her. I just don't want anything to happen to her. I want her to finish school and go on to college. She's really an exceptional kid. She's smart. She's good in sports. She has a great future ahead of her."

Will was clearly very proud of his daughter, and I commented on that. "I am," he said. "She could really be something. I had to drop out of junior college and get a job. I always regretted not having finished. She could go all the way. She's smart enough to get an academic scholarship and talented enough to get scholarships in sports.

"I know I'm too hard on her," he said in a quiet voice. "I'm just afraid for her. She's my baby, and I don't want anything to happen to her. I'm her father, and it's my job to protect her."

"I know," I said. "I have a daughter, too. Right now, more than anything, she needs to know that you believe in her. She wants to know that you trust her to do the right things for herself. And let me tell you something else, man to man, father to father: It isn't easy when our daughters begin to grow up. It's a whole different thing than with our sons." Will looked up and was clearly listening.

"We have to balance our desire to protect with the need to let them learn their own lessons, even if it means they make some mistakes. We have to show them how proud we are of what they do but let them live their own dreams of what they want to become. The most difficult thing for me was to acknowledge that my daughter was becoming a sexual young woman. I had to accept that I worried about boys who might want to be sexual with her before she was ready. I remembered my own desires as a teenager who was mad to have sex as soon as I could convince a girl to go along with it.

"And I had to deal with one of the most confusing and upsetting things a father deals with: his own sexual attraction toward his daughter."

Will looked terrified. "I'd never do anything . . . I'd never touch . . . I don't. . . . "

"I know all that is true," I said. "Most men would never even think of touching their children inappropriately. The truth is that as little girls turn into young women, they become attractive in a way that can excite men— even their fathers.

"I have treated thousands of women who suffer all kinds of psychological trauma connected to their relationships with their fathers. A very small percentage of these women have been sexually abused by their fathers or stepfathers. The largest percentage, however, are women whose fathers became angry or withdrawn when the daughters reached the age of sexual maturity.

"Very few men talk with each other about their conflicted feelings when their daughters mature. Many of us avoid the conflict by withdrawing from our daughters. The result is that a large number of young women grow up feeling a real loss of fatherly love between the ages of 13 and 25. There are an equal number of fathers who move into their middle years feeling the grief of a once wonderful father-daughter relationship that somehow got lost along the way."

Will had tears in his eyes. "I don't want that to happen," he said. "What can I do?"

"Well, you're doing it," I told him. "You're showing the courage to make yourself vulnerable and share your feelings with another man. You're willing to talk to your daughter about the feelings beneath your anger—your hopes, your dreams, your fears, and your love. You may even find that your wife would understand your feelings and could support you and your daughter if she knew what was going on inside you."

Will nodded. A great big smile broke out on his face.

"You're a lucky man, Will," I told him. "You have a great family and hopefully will have many years to learn together and love together."

There is often some degree of discomfort between fathers and daughters as little girls become young women. What distinguishes men like Will who experience IMS from the average father is the degree of frustration, discomfort, and guilt the dads may feel. Some men "act out" in the form of irritability and control. Others "act in" with denial and depression, as I will show in the next chapter.

IRRITABILITY AND ANGER
BETWEEN FATHERS AND SONS

Roland is a 15-year-old young man who was referred to me by the school counselor because he told her that he and his father were always getting into fights. Roland was afraid things would become violent.

"He's always on my case for something. I can't ever do anything right," Roland said, beginning to get worked up as he described the situation. "Why can't he just let me lead my life?"

I asked if he'd mind if I brought his father in so we could see if I could help work things out. "I guess," he shrugged with practiced indifference.

Roland's father, Walter, was tall and well-built, and looked to be about 40. He confirmed that he was 42 and did, indeed, keep in shape. He seemed proud that he was the same weight as he'd been when he played football in college. "Of course, it isn't all muscle like it used to be. But I'm doing pretty well for an old man." I looked over at Roland and watched him squirm and roll his eyes. I imagined that he was uncomfortable with his father's bragging and talking about his body.

"So what's going on that the two of you are fighting all the time?" I asked.

"I can't get him to do anything," Walter exclaimed. "No matter what I ask him to do, he gives me a smart-ass answer or a snotty look. Sometimes, I feel like smacking him.

"Not that I ever would," Walter added quickly. "I want him to keep his room at least somewhat clean. Keep his stuff out of the living room. Pick up after himself. Do his homework without having to be told a million times. He wants me to take him here and there, but he doesn't want to do anything to help. I work hard. I don't have time for this shit."

"So, Roland, what's your view of all this?" I asked.

Roland turned away and slumped farther down in his seat.

"See? That's what I'm talking about." Walter nearly jumped out of his seat. "He never wants to deal with any of this." He was starting to get red in the face. I could see what life must be like at home.

"Walter, please, sit back," I said in as calm a voice as I could muster. "Give Roland a chance to answer."

Turning to Roland, I asked again, "I'm really interested in how you see things. Your dad is entitled to his view. You are also entitled to express your own. How do you see things?"

Roland looked up and began to sit up a bit straighter. "I'd do most of the stuff he's talking about if he'd give me a chance. I just don't want to do it at the moment. I'll get around to it."

"But, you never . . . " Walter was about to jump in, but he stopped when I held up a hand.

Roland continued. "It's like he always wants things his way. If it isn't perfect, just the way he'd do it, it isn't good enough. Well, I have my own way." Roland was starting to find his voice.

Over a period of months, I worked with the whole family. As time went on, the family dynamics began to shift and the anger level in the house began to recede. What the family needed was someone from the outside to act as a mediator and help each member hear what the other felt and needed. As Dad was able to listen more deeply to what Roland was saying, his son could express himself more easily. The more Roland expressed himself directly, the less his dad felt so frustrated and angry. Once a negative cycle is broken, a family often feels the benefit of listening to each other and helping each express his needs more directly.

POINTS OF UNDERSTANDING

• Everyone who has lived with a teenager or remembers what it was like being one knows that I have given only the barest outline of the challenges of adolescence. Sons and daughters generally hit their teens about the same time their fathers (and, often, their mothers) hit midlife. Adolescence and "middlescence" are very similar stages. They both include issues of identity, sexuality, wanting to stay at home and wanting to leave, hormonal changes, and emotional ups and downs. When two or more family members are going through these stages simultaneously, the "normal" turmoil is greatly magnified.

• Both teenagers and parents often need guidance on how to accept themselves, each other, and the fact that they are each in a transition toward a new stage of life.

• There are differences between the ways fathers relate to their daughters and their sons. Dads are often concerned and conflicted about their daughters' emerging sexuality. With their sons, issues of dominance and power are most prevalent. These issues are generally present for all parents and teens but are particularly troublesome for men experiencing IMS.

JAPANESE BOYS "ACT OUT"
THEIR ANGER AND "ACT IN" THEIR PAIN

He is known only as the boy in the kitchen. His mother, Yoshiko, won't say his name, fearful that neighbors in the Tokyo suburb where they live might discover her secret. Her son is 17 years old. Three years ago, he was unhappy in school and began to play truant. Then a classmate taunted him with anonymous hate letters and scrawled abusive graffiti about him across the schoolyard.

One day, he walked into the family's kitchen, shut the door, and refused to come out. Since then, he hasn't left the room or allowed anyone in.

The phenomenon of social withdrawal, or *hikikomori*, was first brought to the attention of the Japanese public following a series of highly publicized crimes. In 2000, a 17-year-old hikikomori sufferer left his isolation and hijacked a bus, killing a passenger. Another kidnapped a girl and held her captive in his bedroom for 9 years. Hikikomori dominated newspaper headlines. (It's interesting that the Japanese have become aware of these kinds of social phenomena. In the 1970s, they identified deaths that occurred as a result of overwork. They call such incidents *karoshi*.)

Though most young men affected by hikikomori are not violent, the frustration that many sufferers experience—the desire to live a normal life but the inability to do so—often expresses itself in anger and aggression toward those around them.[10] The trigger is usually an event such as bullying, an exam failure, or a broken romance.

These seem to be the same kinds of issues that young males face all over the world. When these pressures become too much to handle, as increasingly they do, some kind of breakdown occurs. Some boys act out violently. Others withdraw and turn their aggression on themselves.

There are no easy answers to the psychological and physical aggression associated with the Irritable Male Syndrome. One thing we do know is that there is a strong relationship between the "acting out" that males do as we express our anger toward others and the "acting in" that we do as we focus our unhappiness on ourselves. Like the young Japanese males who suffer from hikikomori, we alternate between outward and inward focus. Given that, in the next chapter we will explore the "acting in" side of things.

CHAPTER 4

"ACTING IN" IMS
Irritability, Depression, and Suicide

Although we're discussing "acting out" and "acting in" in two separate chapters, they're really different faces of the same problem. Some people are more prone to "act out" their pain and unhappiness. Others tend to turn their feelings inward. Some people alternate from one to the other.

My father was a man who alternated between "acting out" and "acting in." At times, he would be expansive and full of energy, overflowing with ideas and projects he wanted to do. At the drop of a hat, his mood could change. He could go from joy to rage very rapidly. He could also flip from aggression to depression.

MY FATHER'S STORY

My father was born in Jacksonville, Florida, on December 17, 1906. He was one of eight children whose parents had been born in Eastern Europe and had come to the United States in the late 1800s. From what I heard when I was growing up, he was emotionally sensitive, artistic, and talented. He wrote stories and poetry and put on little plays for the family.

Unlike most of his brothers and sisters, who either went into business or married businessmen, my father went to New York City to become an actor when he was 18. At first, things looked bright. New York in the 1920s was full of glitter and glitz, a great place to be for a young man seeking fame and fortune. That ended in 1929 with the stock market crash and the Great Depression.

It was in New York that my father first met my mother. They married on her birthday, October 5, 1934, after a somewhat stormy courtship.

Economically, things were difficult. Still, they were together and ready to weather the storm. When all money ran out, they would invite friends and acquaintances to their small apartment, and my father would put on a show—readings from Shakespeare, his own poetry, or short stories. The price of admission was a can of food.

As the economic situation worsened, so did his mood. He would snap at my mother. Small things irritated him. How she cooked, cleaned their apartment, or made the bed became points of discord.

There were increasingly heated arguments and fights. He would accuse her of being interested in other men and sleeping around. She would proclaim her innocence and feel hurt. They would make up and make love, and everything would seem all right. And they would be all right—until the next time. There was always a next time.

My mother was always able to find work as a secretary. She had excellent skills, and even in bad times, people needed her talents and experience. However, there weren't a lot of people looking for my father's skills and talents. Not feeling comfortable at home, my father spent more and more time away. "He'd stay away for hours at a time," my mother said. "Sometimes, he wouldn't come home until early the next morning."

His brothers tried to convince my parents to come home to Florida and sell insurance like they were doing. My father laughed, "I'd rather die first." It was a prophetic outburst. He nearly did die. Most of what I know about his life I learned from my mother and the journals that he kept in the last 3 years before he tried to kill himself.

In the preface to his book *Depression Decade,* author Broadus Mitchell describes the Great Depression this way: "The years of our national economic life here described were crowded with emotion and event. They registered the crash from 1929 super-confidence and the descent into the depression—at first dismaying, then disheartening, then desperate."[1] These last words would be an accurate description of my father's slide into the deep emotional depression that can be the result of untreated IMS as well as male menopause.

Here is a note from my father's first journal, written when he was his old self, full of confidence and joy for life.

> *A traveling troupe is putting on a show not far from us. I know them from earlier times, when I first came to New York. They*

are gay and exciting and have an enchanting flavor of holiday.
I look at Kath and marvel at her sweetness and beauty. You
often forget how lovely feminine youth is. The creamlike tex-
ture of skin, a verve, and a buoyancy. Henry is a perfect type of
company manager. He has great big floppy ears, that inevitable
cigar, and a certain softness. Charm is not the exclusive
province of youth. Henry has it as well as Kath.

I feel full of confidence in my writing ability. I know for cer-
tain that someone will buy one of my radio shows. I know for
certain that I will get a good part in a play. Last night, I dreamt
about candy. There was more candy than I could eat. Does it
mean I'll be rewarded for all my efforts? Has it anything to do
with sex?

Journal number 10 was written 3 years later. The economic depression
of the time and the depression going on within his mind had come together.
His entries are more terse, staccato, and disheartening. I still get tears when
I think about how much was lost in such a short time.

June 4th:
Your flesh crawls, your scalp wrinkles when you look around
and see good writers, established writers, writers with credits a
block long, unable to sell, unable to find work. Yes, it's enough
to make anyone blanch, turn pale, and sicken.

August 15th:
Faster, faster, faster I walk. I plug away looking for work,
anything to support my family. I try, try, try, try, try. I always
try and never stop.

November 8th:
A hundred failures, an endless number of failures, until, now,
my confidence, my hope, my belief in myself has run completely
out. Middle-aged, I stand and gaze ahead, numb, confused, and
desperately worried. All around me I see the young in spirit, the
young in heart, with 10 times my confidence, twice my youth,
10 times my fervor, twice my education.

I see them all, a whole army of them, battering at the same
doors I'm battering, trying in the same field I'm trying. Yes, on

a Sunday morning in early November, my hope and my life stream are both running desperately low, so low, so stagnant, that I hold my breath in fear, believing that the dark, blank curtain is about to descend.

Six days after his November 8th entry, my father tried to kill himself. Though he survived, emotionally he was never again the same.

Over the years, I've treated more and more men who face stresses similar to those my father experienced. The economic conditions and social dislocations that contributed to his feelings of shame and hopelessness continue to weigh heavily on men today.

POINTS OF UNDERSTANDING

• What can begin as irritability, impatience, and blame can lead to more serious problems such as depression.

• In men, depression is likely to be triggered by the loss of status, identity, and self-worth that comes from lack of a steady job.

• Most often, an underlying physiological or psychological imbalance is at the root of serious depression.

• Although not all people who are depressed try to kill themselves, most people who become suicidal suffer from depression. "In fact, some kind of depression is almost ubiquitous in those who kill themselves," says Kay Redfield Jamison, Ph.D., a psychiatry professor at Johns Hopkins University School of Medicine in Baltimore, former director of the UCLA Affective Disorders Clinic, an expert on mood disorders, and one of the world's leading experts on suicide and depression.[2]

• Like my father, many men fluctuate between directing their pain outward onto others and inward onto themselves. In the most serious instances, this is an expression of an illness called bipolar disorder, or manic-depressive illness. My father suffered from this illness, though in the 1930s it was not well-known, and he was never diagnosed or treated. It is one of the biochemical imbalances that can be considered a cause of IMS.

• Some aspects of IMS, such as depression, manic-depression, aggression, violence, and risk taking, tend to run in families. If one family member suffers, it is more likely that other members may also have mood disorders of one kind or another. It's important to look honestly at what you know about your parents, grandparents, uncles, aunts, brothers, and sisters.

• Depression and creativity go together. "The cliché is that creativity and depression go hand-in-hand," says Eric Maisel, Ph.D., author of *The Van Gogh Blues: The Creative Person's Path through Depression.* "Like many clichés, this one is quite true."[3]

"Recent research strongly suggests that, compared with the general population, writers and artists show a vastly disproportionate rate of manic-depressive or depressive illness," says Dr. Jamison.[4]

Many men suffer from less severe forms of mood disorders. They may not be suicidal, but they are not happy. They may not be violent, but their anger causes those who live with them to be continually fearful. In their book *Shadow Syndromes: The Mild Forms of Major Mental Disorders That Sabotage Us,* John Ratey, M.D., and Catherine Johnson, Ph.D., suggest that in our highly complex and demanding society, most of us suffer from normal "craziness." We don't fit all the official criteria for major depression, but we have some of the symptoms.

Drs. Ratey and Johnson offer the example of a woman living with an angry man. The scenario they suggest is typical of many couples dealing with IMS. "Living with him is like living on a fault line," they say. "His loved ones never know when the ground beneath their feet will explode. The children fear him; his wife's blood pressure shoots up the moment she hears his key in the lock. But she loves him because when he is not shouting, he is wonderful."[5]

Drs. Ratey and Johnson go on to describe the case of a person who is pessimistic, worried, and anxious about the future. He may eat too much in response to stress, and his love life is a mess. Yet he has never experienced a true, flat-out, stay-in-bed-with-the-covers-over-his-head crash.[6]

Since depression is the core of the "acting in" type of IMS, let's take a deeper look.

WHAT IS DEPRESSION, AND WHY IS IT VITAL TO UNDERSTAND IT?

"Depression is the flaw in love," says Andrew Solomon, author of *The Noonday Demon: An Atlas of Depression.* "To be creatures who love, we must be creatures who can despair at what we lose, and depression is the mechanism of that despair."[7] When we are depressed, we are unable to give love or to feel the love coming from others.

Depression can be roughly divided into large (major) and small (mild) depression. Solomon offers a useful contrast: "Large depression is the stuff of breakdowns. If one imagines a soul of iron that weathers with grief and rusts with mild depression, then major depression is the startling collapse of a whole structure."[8]

"Small" depression is mild only by comparison with major depression. "On the face of it, 'mild' depression sounds like a quiet problem," say Drs. Ratey and Johnson. "We think of the slightly depressed person as an unassuming soul: melancholic, perhaps shy, a meek and retiring figure standing on the sidelines of life's parade. A person who is more trouble to himself than to anyone else."[9]

As you know if you have ever experienced this kind of depression or lived with someone who has, it is far from minor. "Mild depression is a gradual and sometimes permanent thing that undermines people the way rust weakens iron," says Solomon, a journalist who has personally wrestled with depression throughout his life. "It is too much grief at too slight a cause, pain that takes over from the other emotions and crowds them out."[10] Those suffering from depression are "often stressed, frazzled, angry," say Drs. Ratey and Johnson. "They feel overwhelmed and fed up; they are the people who have 'hit the wall.' They bark at their children; they snap at their mates. They are chronically irritable, and they are having no fun."[11]

In his excellent book, which combines the personal, scientific, historical, and political, Solomon cites important facts on depression taken from the National Institute of Mental Health and other research facilities throughout the world. "Though it is a mistake to confuse numbers with truth, these figures tell an alarming story," he notes.

• More than 19 million Americans suffer from chronic depression. More than 2 million of those are children.[12]

• About 10 percent of all Americans will have a major depressive episode. About 50 percent will experience some symptoms of depression.[13]

• Manic-depressive illness, often called bipolar illness because a person's mood fluctuates from out-of-control highs to the lowest of lows, afflicts 2.3 million. It is the second-leading killer of young women and the third of young men.[14]

• For persons over the age of 5, depression is the leading cause of disability in the United States and abroad.[15]

• Worldwide, depression accounts for more of the disease burden, as calculated by premature death plus healthy life years lost to disability, than anything else but heart disease. Depression claims more years of life than war, cancer, and AIDS combined.[16]

• Depression causes or contributes to other illnesses, such as alcoholism and heart disease, and then is masked by these other diseases. If one takes that into consideration, depression may be the biggest killer on earth.[17]

• Only half of Americans who have had major depression have ever sought help of any kind—even from a member of the clergy or a counselor.[18] (Men are much less likely than women to recognize their depression or ask for help.)

• Among the 50 percent of people who do seek help, about 95 percent go to primary-care physicians, whose expertise in diagnosing and treating depression varies greatly.[19]

• Only about 6 percent of the depressed population gets adequate treatment. (Even fewer men than women get good treatment.)[20]

• Nonetheless, about 28 million Americans—1 in every 10—are now taking selective serotonin reuptake inhibitors, the class of drugs that includes Prozac (fluoxetine), Seroxat (paroxetine), Lustral (sertraline), and Cipramil (citalopram).[21]

• Many of those who get treatment drop out or go off their medications. "It's between 1 and 2 percent who get really optimal treatment," says John Graeden, director of the Mental Health Research Institute at the University of Michigan in Ann Arbor.[22]

WHY MALE DEPRESSION IS HIDDEN: MY PERSONAL EXPERIENCE

There have been a number of times in my life when I have been concerned that my irritability and anger might be related to depression. As a professional therapist, I was well aware of the official symptoms of depression according to the *Diagnostic and Statistical Manual of Mental Disorders— Fourth Edition (DSM-IV)*, the main diagnostic reference of mental health professionals in the United States:[23]

> Five (or more) of the following symptoms have been present during the same 2-week period and represent a change from previous functioning; at least one of the symptoms is either (1) depressed mood or (2) loss of interest or pleasure.

(1) Depressed mood most of the day, nearly every day, as indicated by either subjective report (e.g., feels sad or empty) or observation made by others (e.g., appears tearful).

Note: In children and adolescents, can be irritable mood.

(2) Markedly diminished interest or pleasure in all, or almost all, activities most of the day, nearly every day (as indicated by either subjective account or observation made by others).

(3) Significant weight loss when not dieting, or weight gain (e.g., a change of more than 5 percent of body weight in a month), or decrease or increase in appetite nearly every day.

(4) Insomnia or hypersomnia nearly every day.

(5) Psychomotor agitation or retardation nearly every day.

(6) Fatigue or loss of energy nearly every day.

(7) Feelings of worthlessness or excessive or inappropriate guilt nearly every day.

(8) Diminished ability to think or concentrate, or indecisiveness, nearly every day.

(9) Recurrent thoughts of death, recurrent suicidal ideation without a specific plan, or a suicide attempt or a specific plan for committing suicide.

Every time I checked my own feelings and behavior against these criteria for depression, I concluded I was not depressed. I rarely experienced depressed moods as the official manual defined them. I didn't feel sad or empty or appear tearful. I didn't feel a markedly diminished interest or pleasure in all, or almost all, activities. I noted that irritable mood is considered an indication of depression only in children and adolescents.

Whenever my wife or a close friend suggested I might want to "see someone," I could easily brush them off. "Look, I'm a mental health professional. I've been in practice for more than 30 years. Don't you think I would know if I had a problem? And listen, you don't have to take my word for it. Here, look at this." I'd whip out the professionally accepted, official manual as a reminder that according to the standard guidelines, I wasn't depressed. I didn't qualify. Case closed.

It took me a long time to believe that there might be something going on with me despite what the official manual said. It took me even longer to wonder if the manual might be wrong. As a psychotherapist, I saw a lot of depressed people—primarily women. The criteria in the *DSM-IV* seemed to fit the majority of the depressed women. Though it fit some of the men, it seemed to miss a lot of those whom I believed were depressed.

Furthermore, I couldn't understand why the *DSM-IV* would recognize irritability as a symptom of depression in children and adolescents but fail to recognize it as a symptom in adults. I finally acknowledged that my own unhappiness generally expressed itself through worry, anxiety, hypersensitivity—and irritability.

I also remembered my work with people suffering from substance abuse problems. We used to believe that heroin addicts "got well" if they survived to age 40, because we didn't see them showing up in treatment programs after that age. The problem was that they were showing up in alcohol treatment programs.

Since the two types of programs didn't communicate well with each other, we often didn't notice that the spontaneous cures were anything but that. In fact, most of the addicts who had not fully recovered simply switched to a different drug. I wondered if a similar thing occurred with depressed men. In my work with men who used and abused alcohol and other drugs, I found that many were depressed. Their depression had rarely been recognized or treated because it was covered by their alcohol use. In some ways, the men were self-medicating. Many depressed men use alcohol as a way to deal with their painful feelings.

DEPRESSION UNMASKED: HIS AND HERS

I think of male depression as being masked. Millions of men are depressed but don't know it. Millions more know it but are afraid to show it. It isn't "manly" to be depressed. Many of us consider emotional problems to be "feminine." Mental disability also makes us feel helpless and out of control. So those of us who live with depression wear masks that hide our real feelings from others and even from ourselves. People don't know we are depressed because what they see doesn't look like the kind of depression they are familiar with.

"Because men are raised to be independent, active, task-oriented, and successful, they tend to express painful feelings by blaming others, denying their feelings, and finding solutions for their problems in places outside of themselves," say John Lynch, Ph.D., and Christopher Kilmartin, Ph.D., authors of *The Pain behind the Mask: Overcoming Masculine Depression*.[24] Those around us tend to see us as "bad" rather than "sad." This isn't surprising—our behavior seems more aggressive than passive, more wounding than wounded. We cover our unhappiness with drink, drugs, excessive exercise, overwork, and angry moods. "Hidden depression drives several of the problems we think of as typically male: physical illness, alcohol and drug abuse, domestic violence, failures in intimacy, self-sabotage in careers," says psychotherapist Terrence Real, author of *I Don't Want to Talk about It: Overcoming the Secret Legacy of Male Depression.*[25]

As a result, we don't usually associate the idea of "male" with the idea of "depression." Male aggression, yes. Male depression, no.

The view that depression is more common in women is supported by a number of major research studies worldwide. For instance, Susan Nolen-Hoeksema, author of *Sex Differences in Depression,* found that depression is about twice as common in women as in men.[26]

Similar results were found in two large-scale US studies, the Epidemiological Catchment Area Study (ECAS) and the National Comorbidity Survey (NCS). Both studies are noteworthy in that they interviewed people in the general population rather than people who are already in treatment for depression.

The ECAS, sponsored in part by the National Institute of Mental Health, used trained interviewers to survey samples from five different population centers (New Haven, Connecticut; Baltimore; Raleigh-Durham, North Carolina; St. Louis; and Los Angeles). A total of 19,182 persons were interviewed.[27] The study reported lifetime prevalence estimates of psychiatric disorders by gender. In rates of depression, bipolar disorders, and dysthymia (a milder yet chronic form of depression), women outnumbered men two to one. Interestingly, men outnumbered women five to one in alcohol abuse and dependence and antisocial personality disorders.

The NCS was designed, in part, to minimize gender bias in the reporting of symptoms of mental disorders, including depression. This study sampled a total of 8,098 men and women between the ages of 15 and 54. Although considerably more females than males reported symptoms of depression, the ratio was 1.6 to 1.0 rather than 2.0 to 1.0.[28] It was believed that more men reported symptoms of depression in this study than in the ECAS because the NCS interviews were done in such a way as to counteract the male tendency to forget or underreport symptoms.

Neither the ECAS nor the NCS looked at the possibility that the symptoms of depression may be quite different in men than in women.

So although the generally accepted view is that women are much more likely to be depressed than men, these findings may actually be biased in the following ways:

• Men tend to be less in touch with feelings than women and less likely to discuss feelings when asked. In addition, we often view being "down" as being "unmanly," and hence we are less likely to discuss these specific kinds of feelings.

• Since men don't seek professional help as often as women, there tends to be a bias that women are more likely to be depressed.

• When depressed, women often ruminate and replay situations and feelings in their minds. This makes them more likely to remember and report them. Men tend to project their feelings onto others and avoid or deny their problems. They are, therefore, much less likely than women to describe themselves as depressed.

• Male role conditioning is such that we see ourselves as independent. When we have problems, we are action-oriented and solve them ourselves. We don't focus on our feelings or share them with others. Women are more conditioned toward sharing what is going on inside them, whether or not there is a solution. Tom Golden, Ph.D., an expert on male emotions and the author of *Swallowed by a Snake: The Gift of the Masculine Side of Healing*, recognizes that the ways men and women deal with their emotions, particularly feelings of loss, may be quite different. Women often express their emotions through *talk* and *tears*. Men often express them through *action* and *reflection*.[29]

• Finally, symptoms that characterize female depression may be quite different from symptoms of male depression. Problems that are more common in men, such as alcohol dependence, personality disorders, or acting out sexually, may mask depression.

After seeing hundreds of depressed men and women, I concluded that there are significant differences between the ways men and women generally experience depression. After discussing these differences with clients and colleagues between 1993 and 1997, I wrote about them in my book *Male Menopause*.

Here is how I described the difference: Just as there are two life forces in the natural world, the outer-directed *dynamic* and the inner-directed *magnetic,* I believe there are *dynamic depressions* that are expressed by "acting out" our inner turmoil and *magnetic depressions* that are expressed by "acting in" our pain. Men are more likely to experience dynamic depressions, and women are more likely to experience magnetic depressions. Women often express their depression by blaming themselves. Men, on the other hand, often express their depression by blaming others—their wives and children, their bosses, the economy, the government . . . anyone or anything but themselves.[30]

Dr. Jamison uses an analogy from the animal kingdom to describe the different ways men and women react to the stresses of life. "Young male elephants go out and they are quite solitary," she observes. "The only times males get together is during the breeding period in an adversarial role. They're not talking about anything, they're competing.

"Conversely, the female elephants are drawn together and are constantly communicating with each other. Female elephants have a system set up if one is in distress, and they are more likely to be there to help one another.

"Like male elephants in an adversarial role, human men have an 'irritability' that is part and parcel of depression. It's one of the diagnostic criteria for depression and mania. Emotions get so ratcheted up, it's often we see men with short-tempered fuses. It makes depression difficult for others to be around."[31]

I developed a chart to describe the main differences in how males and females experience depression. I want to emphasize that this is a short summary of thousands of people I have seen. Most depressed people will find they identify with some things on both sides of the chart. Some men will find themselves predominantly on the magnetic side, and some women will find themselves predominantly on the dynamic side. However, most depressed men, I believe, will identify more with dynamic depression and most women will identify more with magnetic depression.

I tend to think of these male/female differences the same way I think of height. What do we mean when we say, "Men are taller than women"? We mean most men are taller than most women. We do not mean all men are taller than all women. As a man who is 5 feet 5 inches (1.65 m) tall, I am constantly reminded of that fact. There are a lot of women who are taller than I am. Think of the chart on the next page as a guide to help explore the general differences between male and female depression.

Magnetic Depression (Female)	Dynamic Depression (Male)
Blames herself for problems	Blames others for problems
Feels sad and tearful	Feels irritable and unforgiving
Sleeps more than usual	Has trouble sleeping or staying asleep
Vulnerable and easily hurt	Suspicious and guarded
Tries to be nice	Overtly or covertly hostile
Withdraws when feeling hurt	Attacks when feeling hurt
Often suffers in silence	Overreacts, then often feels sorry later
Feels she was set up to fail	Feels the world is set up to fail him
Slowed down and nervous	Restless and agitated
Maintains control of anger	Loses control of anger
May have anxiety attacks	May have sudden attacks of rage
Overwhelmed by feelings	Feelings blunted, often numb
Lets others violate boundaries	Maintains rigid boundaries; pushes others away
Feels guilty for what she does	Feels ashamed for who he is
Uncomfortable receiving praise	Frustrated if not praised enough
Accepts weaknesses and doubts	Denies weaknesses and doubts
Strong fear of success	Strong fear of failure
Needs to "blend in" to feel safe	Needs to be "top dog" to feel safe
Uses food, friends, and "love" to self-medicate	Uses alcohol, TV, sports, and "sex" to self-medicate
Believes her problems could be solved if only she could be a better _____ (partner, co-worker, parent, friend)	Believes his problems could be solved if only his _____ (partner, co-worker, parent, friend) would treat him better
Wonders, "Am I lovable enough?"	Wonders, "Am I being loved enough?"

THE MALE DEPRESSION QUESTIONNAIRE

It has only been in recent years that there has been an interest in gender-specific aspects of health. "Until now, we've acted as though men and women were essentially identical except for the differences in their reproductive functions," says Marianne J. Legato, M.D., founder of the Partnership for Gender-Specific Medicine at Columbia University in New York City. "In fact, information we've been gathering over the past 10 years tells us that this is anything but true. Everywhere we look, the two sexes are startlingly and unexpectedly different not only in their normal function but in the ways they experience illness."[32]

Initial differences were in such areas as heart disease, drug metabolism, and the immune system. More recently, we have found differences in problems affecting the nervous system. "When their serotonin levels drop, women tend to withdraw and become anxious and reclusive," says Dr. Legato. "Men, on the other hand, respond to low serotonin levels with aggressive behavior and often increase their alcohol intake."[33] She affirms that a man's symptoms of depression may be quite different from a woman's. "He may increase his drinking or become uncharacteristically short-tempered and abusive, while she may find it difficult to leave the house or may have panic attacks in a crowded department store."[34]

In an article, Laura Young, Ph.D., senior vice president of the National Mental Health Association, described her view of the different ways in which men and women experience depression and why male depression may often be less recognized. "The more commonly identified symptoms of depression—sadness, weeping, feelings of hopelessness, and changes in mood—are things women tend to be more willing to show to the public," she says. "When men experience depression, it is more likely to appear as a loss of concentration, anger outbursts, withdrawal, and sleep disruption. Then these symptoms are identified as stress-related, not depression."[35]

I suggest that the Irritable Male Syndrome is one of the categories where male depression is manifested. This idea has been given additional credibility by two Danish studies indicating that males and females show equal levels of depression when an irritability and aggression component is added.[36] There seems to be a clear need for a questionnaire that speaks specifically to the symptoms that depressed men are most likely to experience. Drawing on my own work as well as on that of other researchers on male depression, what follows is the scale I have found most helpful.[37]

MALE DEPRESSION QUESTIONNAIRE

Just as for the Irritable Male Syndrome Questionnaire in chapter 2, I ask men to look as deeply and honestly as they can at feelings or actions that may be difficult to acknowledge. I ask women, too, to be honest,

1. I become stressed out easily.
2. I feel more stressed than usual.
3. I am more aggressive.
4. I find it more difficult to keep self-control.
5. I feel burned out.
6. I feel empty.
7. I experience inexplicable tiredness.
8. I am more irritable, restless, and frustrated.
9. I have difficulty making ordinary, everyday decisions.
10. I have sleep problems: sleeping too much/too little/uneasily or difficulty falling asleep/waking up early.
11. In the morning, especially, I have a feeling of disquiet/anxiety/displeasure.
12. I overconsume mind-altering substances such as alcohol, caffeine, nicotine, marijuana, or pills.
13. I've become overinvolved with exercise, sports, or working out at the gym.
14. Family, friends, or work associates say I have become more difficult to be with.
15. I have felt gloomy, negative, or hopeless.
16. I have a tendency to feel sorry for myself or feel "pathetic."
17. I am becoming more withdrawn from relationships with family or friends.
18. I have become overinvolved with work.
19. I feel that I have to do things my own way.
20. I avoid asking or allowing others to help me.
21. My interest in sexual encounters has changed, either greatly decreasing or becoming almost compulsive.
22. I have an increased intensity or frequency of angry outbursts.
23. I find I deny my sadness and have an inability to cry.
24. I am very self-critical and often focus on my failures as a provider or protector.

though you may have difficulty recognizing and accepting how much pain your man is experiencing.

Reflect on how often you (or the person you are rating) felt the following emotions during the past month.

	Not at All	Sometimes	Frequently	Most of the Time

(continued)

25. I make impulsive plans to have loved ones cared for
    in case of my death or disability.
26. I have very little emotional energy.
27. I feel I have little of value to give others.
28. I have difficulty concentrating.
29. I have eating difficulties, eating either too much or too little.
30. I think that other people go out of their way to irritate me.
31. I don't like to get bored, so I seek high-stimulation activities.
32. When I'm not active, I like to veg out in front of the TV
    or engage in some mindless activity.
33. I have difficulty in situations where I have to wait.
    I try to avoid long meetings or slow-moving activities.
34. I find it difficult to comply with or go along with what others ask.
35. I find it hard to say I'm sorry even when I feel bad
    about something I've done.
36. I have a tendency to worry needlessly when I'm not actively engaged in
    something else.
37. I have a desire to get away from it all.
38. I engage in fantasies of sex through flirtations,
    pornography, or emotional intrigue.
39. I need to show I'm right and have the last word.
40. I feel suspicious and guarded.
41. I feel jealous.
42. I know I feel hostile even though I don't always let it show.
43. I feel things are stacked against me and others disappoint me.
44. My feelings are blunted and I feel numb.
45. I know I protect my boundaries and push others away.
46. I feel that people don't appreciate what I do.
47. I tend to deny my weaknesses and doubts.
48. I have a strong fear of failure.
49. I believe my life would improve if others treated me with more respect.
50. I have a family history of problems with depression, alcohol, drugs, anger,
    anxiety, obsessive-compulsive illness, or attention-deficit disorder (ADD).

For those emotions felt rarely or not at all, score 0; those felt sometimes, score 1; those felt frequently, score 2; and those felt most of the time, score 3. Your total score can range from 0 to 150.

I developed the following results based on my own clinical experience

	Not at All	Sometimes	Frequently	Most of the Time

with people who took the questionnaire and from the 9,453 people who took the Irritable Male Syndrome and Male Depression Questionnaires on the *Men's Health* magazine Web site.

0 to 25: No signs of depression.

26 to 49: Some indications of depression. May need help or watchful waiting to see if things improve or get worse.

50 to 75: Depression is likely and it is advisable to seek help.

76 or more: Depression is definitely present and getting professional help is most important.

I have found that tests like these can be helpful or harmful. They are not good if we use them to hide what is true and "prove" to others that we don't have a problem. They are also not good if we use them to "prove" to someone else that he does have a problem. They are best used to help us understand what is going on in our lives and how we can make our lives the best that they can be.

Remember that one of the primary symptoms of IMS and male depression is that the problem is usually outside a man's awareness. Either he doesn't see that anything is wrong, he's sure the problem is caused by someone else, or he covers over the problem with things such as excessive work, exercise, alcohol or other mind-altering substances, or continual anger and blame.

SUICIDE: WHEN DEPRESSION TAKES OVER AND LIFE BECOMES TOO PAINFUL

Although most people experience the milder forms of "acting in" IMS, it is useful to explore the outer fringes, where death is a very real possibility. Seeing IMS in its extremes can better help us understand what most people experience. Suicide is still a fearsome and taboo subject, one most people would rather ignore. Yet unless we confront the reality of suicide, too many males will continue to die, too many will experience unremitting suffering, and too many families will be destroyed.

In 2000, suicide claimed the lives of an estimated 815,000 people worldwide, the majority of whom were males.[38] The extent to which male suicides outnumber female varies by country. For instance, in certain parts of China, where people most often kill themselves using chemical poisons found on rural farms, the numbers are nearly equal. In all other countries of the world, males outnumber females. The sex disparity is especially high in countries of Eastern Europe and Latin America. Interestingly, Puerto

ESTIMATED ANNUAL SUICIDE RATE PER 100,000[41]			
Age Range	Men	Women	Male : Female
5–14	1.3	0.4	3.25
15–19	18.5	3.7	5.00
20–24	27.2	4.0	6.80
25–64	25.6	6.1	4.20
65–85	49.4	5.1	9.69
85+	75.0	5.0	15.00

Rico has the highest ratio, with males killing themselves at a rate more than 10 times that of females.[39]

In the USA, the number-one risk factor for suicide is being male. In 1999, the suicide death rate was 18.2 per 100,000 among males, and 4.1 in females. This means that male suicides outnumbered female suicides by a ratio of more than four to one.[40] (Ironically, females *attempt* suicide much more often than males do. Females are simply less likely to succeed in taking their own lives.) The imbalance between the number of males who kill themselves and the number of females who die by their own hands is evident throughout the life cycle, as the table illustrates.

Once thought to be primarily a White male problem, suicide is increasing dramatically in the African-American community. "The staggering growth in the number of Black male suicides over the last 10 years is shocking," says Susan Burks, a writer for the *Denver Post*. "Suicide is now the third-leading cause of death for African-American males ages 15 through 24. Suicide among Black youth, once uncommon, showed a rate increase of 233 percent for boys between the ages of 10 and 14. Black teenagers in this country are killing themselves at a rate of five per day. Sixty-five percent of them are using firearms to do it."[42]

Points of Understanding

• Even for children between 5 and 14 years of age, when rates of suicide are low, males are more than three times as likely to kill themselves as females are.

• For teens between 15 and 19, the ratio nearly doubles, with males killing themselves five times as often as females.

• During the young adult years, 20 to 24, the ratio jumps again, to almost seven times as often.

• In the adult years between 25 and 64, the male rate drops slightly and the female rate increases. The ratio of male to female suicides is still more than four to one.

• In the retirement years, between 65 and 85, the ratio more than doubles, with more than nine men killing themselves for every one woman.

• For the "old, old"—over 85—the female rate drops slightly while the male rate increases dramatically. Among people fortunate enough to be alive after 85, 15 times more men kill themselves than women.

• A number of factors may account for the increased suicide rate as men age. Social isolation, divorce, and widowhood are important risk factors for men.[43]

ALBERT'S STORY

Albert is a 14-year-old boy who was first brought in to see me by his mother and father. His parents had two main concerns. First, Albert was constantly getting into fights with his 12-year-old sister, Angela. Second, he was "always getting into trouble in school." In describing the problem with his sister, they said Albert would sneak into her room and take things. His sister also complained that Albert was giving her "funny looks." At school, the problems seemed relatively minor—teasing girls and getting into food fights with other boys.

When I first interviewed Albert, I saw that he was short for his age and somewhat odd-looking. His ears stuck out and his eyes seemed too close together. When I tried to engage him in talk, his eyes roamed all over my office and he had a difficult time maintaining eye contact. He was fidgety and, like many boys his age, didn't seem comfortable sitting. I suggested we go outside and toss around a ball while we talked. I find that boys generally have a much easier time talking when they are doing something else at the same time.

While we tossed the ball back and forth, I asked Albert what he thought was going on between his sister and him. "She's a creep," he told me. "She's the family pet, and she can do anything she wants. I'm always getting punished for things, but Angela gets away with everything." When asked about school, he was reluctant to talk. It took a number of sessions before he told me that he got teased a lot. "They call me dumbo and numb nuts," he told me. "They say I look like a freak and no girl would want to look at me." I asked if he had told anyone about the teasing. He shrugged his shoulders dejectedly. "Why talk about it? No one can do anything. I just want to leave," he said.

In that session and a number of subsequent ones, I found out how shamed and deeply wounded Albert felt. He talked about wanting to run away and live somewhere else, though he didn't have any real plans for how he'd accomplish that or where he'd go. He also admitted he'd thought about "checking out" permanently.

Many parents are often afraid to talk about the subject of suicide even when their child gives out clear signals that he is extremely unhappy and hints of wanting to "leave." As an adult who has worked for many years with children and teenagers who are depressed and suicidal, I still have a difficult time believing that people so young, with so much life ahead of them, would want to die. I have to remind myself that their youth may be a major risk factor. Since their life experience is limited, they don't know that things change, that despair can turn into hope. For many depressed youth, the despair is all there is, all there was, and all there ever will be.

Adults also fear that they might plant the seed of suicide in a youngster's mind. "If I ask him about it, will that make him start thinking about it?" The answer is no. People who are depressed may think about suicide without any outside help. They won't catch the suicide bug by talking about it. Quite the opposite—talking about it can relieve the pressure of feeling alone and cut off.

I am usually quite direct in my questions. "Albert, you sound really sad and hopeless. Have you ever thought of just wanting to end it all?" Wherever the discussion goes from there, the taboo topic is out in the open. Even if the answer is no, the person knows it's okay to talk about these issues in the future. For Albert, the answer was yes.

Gradually, we began to talk more about the roots of his despair. He told me that he had always felt different, that he had never really fit in. His father played football in college and was an avid sports fan. He was always trying to get Albert interested in sports but that was not where Albert's interests lay. "I've always been interested in drawing," Albert told me. In subsequent sessions, he showed me some of his artwork. It was quite good—intricate patterns, dragons, and a series of big-breasted women.

"My dad thinks I'm a sissy because I don't like sports. He won't even look at my drawings. My mom's all involved with Angela. 'Angela needs this. Angela needs that.' She doesn't have time for me."

When I asked about the pictures of the women, he was shy at first. Eventually, he opened up to a discussion of sexuality. He told me he thought about girls all the time and masturbated a lot. He was quite worried and sure he "did it too much." He said he felt ashamed when he'd sneak magazines into the bathroom. He had found many Internet sites with sexual content and masturbated to those images. Because his mother often came into his room without knocking, he was always afraid of getting caught.

When I told him teenage boys usually masturbate a great deal, he seemed relieved. However, he still felt he was somehow "perverted." He told me he had fantasies about his younger sister, and he wasn't satisfied when I told him that was normal as well. "There's a big difference between having fantasies of sex with your sister and acting that out or touching her," I told him.

What he seemed most worried about was that he would never be able to have a sexual relationship with a girl. "They tease me, too," he told me. "I try to get their attention, but they just laugh at me. Sometimes I feel like. . . . " I could see his anger rising and how difficult it was for him to keep control. "I feel like I want to murder them. I want to wipe those grins right off their faces.

"I'm just a total failure," he told me with a mixture of sadness and resignation in his voice. "I'm never going to get a girl. I'm never going to amount to anything. No one really gives a damn."

"You're here in my office," I reminded him, "and I care. There's a lot you can do to make things better in your life. I want to help. Are you up for the challenge? It won't be easy, but I'll work with you and stick with it if you'll work as well. What do you say?"

Albert looked up and shrugged. "I guess," he said. Coming from a 14-year-old boy in Albert's situation, I took that as a resounding "Yes."

POINTS OF UNDERSTANDING

• Teenage boys are much more likely to express their sadness through anger than are girls.

• Traditional school counseling and therapy are often not best suited for connecting with young males. Finding something to do together makes talking much easier.

• Even though teenagers, and boys in particular, often act hostile or indifferent to our offers to help, they are hungry for someone who really wants to understand them.

• Remember that what seem to adults like small slights can seem huge to teenagers. Teens' self-esteem and connection to others is very vulnerable. It doesn't take much—a negative word, an indifferent stare, a lack of appreciation, a rebuff from a girl—to throw them into a tailspin.

• Being laughed at, teased, or humiliated is one of the most crushing experiences that young people—particularly males—go through. The resulting shame is at the core of much of the violence we see in young males. "I have yet to see a serious act of violence that was not provoked by the experience of feeling shamed and humiliated, disrespected and ridiculed," says James Gilligan, M.D., author of *Violence: Our Deadly Epidemic and Its Causes.*[44]

• Sex, success, and self-esteem are very much intertwined for teenage boys. We need to find ways to reach out to them and discuss these often taboo topics. One of the techniques I used with my teenage son (and, on separate occasions, with my teenage daughter) was to get in the car to go somewhere together. I would always take the long way around and use the time to talk about all the things I wished my father had said to me when I was a teen. Usually, my son would be silent or make disgusted or disgusting sounds. But he couldn't escape. Later, once he became an adult, we joked about those rides. He even told me they were helpful at times.

• While suggestions of suicide should always be taken seriously whenever anyone makes them, we need to be particularly concerned about young males. They are much less likely than young females to let us know that they are becoming increasingly depressed and much more likely to complete a suicide attempt.

A number of researchers who work with boys recognize the different ways boys express their unhappiness. "We see boys who, frightened or saddened by family discord, experience those feelings only as mounting anger or an irritable wish that everyone would 'just leave me alone,'" say

Dan Kindlon, Ph.D., and Michael Thompson, Ph.D., in their book *Raising Cain: Protecting the Emotional Life of Boys.* "Shamed by school problems or stung by criticism, they lash out or withdraw emotionally."[45]

"In so many cases, what in the teenage years may look like a *bad* boy is really a *sad* boy, whose underground pain may lead him to become extremely dangerous to others, or much more likely, to himself," says William S. Pollack, Ph.D., author of *Real Boys' Voices;* co-director of the Center for Men at McLean Hospital in Belmont, Massachusetts; and assistant clinical professor of psychology in the department of psychiatry at Harvard Medical School. "Tragically, boys rarely 'attempt' suicide; when they reach out for a knife, a rope, or a gun, generally they are not crying for help. Rather, they are very much trying to get the job done."[46]

The pain and despair that so many males, young and old, are experiencing is immense. We often avoid looking at the problem because it forces us to confront the anguish we feel for our lost boys and men. We want to understand why males are suffering and what can be done about it. In the next part of the book, we will explore some of the underlying causes of the Irritable Male Syndrome.

PART 2

UNDERSTANDING

"Men have always been afraid that women could get along without them."
—anthropologist Margaret Mead

CHAPTER 5

THE END OF MEN
Are Males an Endangered Species?

The idea that men are in decline and may face extinction would have seemed ludicrous even a few years ago. Now, more and more people are taking it seriously. In November 2001, the prestigious *British Journal of Medicine* published an editorial by Siegfried Meryn, M.D., titled "The Future of Men and Their Health: Are Men in Danger of Extinction?"

The *British Journal of Medicine* is not a publication known for making wild claims. It is one of the most scientifically grounded professional journals in the world. Dr. Meryn is not a "pop psychologist." He is a medical doctor with a worldwide reputation as an expert in the field of men's health. He is professor of medicine at the University of Vienna and chairman and president of the World Congress on Men's Health.

"Although there is still a long way to go in most societies around the world, it is clear that women can perform (and on most occasions outperform) pretty much all the tasks traditionally reserved for men," says Dr. Meryn in his editorial. "In most of the developed world, women are starting to outnumber men in medical schools and making rapid gains in terms of equality in compensation and opportunities in the workforce.

"Will we see the gap in life expectancy between men and women widen as the gaps in social determinants of health become narrower? The answer is probably yes, unless women continue to adopt the same negative behaviors that characterize men today. With the advent of sperm banks, in vitro fertilization, sex-sorting techniques, sperm-independent fertilization of eggs with somatic cells, human cloning, and same-sex marriages, it is also reasonable to wonder about the future role of men in society."[1]

In her book *When Smoke Ran Like Water: Tales of Environmental*

Deception and the Battle against Pollution, top health researcher Devra Lee
Davis, Ph.D., devotes an entire chapter to the serious decline in male reproductive viability that seems to be caused by our destruction of the environment. Dr. Davis, a senior advisor to the World Health Organization,
notes in the chapter called "Save the Males" that men are having increasing
difficulty fathering children and that males are actually in decline. "Now
it looks like something is wrong with baby boys," she cautions. "Fewer
boys are being born today than 3 decades ago, and more of them have
undescended testes and effects in their penis. More young men are getting
testicular cancer than as recently as the early 1990s, and they are developing it at younger ages. Some trendy magazines have even suggested that
male health is an oxymoron."[2]

So what do I mean when I say that men are in danger of extinction?
First, I believe the whole human race is in danger of destroying itself, either
through wars or environmental destruction. Obviously, if we kill off
humanity, the men go as well.

Second, I believe that sometime in the not-too-distant future, as the
world sees a need to regulate population growth, society might decide that
there are too many males and limit the number of males that are born.
Some even suggest that we could eliminate males completely. "Man himself may in the end become redundant," says Steve Jones, Ph.D., a professor
of genetics at University College London and author of *Y: The Descent of
Men,* "for his sperm can be grown in animal testes, and in mice at least an
egg can be fertilized with a body cell from another female, which cuts out
the second sex altogether."[3]

Third, men are killing themselves through suicide, homicide, and wars.
This is another factor that could eventually lead to a severe reduction in the
male population.

Finally, males could continue losing significant roles in society and might
become psychologically extinct, if not physically so.

Whether these possible losses ever come to pass, they still influence our
psyches. If you ask the average guy why he is so irritable, he is unlikely to
say, "Because I'm afraid we're going to blow ourselves up" or "Because
environmental pollution is destroying the quality of my sperm" or
"Because I'm losing my role in society and I might be eliminated from
meaningful involvement in work and relationships" or "Because I'm feeling
depressed and I want to hurt myself or someone else." Most men will

blame their bad feelings—if they allow themselves to feel at all—on such things as the way their wives treat them, job stresses, traffic jams, terrorists, the economy, the government, or general worry about the future.

Certainly, things like family conflict, job stress, and the state of the economy can cause anyone to become irritable. But there is more going on than meets the eye. If we are going to help ourselves and each other prevent and treat IMS, we have to have a better understanding of the causes of male insecurities.

As we go through the ways in which men feel endangered and insecure, remember that we aren't speaking of all men. We nevertheless need to recognize the ways in which these underlying issues affect all men's sense of security. We might think of these things as the foundation of manhood. There are many ways in which the foundation itself is weak, beginning with our genetic makeup and extending to our upbringing and socialization.

WHAT DOES IT MEAN TO BE MALE?

Nothing is closer to one's sense of self than a sense of "maleness" or "femaleness." When a baby first emerges from the womb, the mother (and increasingly, the father, who is in the delivery room) hears, "Congratulations, it's a boy" or "It's a girl." Many parents-to-be say that they would be happy with either a boy or a girl, but none can ignore the fact that boys and girls are not alike.

An increasing body of evidence accumulated over the past 25 years shows that males and females are different in many ways. According to Bobbi S. Low, Ph.D., a professor of resource ecology at the University of Michigan in Ann Arbor, "New research in evolutionary theory, combined with findings from anthropology, psychology, sociology, and economics, supports the perhaps unsettling view that men and women have indeed evolved to behave differently—that, although environmental conditions can exaggerate or minimize these differences in male and female behaviors, under most conditions each sex has been successful as a result of very different behaviors."[4]

We will see that a good deal of what leads to the Irritable Male Syndrome can be understood in terms of the ways the biology of being male interacts with the environment in which we find ourselves. It isn't a question of nature versus nurture. Our biological nature has an influence on our environment, and our environment can have a profound impact on our biology. Let's take a look at some of these male attributes and see how they make men so vulnerable to stresses that can lead to increased irritability.

MAKING BABIES: "WILL MY GENES BE CARRIED ON?"

None of your direct ancestors died childless. Think about that for a moment. It's obvious that your parents had at least one child. Your mother's parents and your father's parents had children. If you could look backward and trace your ancestors as far back as you could go, you would find an unbroken chain of reproductive success. Over a period of 5 million years, not one of your family members dropped the ball. You are a product of their reproductive success, so you can bet that what it takes to pass on your genes to the next generation is built into your attitudes, desires, and behaviors. From an evolutionary perspective, whatever contributes to your genetic success makes you feel good. Whatever stands in the way of your evolutionary success makes you feel irritable, angry, and depressed.

"The goal of an animal is not just to survive but to breed," says Matt Ridley, author of *The Red Queen: Sex and the Evolution of Human Nature*. "Indeed, where breeding and survival come into conflict, it is breeding that takes precedence; for example, salmon starve to death while breeding. And breeding, in sexual species, consists of finding an appropriate partner and persuading it to part with a package of genes."[5]

THE DATING AND MATING GAME: SMALL SPERM, LARGE EGG

Biologists have very simple and useful definitions of *male* and *female*, whether they are studying ferns, fish, or human beings. An individual can make either many small gametes (sex cells) or fewer but larger gametes. Individuals that produce smaller gametes are called males, and ones that produce larger gametes are called females.

The small gametes are designed to fuse with a large one, and the large ones are designed to fuse with a small one. Although the human egg is microscopic, it is large enough to house 250,000 sperm. An individual must invest in either a few large eggs or millions of sperm. So the female strategy produces gametes that have a higher rate of survival and fertilization.

A woman ovulates about 400 eggs in her lifetime. The male strategy is to produce as many gametes as possible, to increase the chances of finding a large one. A healthy male produces 500 million sperm per day.

Thus, there will always be many times more sperm than there are eggs. Consequently, sperm must compete for access to those rare eggs. This makes a huge difference in how we act as males. Generally, it is easier to move the smaller sperm to the larger egg than vice versa, and so it is the male who seeks out the female and the female who makes a selection from among those males who come courting. "Males are in flux in almost every way: in how they look and how they behave, of course," says Dr. Jones, "but, more importantly, in how they are made. From the greenest of algae to the most blue-blooded of aristocrats, their restless state hints at an endless race in which males pursue but females escape."[6]

This is one of the reasons that there will always be more irritable and insecure men than women. Because they carry the larger, scarcer, valuable eggs, women will always be sought after more than men. Men will always have to take the initiative, and women will always get to choose the most attractive male from among those who present themselves, rejecting the others. This also helps explain why young men, more often than young women, take risks that put their lives in danger. During the key reproductive years, males must compete against other males for access to females. Bull moose and bullheaded 20-year-olds must be willing to fight other males or take other risks in order to have the best chance of having sex with the most attractive females available. In the game of life, women hold more of the evolutionary valuable cards.

Reproductive strategy also helps us understand why older men are more likely than older women to have affairs or leave their partners. Rarely do older men hook up with women the same age as their wives. They almost always choose younger women. Why? Older men have the biological potential to have more kids. If they stay with their 50-year-old postmenopausal wives, their genetic potential is limited. If, on the other hand, they find 35-year-old or 25-year-old women to have sex with, the men's genetic success can be increased.

Remember, this does not occur on a conscious level. Few men say to themselves, "I'd like to increase the success of my genes, so I think I will leave my 50-year-old wife and date two 25-year-olds in the hope that I might have more children to carry my genes." More often, this urge expresses itself as, "I love my wife, but we just don't have the old spark we used to. We fight all the time. She just doesn't like to do the things that I like to do. And, well, there's this woman at work. . . . "

Let me be very clear here: I'm not saying that, because men have a genetic urge to leave their wives or have affairs with younger women, acting on these urges is a good thing. I'm not saying that we are prisoners of our genes and have no power to decide what is right or wrong. I am simply saying that our biological urgings to reproduce and pass on the most genes to the next generation is powerful. If we are not aware of the strength of these desires, we will have less success controlling them.

Remember, too, that for every older man who hooks up with a younger woman, there is a younger woman who wants to connect with an older man. As we will discuss later in the chapter, women have a biological attraction to successful men with resources to share with them and their children. These are often older men, who have had a chance to become successful in the world.

Yet biology is not destiny. Older men don't have to leave their wives and have affairs. Younger women don't have to go after the husbands of those older wives. We all can choose, but the choices aren't always easy.

We may not like the ways our genes influence us, but we better pay attention to their pull. "Genes never sleep," say Terry Burnham, Ph.D., and Jay Phelan, Ph.D., two experts on genetic influences and the authors of *Mean Genes: From Sex to Money to Food—Taming Our Primal Instincts.* "Instead of a blissful 'They got married and lived happily ever after,' gene fairy tales end with offspring and more offspring—any way the genes can get them."[7] In order to further our understanding of the ways males are losing position in the game of life, we need to look more deeply at the differences between males and females.

"Y AM I LIKE THIS?"

According to UN statistics, compared with women, men have higher death rates for all 15 leading causes of death and die 6 years younger. In fact, from the moment of conception, males are more fragile and vulnerable than females.[8] Part of the reason is the biology of the male fetus, which is little understood and not widely known. More male than female embryos are conceived, possibly because the sperm carrying the Y, or male, chromosome swim faster than those carrying the X, or female. The advantage is, however, immediately challenged. External maternal stress around the time of conception is associated with a reduction in the male-to-female sex ratio, suggesting that the male embryo is more vulnerable than the female.[9] The male fetus is at greater risk of death or damage from almost all the obstetric catastrophes that can happen before birth.[10] Perinatal brain damage,[11] cerebral palsy,[12] congenital deformities of the genitalia and limbs, premature birth, and stillbirth are more common in boys.[13] So although 120 male babies are conceived for every 100 females, the ratio of live births falls to 105 boys per 100 girls.[14]

By the time a boy is born, he is, on average, developmentally some weeks behind a girl of the same age. According to a study reported in the journal *Behavioral Brain Science,* "a newborn girl is the physiological equivalent of a 4- to 6-week-old boy."[15]

So we see that right from the moment that sperm penetrates the egg, males begin to experience problems. Some of us don't make it. We die off early. Others survive to make it into the world but are at a greater handicap than our female counterparts.

THE PSYCHOLOGICAL HAZARDS OF BEING MALE

William S. Pollack, Ph.D., and Ronald F. Levant, Ed.D., have spent a great deal of their professional careers working with males. Dr. Pollack is the co-director of the Center for Men at McLean Hospital in Belmont, Massachusetts; assistant clinical professor of psychology in the department of psychiatry at Harvard Medical School; and author of *Real Boys' Voices.* Dr. Levant is dean and professor of psychology at Nova Southeastern University in Fort Lauderdale and founder and former director of the Boston University Fatherhood Project. In their excellent book *A New Psychology of Men,* Drs. Pollack and Levant describe the behaviors that are often at the core of male susceptibility to later problems in life. Men suffer under a code of masculinity that requires them to be:

- Aggressive
- Dominant
- Achievement oriented
- Competitive

- Rigidly self-sufficient
- Willing to take risks
- Adventure seeking
- Emotionally restricted
- Constituted to avoid all things, actions, and reactions that are potentially "feminine"[16]

We must remember that a good deal of this male behavior has genetic roots and evolutionary survival value: Aggressive, competitive, stoic men who take risks are more likely to reproduce. The problem is that men in our culture, according to Dr. Pollack, are pretty much limited to a menu of three related feelings: rage, triumph, lust. "Anything else and you risk being seen as a sissy," says Dr. Pollack.[17] He blames this perception on the persistent image of the dispassionate, resilient, action-oriented male—the Marlboro Man who is self-sufficient and self-absorbed. Although in the past 10 years there has been progress in helping men expand our range of emotions, for most men, our ancestral heritage and the training we grew up with still restrict us.

In his book *Real Boys: Rescuing Our Sons from the Myths of Boyhood*, Dr. Pollack proposes that boys "lose their voice, a whole half of their emotional selves," beginning at age 4 or 5. "Their vulnerable, sad feelings and sense of need are suppressed or shamed out of them"—by their peers, their parents, the great wide televised fist in their face.[18] "If you keep hammering it into a kid that he has to look tough and stop being a crybaby and a mama's boy, the boy will start creating a mask of bravado," says Dr. Pollack.[19]

In his book *The Hazards of Being Male: Surviving the Myth of Masculine Privilege*, psychologist Herb Goldberg summarizes what many have come to believe about men. "The American man an endangered species?" he asks. "Absolutely! The male has paid a heavy price for his masculine 'privilege' and power. He is out of touch with his emotions and his body. He is playing by the rules of the male game plan and with lemming-like purpose he is destroying himself—emotionally, psychologically, and physically."[20]

WHAT HAVE WE DONE TO OUR SONS?

In the past 10 years, a lot of attention has been paid to the stresses placed on girls growing up. More recently, we have begun to recognize what is happening to our boys. "In-depth research shows that girls and boys each have their own equally painful sufferings," says psychologist Michael Gurian, author of *The Wonder of Boys*. "To say girls have it worse than boys is to put on blinders."[21]

Boys who have trouble grow into troubled teens and become adults who are much more likely to suffer from the Irritable Male Syndrome. "If there's one thing we've learned," say Dan Kindlon, Ph.D., and Michael Thompson, Ph.D., in their book *Raising Cain: Protecting the Emotional Life of Boys*, "it's that, unless we give him a viable alternative, today's angry young man is destined to become tomorrow's lonely and embittered middle-aged man."[22]

Understanding what our boys experience can help us better deal with IMS in our teenagers. It can also make us aware of the stresses many adult males experienced growing up. Understanding our boys can also alert us to the kinds of stresses that will form the character of the men of the future.

SCHOOLS ARE LEAVING OUR BOYS BEHIND

In 1990, psychologist Carol Gilligan, co-editor of *Making Connections: The Relational Worlds of Adolescent Girls at Emma Willard School*, announced to the world that America's adolescent girls were in crisis: "As the river of a girl's life flows into the sea of Western culture, she is in danger of drowning or disappearing."[23] A number of other popular books focused on the problems our daughters were experiencing in school. "Something dramatic happens to girls in early adolescence," said Mary Pipher, author of *Reviving Ophelia*. "Just as planes and ships disappear mysteriously into the Bermuda Triangle, so do the selves of girls go down in droves. They crash and burn."[24]

These concerns were taken up by women's groups and organizations concerned about the effect of society on the success of our daughters. As a result, money was poured into the schools to make changes that would help girls. Some researchers feel that the data supporting the view that girls are being shortchanged is suspect and that many of the changes that are meant to be "girl friendly" in fact discriminate against boys.

Interestingly, it is a woman who is one of the strongest advocates for boys. Christina Hoff Sommers has a Ph.D. in philosophy from Brandeis University in Waltham, Massachusetts, and was formerly a professor at Clark University in Worcester, Massachusetts. "The research commonly cited to support the claims of male privilege and sinfulness is riddled with errors," she says. "Almost none of it has been published in professional peer-reviewed journals. . . . A review of the facts shows boys, not girls, on the weak side of an educational gender gap."[25]

I don't find it helpful to debate whether females or males have a worse time of it. My experience raising both male and female children is that each sex has unique strengths and unique difficulties. Having worked in the classrooms when my son and daughter were growing up, it seems to me that both girls and boys are getting shortchanged. Here, though, I want to focus on boys since a great deal of attention is already being focused on girls and since educational programs seem to be geared more to the success of our daughters.[26]

Data from the U.S. Department of Education, and from several university studies worldwide, show that boys are falling behind in their education. Girls get better grades.[27] They have higher educational aspirations.[28] They follow a more rigorous academic program and participate in greater numbers in the prestigious Advanced Placement program.[29]

"A 1999 *Congressional Quarterly Researcher* article about male and female academic achievement takes note of a common parental experience; 'Daughters want to please their teachers by spending extra time on projects, doing extra credit, making homework as neat as possible,'" notes Dr. Sommers. "'Sons rush through homework assignments and run outside to play, unconcerned about how the teacher will regard the sloppy work.' In the technical language of education experts, girls are academically more 'engaged.'"[30] Dr. Sommers also cites studies that have found that "engagement with school is perhaps the single most important predictor of academic success."[31]

It should not surprise us, then, that girls read more books.[32] They outperform males on tests of artistic and musical ability.[33] More girls than boys study abroad.[34]

Conversely, more boys than girls are suspended from school. More are held back and more drop out.[35] Boys are three times as likely as girls to be enrolled in special education programs and four times as likely to be diagnosed with attention deficit disorder (ADD).[36]

"Demographers predict that by 2007, 9.2 million American women and only 6.9 million American men will be enrolled in college," says anthropologist Helen Fisher, Ph.D., in her book *The First Sex: The Natural Talents of Women and How They Are Changing the World.* "The contrast is even greater among part-time, adult, and minority students. Women are also gradually closing the education gap in much of the rest of the world."[37]

In 1998, the Horatio Alger Association, a 50-year-old organization devoted to promoting and affirming individual initiative and the American dream, released a survey that contrasted two groups of students: the highly "successful" (approximately 18 percent of American students) and the "disillusioned" (approximately 15 percent of students). They noted that the students in the successful group work hard, choose challenging classes, make schoolwork a top priority, get good grades, participate in extracurricular activities, and feel that their teachers and administrators care about them and listen to them. According to the report, the successful group is 63 percent female and 37 percent male.

At the other extreme, the disillusioned students are pessimistic about their own futures, get low grades, have minimal contact with their teachers, and believe that there is no one they can turn to for help. We would certainly say the disillusioned group has become demoralized. According to the report, "nearly 7 out of 10 are male."[38]

These are the young men who will suffer from the Irritable Male Syndrome. They will be more likely to drop out of school, get involved with alcohol and drugs (more boys than girls are involved in crime, alcohol, and drugs[39]), have difficulty finding good employment opportunities, have very chaotic marriages, and engage in violent or suicidal behavior (between the ages of 15 and 24, males kill themselves nearly six times more often than females[40]).

If we pay attention to our young men, they will have a better chance of growing up to be responsible and loving adults. Whether or not we help them, those who avoid falling victim to societal or self-inflicted violence will grow up—and the great majority of them will go on to find partners, start families, and likely pass on their experiences to the next generation of young males.

MALES ARE BECOMING THE NEW SECOND SEX

In her book *The First Sex,* Dr. Fisher uses her considerable talents to survey the world of the 21st century, concluding that women will increasingly find their talents and skills to be useful while men, unless there is considerable change, will find themselves falling farther behind. She finds that the differences in the way males and females think will favor women. Women, she says, more regularly think contextually. They take a more holistic view of issues. Men, on the other hand, tend to compartmentalize their attention. Their thinking is more channeled and focused.[41] In a world that is becoming increasingly complex, where context is everything, men are at a considerable disadvantage.

Power in the world is shifting and will continue to do so. Countries like the Soviet Union have come apart. Huge corporations like Enron have folded. The power of the United States government is being challenged from within and without. Centralized, top-down power is shifting everywhere toward a more egalitarian, shared power.

This way of being is familiar to women and often foreign to men. "Men regularly associate power with rank and status," says Dr. Fisher. "Women more often see power as a network of vital human connections." We can witness this in children on the playground. Boys play war games and sort themselves into hierarchies. They compete to see who will be the leader, the team captain, the top dog. Girls are more interested in the relationships that they form through play. They care about each other's feelings more than boys do.

"If girls want to be liked," says Dr. Fisher, "boys want to be respected."[42] The need for respect is at the core of manhood. From an evolutionary point of view, a man who wasn't respected among his peers didn't get the opportunities to participate fully in male-oriented activities such as hunting. If he wasn't a good hunter who could earn the respect of his peers and provide for a mate, he was less attractive to women and less likely to reproduce. For a man, this is evolutionary death. This is why some men, in extreme situations, feel that they would prefer physical death to dishonor and loss of respect.

In our modern world, this male need for respect is becoming increasingly difficult to fulfill. Career advancement has always been a part of men's feeling of self-respect, and as we've seen, more and more men lack the education to compete for the best jobs.

Compounding this challenge, women's way of communicating is becoming the business model of the future, according to Edie Weiner, president of Weiner, Edrich, Brown, a leading American futurist consulting group. Dr. Fisher agrees: "Trends toward decentralization, a flatter business structure, team playing, lateral connections, and flexibility favor women's way of doing business."[43]

Women have always been better than men at "people skills." They tune in to others' feelings and are more empathic. This has enabled women to be good mothers and, increasingly, excellent employees. Surprisingly, it was John D. Rockefeller who said, "The ability to deal with people is as purchasable a commodity as sugar or coffee. And I pay more for that ability than for any other under the sun."[44]

Simon Baron-Cohen, Ph.D., a professor of psychology and psychiatry at Cambridge University in England who has been researching sex differences for over 20 years, details the latest research in his fields in his book *The Essential Difference: The Truth about the Male and Female Brain*. His findings substantiate the fact that males and females are different, in large measure because of the different ways our brains are structured. "The female brain is predominantly hard-wired for empathy," he says. "The male brain is predominantly hard-wired for understanding and building systems."[45]

Neuroscientists currently believe that interpersonal sensitivity, a conglomerate of aptitudes they call "executive social skills" or "social cognition," resides in the prefrontal cortex, the area of the brain behind the brow. Someone with a well-functioning prefrontal cortex is aware of the feelings of others, picks up on emotional expressions and body language, and is adept at maintaining good social relationships. Neuroscientist David Skuse believes that women are more likely than men to acquire the genetic endowment for developing these vital social skills. The reason, he believes, is that a specific gene or cluster of genes on the X chromosome influences the formation of the prefrontal cortex. He found that this gene or gene cluster is silenced in 100 percent of men but active in about 50 percent of women. Hence, about half of all women—and no men—have the brain architecture to excel at the nuances of social interplay.[46] This doesn't mean that the other 50 percent of women and all men can't learn these skills. It just means we have to work harder at them.

All these factors cause men to increasingly feel that they may lose their positions of power in the work world. Though they may act like they are in charge and confident, many harbor deep insecurities that they often express through irritability and anger. "Hell hath no fury like a man devalued." These are the opening words of the book *Eve's Seed: Biology, the Sexes, and the Course of History* by historian Robert S. McElvaine.[47] They could also be the words of the millions of men today experiencing the Irritable Male Syndrome.

EMOTIONS GUIDE OUR DIRECTION IN LIFE—
AND MEN ARE EMOTIONALLY ADRIFT

The various mental states we call emotions have evolved through time to help us meet life's challenges. It is our emotions that let us know when we are on the right path in life. "Negative emotions—fear, sadness, and anger—are our first line of defense against external threats, calling us to battle stations," says psychologist Martin Seligman, Ph.D., in his book *Authentic Happiness*. "Fear is a signal that danger is lurking, sadness is a signal that loss is impending, and anger signals someone trespassing against us."[48]

These emotions are essential to a man's survival, and we have all evolved to be able to feel them. The problem for men is that we often have difficulty getting in touch with our feelings and articulating them. We also tend to overemphasize feelings of anger and deny feelings of sadness and fear. I suspect that this tendency is built into our genetic heritage. For millions of years, men had to leave their wives and children and go out for days on end to hunt. An ability to suppress their feelings would have made it easier for them to leave and easier for them to kill.

The men who allowed their feelings for their wives and children to come to the surface, the men who broke down when their children called, "Daddy, daddy, don't leave," the men who couldn't make themselves "be strong" were the men who didn't hunt and didn't bring home food for the family. In the long run, the children of these men were not as successful. These men didn't pass on a lot of their genes to the next generation. We are descended from the men who submerged their feelings and went off with the other men.

Our female ancestors, on the other hand, took the major responsibility for nurturing young children. An ability to read and respond to a baby's emotions would have been a great advantage.

As men become more nurturing and are required to be away from their families less, we are learning to more easily express our feelings. Yet millions of years of evolutionary history continue to have an impact on the differences in emotional expression between men and women. This seems to be true everywhere in the world. After Gallup pollsters asked people in 22 societies which sex was more emotional, they concluded, "More than any other trait, this one elicits the greatest consensus around the world as more applicable to women than men. Eighty-eight percent of Americans think women are more emotional, as do 79 percent of the French, 74 percent of the Japanese, and 72 percent of the Chinese."[49]

This evolutionary difference may have a hormonal basis. Prior to puberty, both sexes express their emotions fairly equally. As boys mature and their testosterone levels increase, however, they begin to mask feelings of vulnerability, weakness, and fear. It usually is during adolescence that boys first refuse to discuss their feelings. "They become fluent at 'joke-speak,'" says Dr. Fisher, "all of the quips and gags and seemingly offhand remarks that boys and men employ to mask their emotions."[50]

Emotions give color to our lives. Feeling our feelings and sharing them with others creates the bond that is the foundation of love. Yet most men I know are very limited in their abilities to experience a range of feelings, let alone to put those feelings into words. As we've seen, women, on average, are more aware of their emotions, show more empathy, and are more adept interpersonally. One of the most common questions a woman will ask a man when she wants to get closer to him is "What are you feeling?" For most men, the response is "I don't know."

The inability to describe emotions in words is a condition called *alexithymia*. Frequently, alexithymic individuals are not even aware of what their feelings are. Dr. Levant coined the technical term *normative male alexithymia* to describe the general emotional restriction most men experience. He used the adjective *normative* because his research shows that this limited dual response of anger or sex is the norm for men. His research and that of many others indicates that most North American males suffer to some degree from the cultural conditioning that causes men to be under-developed emotionally.

Dr. Levant's research shows that men have developed two primary responses to emotional issues. For vulnerable feelings, including fear, hurt, and shame, he sees men using anger as the "manly" response. For nurturing feelings, including caring, warmth, connectedness, and intimacy, he sees men channeling these feelings through sex.[51]

So most men are playing an instrument with only two strings. We alternate between the notes "I'm pissed off" and "Let's have sex." It's a pretty limited repertoire, made even worse when we are going through IMS.

Men often have the most difficulty in our most intimate relationships. Many combine their anger with their desire for sex. Since most women are turned off by anger, these men are not likely to get a positive response. This in turn makes men more angry, negative, and irritable.

"When we are in a positive mood, people like us better, and friendship, love, and coalitions are more likely to cement," says Dr. Seligman.[52] So men suffering from IMS find that their negative mood undermines their love relationships and friendships. Even men who are not suffering from IMS are often emotionally inept. Because social connection is one of the key factors that determine health and longevity, men's failure to express ourselves emotionally may account for the fact that, on average, we die 6 years sooner than women.

Emotions are what we experience during gaps in our thinking. If there are no gaps, there is no emotion. Men often mistake thoughts for emotions.

I once had a man in my office who was obviously feeling a mixture of emotions: anger, hurt, fear, confusion, worry, sadness. He had been injured on the job and had been referred to me by his wife because he was becoming increasingly depressed. He hadn't been able to work for the previous 6 months, and the medical procedures he had undergone weren't working. After getting some history, I asked him how he was feeling. "I feel like I want to get back to work," he said.

"I know you want to get back to work, but how are you feeling?" I asked.

He thought for a moment and replied. "I feel like I need to do something, but I don't know what to do."

When I kept pressing for his feelings, he just looked at me and was obviously mystified. It took many sessions to help him tune in to the sensations in his body, to recognize the feelings that went with the sensations, and to put words to the feelings. He finally exploded with feelings and said, "I'm really, really pissed off." I cheered, and we both laughed.

Tom Golden, Ph.D., a psychotherapist who works extensively with men and the author of *Swallowed by a Snake: The Gift of the Masculine Side of Healing,* suggests that asking a man to tell you how he feels may not be the best way to find out what's really going on inside him. "When a man had suffered a loss, I started asking not what he was *feeling* but what he was *doing* about it," says Dr. Golden. "I was delighted at that point to see that when I asked the right questions, in the right manner, I started seeing things in a very different light. The men started talking to me about what they were doing. This was familiar territory. As the men talked of their endeavors, the emotions flowed in a comfortable manner."[53]

When men do tap in to their feelings—especially in to powerful ones such as fear, anger, sadness, or anxiety—they are more likely than women to be swamped by these emotions, a condition that author and psychologist John M. Gottman, Ph.D., calls "emotional flooding."[54] As I first mentioned in chapter 4, we often close down and refuse to talk to our partners not because we are being stubborn or emotionally stingy but because we are overwhelmed by our emotions. This emotional handicap often keeps us from participating fully in a relationship and may lead to IMS as these feelings "leak out."

Feelings are like water held in a cracked vessel. No matter how much we try to contain them, they find a way to come out. And when they do, they are often distorted. Feelings of worry or fear, for instance, can come out as impatience or irritation. And just as our feelings become distorted, so, too, does our sense of male identity.

BECOMING A MAN: "THE BIG IMPOSSIBLE"

It isn't easy being a man today. We have the same evolutionary needs that we've always had, but the world has changed in such a way that it is more difficult for many men to meet these needs. In his book *Manhood in the Making,* anthropology professor David D. Gilmore reports on his cross-cultural exploration of what it means to be a man. In cultures as diverse as hunter-gatherers, horticultural and pastoral tribes, peasants, and post-industrial civilizations in the East and West, he found a similar vulnerability in all men. "Among most of the peoples that anthropologists are familiar with," says Gilmore, "true manhood is a precious and elusive status beyond mere maleness."[55]

Gilmore found that, in every culture he examined, masculinity is a much more uncertain concept than femininity. As author Norman Mailer recognizes, "Nobody was born a man; you earned manhood provided you were good enough, bold enough."[56] Mailer could be speaking about the universal man, not just men in contemporary Western cultures. For instance, in aboriginal North America, among the Fox tribe, manhood was seen as being "the Big Impossible," an exclusive status that only the nimble few could achieve.[57]

"A man must prove his manhood every day by standing up to challenges and insults," says Oscar Lewis, author of *The Children of Sanchez*, "even though he goes to his death 'smiling.'"[58] How many young men in our schools and neighborhoods would rather go to their deaths smiling than risk an insult to their manhood?

In the modern world, men are finding it harder to fulfill women's desires. We're falling farther behind. We begin with many biological disadvantages and increasingly experience social stressors as well. At all stages of life, boys, teens, and adult men are losing out. As we've seen, this is most apparent in the two critical areas of life: production and reproduction. Boys face challenges in school that lead to challenges in the workforce. Without good jobs, men have trouble being productive in the world. Men who are not good producers and providers have difficulty developing and sustaining relationships with women and, consequently, their own children. As we will see in the next chapter, this trend is having devastating effects on men, women, children, and society, and is a major factor in understanding the Irritable Male Syndrome.

CHAPTER 6

IRRITABILITY, LOVE, AND WORK
Are Men Becoming the Second Sex?

Sigmund Freud, the father of psychoanalysis, was once asked what he thought a normal person should be able to do well. The questioner probably expected a complicated answer. But Freud, in a curt reply, is reported to have said, "*Lieben und arbeiten*" ("To love and to work"). In the previous chapter, I suggested that many males have the experience of going downhill in today's society. They feel they are swimming against the tide and falling farther and farther behind. As Freud suggested, when a person doesn't feel successful at love and work, he doesn't feel fully human. This is increasingly a problem for many men.

Ask most guys what it means to be a man and they will give you characteristics of what, in their minds, it *doesn't* mean to be a woman. Men are (and women aren't) cool, stoic, logical, aggressive, hairy, muscular, outspoken, rugged, tough, warlike.

There are three primary problems when men define themselves in opposition to women. The first is that we never develop any deeply felt understanding of what it means to be a man. The traditional roles that men have maintained, breadwinner and protector, are much less secure than the female roles of nurturer and nourisher. Over the years, I have continuously heard from men both young and old who tell me, "I don't know how to act. I've never really learned what a man is."

Second, we give a lot of our power to women. Our sense of self-esteem and value depends totally on their view of us. We become "nice guys" who are forever trying to please the women in our lives. Or we become controlling and mean as we take out our anger on the women we are so dependent upon.

Third, as women's roles change, men are thrown off balance. "If a woman stops acting like a woman," we wonder in terror, "how will I know what a man is supposed to do? If my wife has her own job and brings in money, where does my breadwinner role go? Worse, what if I can no longer bring money in? Who am I? What am I? What will I do?" These are questions that men are asking more and more these days.

"I . . . FEEL . . . I'VE . . . BEEN . . . CASTRATED"

In her book *Stiffed: The Betrayal of the American Man,* Susan Faludi concludes that male stress, shame, depression, and violence are not just a problem of individual men but a product of social betrayal of men that occurred after World War II.[1] Men feel betrayed by fathers who had told them that living by the rules—getting a good education, getting a good job, marrying, and having children—would ensure success and happiness. Somewhere along the way, the rules changed. Men need a different kind of education for the world of the 21st century—an education much better suited for women. Job security has become a thing of the past, marriages end, and children mostly stay with their mothers.

In concluding her book, Faludi reflects back on the men she interviewed. "That layer of paternal betrayal felt, for many of the men I spent time with, like the innermost core, the artichoke's bitter heart. The fathers had made them a promise, and then had not made good on it. They had lied. The world they had promised had never been delivered."[2]

Faludi describes in detail the dream men were asked to buy into and what happened to the men when it died. "Implicit in all of this," she says, "was a promise of loyalty, a guarantee to the new man of tomorrow that his company would never fire him, his wife would never leave him, and the team he rooted for would never pull up stakes. Instead, the average man found his father was an absent father, the job market had no place for him, women were ashamed of his inability to make a decent living, and his favorite sports team abandoned him."[3]

One of the men Faludi quoted in her book, Don Motta, could be speaking for millions of men in this country who have been laid off, downsized, or part of a company that has gone under. "There is no way you can feel like a man. You can't," says Motta in Faludi's book. "It's the fact that I'm not capable of supporting my family. . . . When you've been very successful in buying a house, a car, and could pay for your daughter to go to college, though she didn't want to, you have a sense of success and people see it. I haven't been able to support my daughter. I haven't been able to support my wife.

"I'll be very frank with you," he said slowly, placing every word down as if each were an increasingly heavy weight. "I . . . feel . . . I've . . . been . . . castrated."[4] Motta is clear about the connection between manhood, work, and sexuality. A man who can't work and support his family is a man without balls—not really a man at all.

Men's feeling of disconnection from the world of work is increasing as politics and big business interact. In his book *Dude, Where's My Country?*, Michael Moore describes the frustration that many of us feel. "The whole destruction of our economic future is based solely on the greed of the corporate mujahedeen," he tells us. "There is a master plan, my friends, each company has one, and the sooner you can get over not wanting to believe it, or worrying that to believe it puts you in the ranks of the nutters who thrive on conspiracy theories, then the sooner we have a chance of stopping them. Their singular goal is to take enough control over our lives so that, in the end, we'll be pledging allegiance, not to a flag or some airy notions of freedom and democracy, but to the dictates of Citigroup, Exxon, Nike, GE, GM, P&G, and Philip Morris."[5]

JOB LOSS WILL BE A MORE DEVASTATING PROBLEM THAN THE VIETNAM WAR

Mary Furlong, Ph.D., is a leading authority on technology and aging and an expert on the impact of the baby boom on society. She founded ThirdAge, a Web site for boomers, as well as SeniorNet, a nonprofit membership organization dedicated to educating older adults about computer technology. According to Dr. Furlong, job loss will become a more devastating problem than the Vietnam War.

We are seeing an emerging pattern throughout the industrial world, says anthropologist Lionel Tiger, author of *The Decline of Males*. "Men and women may not discern it clearly, but the pattern underlies their experience in industrial society. It is a pattern of growth in the confidence and power of women, and of erosion in the confidence and power of men."[6]

This is evident in the major shifts we see in the workforce. Women are moving in and men are moving out. Women currently make up 40 percent of the labor force throughout the industrialized world.[7] During the past 2 decades, more women have begun to work outside the home, while men's participation in the labor force has declined.[8]

If any picture can truly capture thousands of words, it is the photo on the cover of the book *Mismatch: The Growing Gulf between Women and Men* by Andrew Hacker, Ph.D., a political science professor at Queens College, The City University of New York. It shows a woman and a man facing each other but reveals them only from the knees down. We are drawn to their equally shiny black shoes. It is he, however, not she, who is standing on tiptoe so the two can come eye to eye.

"As women are becoming more assertive, and taking critical stances toward the men in their lives, they are finding that all too many men lack the qualities they desire in dates and mates," says Dr. Hacker. Thus throughout the Western world, there is a greater divide between the sexes than at any time in living memory. "The result will be a greater separation of women and men, with tensions and recriminations afflicting beings once thought to be naturally companionable."[9]

This changing trend in the status of women and men can be seen in the changes within various occupations. Dr. Hacker notes the following shifts:

• In 1970, 29.6 percent of insurance adjusters were women. In 2001, that number had increased to 72.1 percent.

• Also in 1970, 26.6 percent of publicists were women. In 2001, 60.2 percent were women.

• Women accounted for 12.1 percent of pharmacists in 1970, compared to 48.1 percent in 2001.

• In 1970, less than 5 percent of lawyers were women. By 2001, that number had increased nearly six times, to 29.3 percent.

• The number of female physicians increased threefold from 1970 to 2001, with women accounting for 29.3 percent of doctors in the latter year.[10]

Men maintain their positions of power in traditionally male jobs. But that may not be a real benefit. In the 2002 *Jobs Rated Almanac,* author Les Krantz rated the nation's 10 best and 10 worst jobs. The criteria to determine the most and least appealing career opportunities included environment, income, employment outlook, physical demands, security, and stress. Each occupation was ranked using data from such sources as the U.S. Bureau of Labor Statistics and the U.S. Census Bureau as well as studies conducted by a wide range of trade associations and industry groups.[11]

The 10 best jobs were biologist, actuary, financial planner, computer-systems analyst, accountant, software engineer, meteorologist, paralegal assistant, statistician, and astronomer. The 10 worst jobs included lumberjack, commercial fisherman, cowboy, ironworker, seaman, taxi driver, construction worker, farmer, roofer, and stevedore. Picture people engaged in the jobs listed above. Who comes to mind—men or women? Do we see a pattern here in terms of gender? The worst jobs are ones in which men still dominate. Although the Monty Python comedy troupe made famous the song, "I'm a Lumberjack and I'm Okay," the life of professional lumberjacks couldn't be much rougher. I live in a town where men still cut trees and work in the lumber mills. They all know a colleague who has died over the years, and every lumberjack I know has sustained serious injuries. Those occupying the other professions don't do much better. In fact, psychologist Warren Farrell, Ph.D., author of *The Myth of Male Power,* calls these jobs the "death professions."[12]

Even the average man with a comparatively safe desk job feels the pressure. *Time* magazine's May 26, 2003, cover story has a picture of a worried man holding a tiny paycheck with tweezers. The cover says, "Paychecks are shrinking for millions of Americans. What that means for your future." The article highlights some of the new realities for those holding on to their jobs:[13]

• Shrinking paychecks and benefits are the reality for many Americans.

• Global markets and a weak economy are forcing many companies to tighten their belts.

• Adjusted for inflation, median weekly earnings fell 1.5 percent in the first quarter of 2003—the biggest drop since the early 1990s.

• Financial services firms say they plan to transfer 500,000 U.S. jobs to foreign countries by 2008.

• Eighty percent of large employers made workers pay more for health coverage in 2003.

MEN AND WOMEN IN THE WORKPLACE: STRESSES AND STRAINS

The economic realities I've mentioned mean that, increasingly, both men and women must work in order to provide financial support for their families. In 2002, the U.S. Department of Agriculture, which conducts annual Consumer Expenditure Surveys on the cost of raising children, estimated that families making $65,800 a year or more will spend a whopping $249,180 to raise a child from birth through age 17.[14]

Though not as steep, the figures for lower-income families are just as unsettling: $170,460 for families earning $39,100 to $65,800 and $124,800 for families making less than $39,100.[15] These rising costs of raising children cause anxiety, worry, and irritability—especially among men, who have traditionally been their families' breadwinners. These stresses contribute to the Irritable Male Syndrome.

We might think that having enough money to eliminate worry about these expenses would take the pressure off men. But even a job at the top of the professional ladder may be deadly. In a 2003 issue of *Psychology Today*, writer Hara Marano described the plight of many seemingly successful men who occupy the executive suites. "For a shocking number of CEOs, getting to the top brings only crippling emotional bleakness," says Marano.[16] As a prime example, he cites the experience of Philip Burguieres, once the youngest CEO of a Fortune 500 company. Burguieres spent 5 years building Weatherford Industries into a major contender in energy services. Then, in 1996, at the age of 53, he abruptly resigned as CEO and entered a mental hospital to be treated for suicidal depression.

In counseling thousands of men in positions of power, I have found that a number of factors can contribute to stress and depression such as that experienced by Burguieres. Many men who make it to the top of their businesses have to continually drive themselves. When they are successful, they feel the need to become even more successful. They often don't take care of themselves physically or emotionally.

And along with privileges, power also has its responsibilities. Many men feel that they must take care of others—not only their families but also their employees, customers, and stockholders. Probably the most damaging factor is that many of these men think they must always be strong and silent. They have a great deal of fear about letting others know about their stress. They hold it inside until it finally causes a breakdown.

Burguieres came through his dark night of the soul and now speaks about his experiences to others. He is breaking the silence. He has been called on to address stateside and international meetings of the World Presidents' Organization, a group of 3,300 current and former CEOs. Many high-powered men seek him out privately to share their own stories and seek support from someone who has been there. From his exclusive vantage point, Burguieres is convinced that estimates of the prevalence of mental disorders are on the low side. "At some point in their careers, fully 25 percent of top-level executives go through a severe depression," says Burguieres, in Marano's article. "You would be shocked at the number of CEOs, now running big companies, who are suicidally depressed."[17]

Another on-the-job stressor for men is interaction with female co-workers. For most of human history, men and women worked in separate spheres. Men hunted and women gathered. Even in modern times, women's work and men's work remained quite separate. Now, men and women are spending significant amounts of productive time in close proximity with each other.

We spend 8, 10, 12 hours a day together. We dress up for work and wear perfumes and colognes. We may socialize together at business gatherings or after work at a local bar. We may even travel together and stay in nearby rooms at the hotel. In other words, men and women are in perfect proximity to be drawn to each other.

In the past, when men controlled the workplace, the ways they showed romantic or sexual interest predominated. If a woman felt offended, it was her problem, not his. As women have gained power in the workplace, however, things have changed. Men tell me they feel like they are walking on eggshells whenever they are around women co-workers. In the office setting, men worry about telling the wrong kind of joke or that a show of friendliness will be construed as a come-on.

Since men and women spend more time at work and often have little time to find other situations where they might meet each other, much of the dating and mating goes on between workmates. But the rules are unclear. When is a show of interest "courting" and when is it "harassment"?

Dr. Farrell points out the bind that many men feel at the office. In workshops he conducts throughout the country, he found that two-thirds of married working women met their husbands at work. Another 15 percent had lived with or had long relationships with men they met on the job.[18]

Here's the bind: The majority of the men these working women married were above them in the status hierarchy. Additionally, almost all the men took the initiative in making their interest known to the women. Yet sexual initiatives by men toward women who have less powerful positions in the work environment constitute the most frequent definition of sexual harassment. "When it works, it's called courtship," concludes Dr. Farrell. "When it doesn't work, it's called harassment."[19]

Clearly, there needs to be some balance and common sense in how we deal with these issues. Men and women both want and need to be productive. Women will continue to enter the workforce in increasing numbers. Men need to accept these realities. At the same time, we have to find ways that men can feel free to express themselves without constant worry. Otherwise, men will continue to feel devalued, irritable, and aggressive, or sullen, irritable, and withdrawn. That is not good for men or women.

PRODUCTION AND REPRODUCTION: MEN ARE LOSING OUT ON BOTH FRONTS

With male economic prospects declining and female prospects rising, women are less likely to marry and have families with men who aren't on the track for success. Throughout the industrialized world, the education gap is having a profound effect on marriage and family life. According to Paul Harrington of Northeastern University's Center for Labor Market Studies in Boston, we are now seeing a "marriage gap," where educated women are finding it more difficult to find partners whom they consider equals.[20]

The complaint that there aren't enough "good men" available is particularly common among college-educated African-American and Hispanic women. African-American men receive about half as many college degrees as Black women do, and Hispanic men are outpaced 40 percent to 60 percent by Hispanic women.[21]

What has been true for minority women for some time is now becoming true for all women. Sylvia Ann Hewlett, author of *Creating a Life,* says that the more financially successful the woman, the more difficult it will be for her to find a mate or bear a child.[22]

From a man's point of view, his prospects are diminishing. Without a good education, he can't get a good job. Without a good job, he can't get a good woman who wants to settle down and create a family with him.

Without a family, a man can become increasingly isolated, irritable, angry, and depressed.

In losing out in the world of work, men are losing a role that has always been at the heart of what it means to be a man. "It is no longer possible for men to hunt for their daily bread and bacon in literal terms," says Tiger. "Man the Hunter is profoundly unemployable at the job he did well for hundreds of thousands of years."[23]

There are women who say that they don't need men who are able to successfully move up the monetary success ladder. When women do well economically, they claim that this allows them to connect with men who may be wonderful in many other ways besides advancing in the business world. After all, women say they would like to marry men who are less driven, more interested in emotional connection, and more dedicated to family.

And there are many men who would love to get off the economic fast track and find women who would love them for qualities other than their financial prospects.

All of this is nice in theory. Research findings, however, show that successful women do not tend to seek out men who may be wonderful in ways other than career success. Psychologist Douglas Kenrick, Ph.D., and his colleagues at Arizona State University in Tempe, devised a useful method for revealing how much people value different attributes in marriage partners.

They asked men and women to indicate the "minimum percentile" of each characteristic they would find acceptable in a long-term partner. In their studies, American college women indicated that their minimum acceptable percentile of earning capacity they would want in a husband is the 70th. In other words, for a young man to even be eligible for consideration as a possible marriage partner, he must have an earning capacity *higher* than 7 out of 10 other men.[24]

Put yourself in his shoes. How would you feel if you were a young man going up against those odds in the economic climate we face? What happens to the 7 out of 10 men who don't measure up?

Certainly, what women say they want is not always what they get. Although some women refuse to compromise, holding out for men who meet their high economic standards, most eventually choose mates who do not perfectly meet all their ideal criteria. Therefore, even a man who finds a mate may fear that he isn't what she truly wanted and that she might leave if someone "better" came along.

In his book *What Women Want—What Men Want*, John Townsend described Gwen, a successful woman who married a hard-driving, achievement-oriented medical student. After her husband completed his medical training, Gwen found out he had been having a series of affairs. "He's successful, exciting, drives a race car, but he's so wrapped up in his own pursuits he can't really love anyone," she's quoted as saying in Townsend's book. "He won't open up and let love in."[25]

After divorcing that guy, Gwen met and married a different kind of man—one who had all the qualities she thought she wanted in a partner. "Sal was from an Italian background and was very warm and expressive. In fact, he was the most sensitive and loving man I've ever known, and I had the best sex with him that I have ever had. That relationship lasted about 2 years. I finally broke it off. I couldn't really complain about the way he treated me. He was very sweet. But he just didn't seem to be going anywhere. He was from a working-class background and he lacked the ambition and drive to escape it. I mean he could have supported a family, but in what style?"[26]

Can we blame such a man if he feels confused, frustrated, and angry? I can just imagine him thinking to himself: "Let's see, I'm the most sensitive and loving man she's ever known. She's experiencing the best sex she ever had. I am sweet, I treat her well, and I have a good enough job to support a family. But she still leaves me because I'm not going anywhere, I lack ambition, and I don't want to escape my working-class background? What the hell does it take to get a woman these days?"

Women seem to want it all. They want men who are highly successful in the outside world and also sexy, loving, and sensitive at home. Like men who want loving wives who stay at home, take care of the kids all day, clean the house, prepare the meals, and act like pussycats when husbands need nurturing and tigers when men want sex, women, too, are bound to be disappointed.

Gwen, like the women in *Sex and the City,* is successful at work and disappointed in love. Townsend concludes his description of his typical successful woman with these words: "Gwen now earns over $50,000 a year as a buyer for a department store chain. She has no children and does not feel forced by economic necessity to compromise her standards. Statistically, she has a very slim chance of finding what she wants."[27] He doesn't say what happened to Sal, the loving Italian from a working-class background, but it wouldn't surprise me to learn that he was exhibiting severe symptoms of the Irritable Male Syndrome.

THE DECLINE OF MEN IN THE FAMILY

"The most destabilizing geopolitical force in the world today is the vast number of young men without jobs and other opportunities," says Edie Weiner, president of Weiner, Edrich, Brown, a leading American futurist consulting group.[28] As we have seen, underemployment makes it difficult for young men to attract mates. And one of the leading predictors of violence in countries throughout the world is the percentage of young men between the ages of 20 and 29 who are not married.

Countries with large percentages of young, single men include Iraq, Iran, Algeria, Turkey, Egypt, India, Afghanistan, China, and Israel.[29] We don't have to be experts in world politics to know that these countries are also the ones where war and violence are constant concerns. The place where a large population of unmarried males is most evident is China. Chinese traditions, a tough one-child-per-couple policy, modern medical technology, and a more educated population of women who have higher standards for the men they will marry, have combined to create a demographic nightmare that could pose a threat to the stability of China and is likely to impact the rest of the world. Over the next two decades, as many as 40 million young Chinese men won't be able to marry, settle down, and start families.[30]

Researchers say growing numbers of lonely men in migrant shantytowns and isolated farm villages will pose a threat to social order. These young, unmarried men are known in Chinese as *guang guan*, meaning "bare branches" or "bare sticks." As is true on a smaller scale in countries throughout the world, most of the men who will go unmarried over the next two decades are China's "losers in societal competition," says a report by Hudson and Andrea Den Boer of Great Britain's University of Kent.[31]

These young men complain that modern women are too picky. "Before, it was men choosing women," says Liu Xicheng, 21, a migrant worker who came to Beijing from nearby Nebei Province. "Now it is women choosing men. Some have high-quality standards. It is hard to marry them."[32]

In deciding on a potential mate, department store salesperson Yang Wen, 20, says, "he needs a stable job and to be well-educated." Chinese men, like men throughout the world, are having a difficult time keeping up. Among rural men, for example, 97 percent never finish high school and 40 percent are illiterate.[33]

The Chinese government is alarmed at the surplus of bachelors. "This is a seriously dangerous ratio," Ren Yuling, a delegate to the Chinese People's Political Consultative Committee, told *China Youth Daily.* "The numbers mean that some people will never have their needs for a spouse met, so they move into dangerous territory." The Chinese magazine *Beijing Luntan* predicted as early as 1997 that "such sexual crimes as forced marriages, girls stolen for wives, bigamy, visiting prostitutes, rape, adultery, homosexuality, and weird sexual habits appear to be unavoidable." Crime is on the rise. Prostitution is already epidemic in Chinese cities. Bride trafficking is common in the countryside. Kidnapped brides have fetched $600 apiece in rural provinces.[34]

These are symptoms of irritable males at the very extremes.

As the number of unmarried young males grows, problems are sure to increase. The Den Boers write that those "bare branches" provide kindling sufficient to turn the sparks into a fire larger and more dangerous than anything we have seen so far.

One of the traditional ways in which countries handle large populations of young men is to send them off to war. Researchers predict that India and Pakistan, both of which have large surpluses of unmarried men, may have little incentive to create a lasting peace. An increasingly assertive China might create a firestorm that could affect the whole planet.[35]

Meanwhile, individual men continue to suffer. They are cut off from the twin roles of production and reproduction that are at the center of life on the planet. *Beijing Luntan* concludes that many poor young men will have no choice but to get used to the single life. They must learn to "handle the punishment they have received as a result of the mistakes of the previous generation."[36]

What we see in China may be an increasingly common trend throughout the world. Few will easily "handle their punishment." Men who are isolated from family life become more irritable, depressed, and suicidal. In my career as a psychotherapist, I have found that one of the primary reasons men become depressed is a lack of connection with wives and children.

WHERE HAVE ALL THE FATHERS GONE?
THE RISE OF SINGLE MOTHERHOOD

Even when men do find women to mate with, those women may choose to raise children without the men's involvement. "Men have been decreasingly successful in the labor force," says Tiger. "Partly for that reason, many have been 'fired' as potentially useful fathers by women who expect that as mates they will be a burden, not a help. They will consume resources, not bring them in. They will import problems, not defend against them. They may well be nothing but chronic trouble. Who needs them? Why bother?"[37] The belief that they are superfluous or may become superfluous is a fear that drives more men in our society and lies at the center of the Irritable Male Syndrome.

"More women are having children without men, and therefore more men are without the love of families," says Tiger.[38] "Meanwhile, men fade out of the picture."[39] Further, more women are deciding to leave unhappy marriages, even when they have children to raise. With more economic power, they don't need to rely on men's earnings to support them and their children.

"The United States is becoming an increasingly fatherless society," says David Blankenhorn, author of *Fatherless America*. "A generation ago, an American child could reasonably expect to grow up with his father. Today, an American child can reasonably expect not to."[40]

This phenomenon is not restricted to the United States. It is occurring all over the world. In Thailand and Brazil, for example, 20 percent of households are headed by women; in the Dominican Republic and Hong Kong, the figure is 26 percent; in Ghana, it is 29 percent.[41]

As men become separated from their roles as husbands and fathers, they lose the incentive to fulfill the roles of breadwinners, protectors, nurturers, teachers, and mentors. In the foreword to the American translation of German writer Alexander Mitscherlich's 1963 book *Society without the Father*, Robert Bly describes the key focus of the book. "The father society has collapsed," says Bly. "It's not so much that the father doesn't talk or pay support or has left the house, but rather that the image of the working, teaching father has faded from the mind. . . . The disappearance has happened so abruptly—so unexpectedly from the centuries' viewpoint—and the implications are so immense—that we really turn our heads away, we can't take it in."[42]

As is often the case, when there are social changes that we don't understand, we tend to blame the victim. "Because he no longer teaches as he
works," says Bly, "we in our rage call him a nuisance, a curse, a survival
from archaic times, an enemy, or a virus, some persistent strain in the
bloodstream."[43] Without realizing it, we have begun to eradicate the male
experience from our collective consciousness. It's as though we had an auto-
immune disease that attacked our own bodies.

In losing fathers, we are losing one of the very characteristics that make
us uniquely human. Pair-bonding is really quite rare in nature, particularly
among mammals. "Only about 3 percent of all mammals form a long-term
relationship with a single mate," says anthropologist Helen Fisher, Ph.D.,
author of *The First Sex: The Natural Talents of Women and How They Are
Changing the World*.[44] Humans are among that small percentage because,
in our evolutionary past and up to the present time, there was an advantage to women and men staying together at least long enough to raise children. Humankind is in the midst of a social reversal that is taking us *away*
from what makes us who we are. Without our conscious intent, the culture
is returning to our pre-human, mammalian roots.

This trend is having a devastating impact on men, women, and especially
children. It is the most significant and harmful demographic that we have
ever faced. "It is the leading cause of declining child well-being in our
society," says Blankenhorn. "It is also the engine driving our most urgent
social problems, from crime to adolescent pregnancy to child sexual abuse
to domestic violence against women."[45]

MEN, DIVORCE, AND SUICIDE

Children offer joy and meaning in men's lives, just as they do in women's.
When men are not allowed to fulfill their roles as fathers, they become
increasingly angry and violent. Many lose the desire to live. Divorced or
separated men are more than twice as likely to kill themselves as men who
remain married. Among women, a marital split is not a significant risk
factor for suicide.

These are the findings of one study of suicide and divorce. "We knew
from past research that divorce was linked to increased risk of suicide,"
says Augustine Kposowa, the author of the study, which appeared in the

Journal of Epidemiology and Community Health. "What we didn't know was the difference between men and women in this respect."[46]

Kposowa, a professor of sociology at the University of California, Riverside, analyzed the causes of death for almost 472,000 men and women over a 9-year period, starting with 1979. He believes that one of the primary reasons for divorced fathers' higher suicide rate may be that they feel so alienated from their children. "A man may not get to see his children, even with visitation rights," Kposowa says. "As far as the man is concerned, he has lost his marriage and lost his children and that can lead to depression and suicide."[47]

The revolutionary sociologist and economist Karl Marx said about the industrial system that people are profoundly alienated from the means of *production*—jobs. If Charles Darwin, the father of evolutionary theory, were alive today, he might comment that men are profoundly alienated from the means of *reproduction*—women.[48] Freud might point out that men have become alienated from both basic needs, *lieben und arbeiten*— to love and to work. Until we can abolish this alienation and help men fulfill those needs, the Irritable Male Syndrome will become an increasingly common phenomenon in our world.

CHAPTER 7

IMS AND STRESS
Why Men Want to Get Away from It All

We all know the feeling. You've had another one of those days at work. One deadline after another, and there isn't enough time to breathe. Someone always seems to be making more demands, and no matter how hard you try to stay on top of things, you seem to be getting farther behind. You eat at your desk to try to catch up. Working while eating, you spill coffee on the report you're working on. "Goddamn it," you yell, grabbing a newspaper to wipe up the spill before it spreads over the desk.

You try to get home before 6:00 in the evening because your child is in a school play that you promised to attend. The traffic is worse than ever. You pound on the steering wheel, knowing it won't help. You're sure the guy that just cut in front of you did it because he wants you to run into him so he can collect the insurance money, even though you know it's an irrational thought. It seems like the world is conspiring to make your life miserable. You have fantasies of chucking it all and just taking off to parts unknown.

By the time you scramble in the door, your wife greets you with a quick peck on the cheek. "Hurry, dear," she says with a smile. "Sit down and eat so we won't be late." You'd like to punch her lights out, but you don't know why. She's just trying to be helpful. You feel like screaming at her to shut up and give you a minute to unwind. Instead, you grunt and follow her into the dining room, where you pretend to have a nice dinner with the family before jumping in the car and racing to your kid's school to see them in the performance.

Why is your mood so black? Why do you see red when you experience the slightest upset? You know the answer. You are overstressed.

In my experience as a psychotherapist, I have found that stress underlies most of the psychological, social, and medical problems that people face in contemporary society. One of the questions on the Male Depression Questionnaire that was filled out online by nearly 3,500 men ranging in age from 16 to 75 was "Have you become stressed out more easily?" Eighty-seven percent of respondents answered that they have.[1] On the Irritable Male Syndrome Questionnaire filled out by nearly 6,000 men, 91 percent of respondents said they were experiencing some degree of stress in their lives.[2]

Less than 9 percent of the people taking the Irritable Male Syndrome Questionnaire said they were almost never stressed. It is not an exaggeration to say that stress is the most contagious plague of modern society.

WHAT IS STRESS?

For most of us, stress is synonymous with worry. If something makes us worry, it's stressful.

Our bodies have a much broader definition of stress. Physically, stress is synonymous with change. Good changes and bad changes are both stress. When you find your dream home and get ready to move, that's stress. If you get a divorce, that's also stress. Even imagined change is stress. If you think that you may receive a promotion at work, that's stress, even though it hasn't happened yet and it would be a good change if it did.

"In its medical sense, *stress is essentially the rate of wear and tear in the body*" (italics in the original), says Hans Selye, M.D., the father of modern stress research. "Anyone who feels that whatever he is doing—or whatever is being done to him—is strenuous and wearing knows vaguely what we mean by *stress*. The feelings of just being tired, jittery, or ill are subjective sensations of stress. But stress does not necessarily imply a morbid change: normal life, especially intense pleasure and the ecstasy of fulfillment, also cause some wear and tear in the machinery of the body."[3]

We can't avoid stress, nor would we want to. Stress is unavoidable, necessary, invigorating, and life-enhancing, because life is change and change is life. The problem arises when there is too much change in too short a time. We might think of stress that leads to the Irritable Male Syndrome as "distress" or "overstress." These can cause untold problems if not understood and prevented.

WHAT GOOD IS STRESS?

In order to understand our bodies' reactions to stress, we need to remember that it has been part of our ancestral heritage since we were living as hunter-gatherers on the savannas of Africa. Picture the scene: You and your family are having a peaceful meal around the campfire. You and the other men are telling stories about the last time you were out hunting for wildebeests. Your wife is mending your moccasins. The children are chasing each other around the camp, much as children do today.

Suddenly, a leopard runs into the camp and heads right for you and your family. Other families scatter. Your wife grabs the children and starts to run. You lunge for your spear and prepare to defend yourself and those you love. The leopard attacks. You, being the warrior you are, kill her, saving the day. Or in another scenario—the one written by the leopard—you and your family are lunch for the big cat and her family.

Regardless of how the encounter ends, from the moment you first become aware of the danger, your body goes through characteristic changes. When your brain consciously or unconsciously perceives a threat, it triggers an automatic nervous system response that prepares your body to either fight or flee. The autonomic nervous system is the portion of the central nervous system that regulates bodily functions you don't normally consciously control. When you're stressed, the rate of all these bodily functions increases dramatically to give you the physical strength to protect yourself against an attack. For instance, blood is diverted away from the stomach and digestive tract and sent to the major muscle groups. This is why you may get indigestion if you try to eat when you are anxious or scared. Scientists call this type of autonomic nervous system response *sympathetic activation*. It is the biological basis of the fight-or-flight response.

A second stress system is the hypothalamic-pituitary-adrenocortical system, or HPA for short. You don't feel the HPA response in your body to the degree that you feel the sympathetic arousal. The HPA activation touches your emotional sense of danger. You feel that sense of anxious worry. You have a sense of terror and dread. You become a bit paranoid, wondering whether someone or something is after you. These reactions are quite important if there is a leopard on the prowl.

When the area of the brain called the hypothalamus perceives that extra energy is needed to fight a stressor, it stimulates the adrenal glands to release the hormone epinephrine, also called adrenaline. Epinephrine causes more blood to be pumped with each beat of your heart, dilates the air sacs in your lungs to increase oxygen intake, increases your breathing rate, stimulates your liver to release more glucose, and dilates your pupils to improve visual sensitivity. Your body is then poised for immediate action.

All the changes that occur are vitally necessary for fighting the leopard or running for your life. Without this kind of stress reaction, our ancestors would have been eaten more often than not. Few of them would have survived to pass on their genes.

Obviously, the stress response served us well in the past. The problem is that the kinds of stressors we were designed to deal with no longer exist— and the new stressors are ones that our ancestors never dreamt of facing. The stress response works wonderfully for the stressors it was designed for. It causes great problems in the face of the stressors of modern life.

THE PROBLEMS WITH MODERN-DAY STRESS

The first problem with modern-day stress is that it is primarily psychological, not physical. We worry about whether we'll get good jobs, whether we'll find loving mates, and whether we'll have to go fight a war. We think about whether our children will stay healthy and happy. We are concerned about the future of the environment. Will there be good air to breathe, water to drink, fish to catch, old-growth forests to remind us of the splendor of life? We worry about whether our employers will still be around in 10 years and whether we will ever have enough money to retire.

Between raising children who seem to need more support for more years and taking care of parents who live longer, we wonder if there will ever be any time for us.

We wonder if we have done anything of real value in our lives. Would anyone really care if we were no longer here? We worry about more abstract things—the economy, the state of the world, terrorism, war. In so many areas of our lives, there seem to be more questions than answers.

The body doesn't know the difference between an attacking leopard and a criticizing boss. It can't even tell the difference between a real threat and an imagined one. When stress strikes, whatever the source, the body mobilizes, thinking it's under attack. Body, mind, and spirit are set for action, be it fighting or fleeing. The body reacts with an outpouring of hormones (adrenaline, norepinephrine, and cortisol) that increase heart rate and respiration, send more blood to skeletal muscles, dull pain, stimulate the immune system, and turn sugar and fat into energy.

The physical reality of fighting an attack or running away from one provides an outlet through which to express anger and fear. When the threat is resolved, the body returns to normal. But when the boss yells or a guy cuts you off on the freeway, you can neither run away nor chase them down and kill them. So all those neurochemicals and hormones continue to be released. They have no place to go, and eventually they cause damage to your body.

Furthermore, even our ancestors in the wild rarely had to put their lives on the lines fighting leopards. Most of the time, they enjoyed stories, fun, food, laughter, and preparing for the next hunt. We, on the other hand, experience stressors almost constantly.

The anxiety and depression that are at the core of the Irritable Male Syndrome are closely related. When stress first starts to come on, we are invigorated by the opportunity to solve a new problem and deal with a new threat to our stability and balance. However, as stress continues to mount, we become hypervigilant and anxious, and we frantically try to regain control. As the stress continues, we become overwhelmed and sink into hopelessness and depression.

"If anxiety is a crackling, menacing brushfire, depression is a suffocating heavy blanket thrown on top of it," says stress researcher Robert M. Sapolsky, Ph.D., a professor of biological sciences and neuroscience at Stanford University.[4] He believes we must learn how to lessen stress in our lives. "We must find ways to heal a world in which so many people learn that they must always feel watchful and on guard or that they must always feel helpless."[5]

FIGHT OR FLIGHT VERSUS TEND AND BEFRIEND

Just as men and women experience depression quite differently, so too do they have different responses to stress. This might seem obvious, but it has only recently been recognized. Most everything I have read about stress over the years discusses the fight-or-flight response and the ways the body prepares to deal with danger. It has been assumed that men and women faced the same kinds of dangers and responded in similar ways. We are now finding that this is only part of the story.

"A team of NIMH-supported scientists has formulated a theory that characterizes female responses to stress by a pattern they term 'tend-and-befriend,' rather than by 'fight-or-flight,'" says the National Institute of Mental Health (NIMH). "They believe that female stress responses have selectively evolved to simultaneously maximize the survival of self and offspring. Thus, the 'tend-and-befriend' pattern involves females' nurturance of offspring under stressful circumstances, the exhibition of behaviors that protect them from harm (tending), and befriending—namely, creating and joining social groups for the exchange of resources and to provide protection."[6]

Remember, the way the body/mind is built to respond to stress has been part of our makeup since humans lived on those African savannas tens of thousands of years ago. Picture that scene of the attacking leopard again. Imagine what happens to men and women as the big cat bounds into camp. The stress reaction begins the same for both sexes. There is an arousal reaction as our eyes open wide, our hearts begin to send blood to the muscles, our guts shut down, and we get ready to act. But the actions taken by the men and women would likely be different.

The men would prepare to fight. They might also flee if they thought it would cause the leopard to follow them away from the camp so that the women and children would be safe. We recognize these actions as the traditional stress response of fight or flight. What would the women do? It's unlikely that they would run away and leave their children or risk leaving the children motherless by leaping into battle. More likely, they would take the children to safety, and hold and comfort them. They might quietly soothe them so that they wouldn't cry and attract the leopard to their hiding place. They would join with other women to shield themselves and the children from harm.

This was the likely origin of women's response to stress. "Women turn to the social group in times of stress, and so we looked for patterns of 'befriending,'" says Shelly Taylor, Ph.D., the leader of the NIMH research team; professor of psychology at the University of California, Los Angeles; and a world-renowned researcher on stress and health. "We constructed our theory around these two pivotal observations about female responses to stress—protecting offspring and turning to others—and accordingly called it 'tend and befriend.'"[7]

The difference between the fight-or-flight and tend-and-befriend responses can be seen in research showing that men and women differ in what causes them to feel stress. A study of 2,000 male and 670 female workers in an American manufacturing plant found that men experienced depression, anxiety, and sleeplessness when they felt a lack of control over what they were doing at work. Women became stressed when they felt they lacked social support.[8]

THE IRRITABLE MALE
AND HIS INABILITY TO RELIEVE STRESS

I would like to suggest that the unique ways in which women have learned to relieve stress are more readily available than those stress relievers that come naturally to men. Even with the different kinds of stressors that women face in today's world, they still have many opportunities to "tend and befriend."

But how about men? What do we do when the boss is breathing down our necks, when our company is downsized and we lose our jobs, when terrorists attack our country, when our children start running with a bad crowd, when our wives go through menopause, when the doctor tells us our high cholesterol is killing us? What actions can we take? Whom do we kill? How do we lure danger away from our families?

We can't use the stress relievers that were built into our bodies and minds over our ancestral history. The result is that the stress increases, we seethe with anger, we wither with despair.

The positive ways women deal with stress and the negative responses that are so common in men are illustrated by an elegant experiment that was conducted by Rena Repetti, Ph.D., a developmental and clinical psychologist at UCLA.[9] Dr. Repetti began the research by asking working parents to fill out detailed questionnaires about the events of specific workdays and their subsequent activities at home. She also asked their children to fill out questionnaires about their own experiences each day, particularly their parents' behavior toward them.

As we might guess, stressful days took a toll on the families. Some days were just busy—too much work with too little time to get it done. Other days were filled with conflict—disputes with the boss or an angry outburst from a co-worker. Interestingly, Dr. Repetti found that the nature of the stressful day—whether it was merely busy or filled with conflict—made a big difference in how fathers behaved with their families.

When dads came home after a particularly busy day, they just wanted to be left alone. They would withdraw behind a newspaper, zone out in front of the TV, or go into the home office and close the door. This is what fathers said they did after a day with too much to do, and the children confirmed it. "Dad wants to be left alone. He's tired."

When they'd had a day filled with conflict, however, these same men would become irritable and pick at their wives and children. "Why isn't your homework done? Can't you clean up that mess in the kitchen? Turn down that damn music." Fathers at these times were clearly blaming and shaming their families because of the frustrations of the day, without usually being aware of it. In their minds, their children were "trying" to irritate them, their partners were going out of their way to stir up bad feelings.

The evidence is clear. Reading the fathers' logs of the kind of day they had and comparing them to the ones the children kept shows a clear correlation: When there was conflict at work, dads took out their anger on their families at home. The children learned to pick up the signs and act accordingly. "Stay out of Dad's way. He's in one of his moods."

So the kind of stress at work determines men's fight-or-flight response. When stress is from overwhelming work, we try to flee and find some peace and quiet. When stress is from conflict, we come home in a "fight" mode and take out our anger on those we love. Neither response is adequate to the situation.

Men often complain that they never have enough time at home to relax and be by themselves. When they take time, they often feel guilty. "I know my kids want to be with me," one overworked man told me, "but I have to have some downtime when I get home. I'm always feeling pulled by the needs of the family and my need to relax."

Men who take out their anger on their families also end up feeling unhappy and frustrated. "I know it isn't all their fault," another man told me. "It's just that they do such stupid things that drive me up the wall. I guess the stress I'm feeling at work has something to do with it, but what can I do? If I get mad at my boss, I'll get fired. What would happen to my family if that happened? I feel I'm caught between a rock and a hard place."

The mothers in Dr. Repetti's studies behaved quite differently. When the moms had a bad day, they were *more* involved with and *more* affectionate with their children. They hugged them, spent time with them, and told them they loved them. In other words, the mothers "tended" to them.

The mothers were often not even aware that on particularly difficult days at work, they came home and reached out to their children in a positive and caring way. As we might guess, the children responded in a more positive and affectionate way to their moms. The result is that there was also a lot of "befriending" going on.

For women, the kind of stress relief that they were built for in their ancestral environment still works well today. When things happen that cause women to become afraid, they reach out for their children or they call up one of their girlfriends.

For men, however, things have changed dramatically. We can no longer engage in battle to physically defeat the threat. All of our fight-or-flight chemicals surge through our systems without being dissipated through action. In the short run, we become hypersensitive, irritable, anxious, and frustrated. We take out our frustrations either on ourselves, becoming increasingly withdrawn and depressed, or on others, becoming angry and blaming. In the long run, continuous stress, with no ability to relieve it, leads to breakdown and sickness.

IRRITABILITY, WITHDRAWAL, AND ILLNESS

Thirty scientific studies worldwide have shown that women draw on their social connections to friends, relatives, neighbors, and family more often than men do. This is true whether the stress results from unemployment, cancer, fear of crime, a death in the family, or simple sadness.[10]

And study after study has shown that feeling connected with other people is extremely important for physical and mental health. A massive study of 4,725 randomly selected residents of Alameda County in California found that those with the fewest close friends, relatives, and social connections had mortality rates that were two to three times higher than those of people with high levels of social connectedness. Also, life expectancy tables show a difference of 9 years between people with very poor social connections and those with very good ones.[11] Problems such as suicide, alcoholism, and mental illness rates are also much higher among people who live alone.[12]

Are men doomed to suffer stress-related illnesses, including IMS, because of our lack of connection? Not at all! We all know women who are shy and have great difficulty socializing with others. We also know men who have lots of friends and companions and reach out to them when they are in pain or under stress.

FUTURE SHOCK AND IMS

Futurist Alvin Toffler was one of the first people to recognize the effect of stress on society as a whole. "I coined the term 'Future Shock,' in 1965," says Toffler, "to describe the shattering stress and disorientation that we induce in individuals by subjecting them to too much change in too short a time. . . . This psychobiological condition can be described in medical and psychiatric terms. It is the disease of change."[13]

Although I wasn't aware of the connection at the time I first read *Future Shock,* Toffler goes on to describe men experiencing the Irritable Male Syndrome. "Its victims often manifest erratic swings in interest and lifestyle, followed by an effort to 'crawl into their shells' through social, intellectual, and emotional withdrawal. They feel continually 'bugged' or harassed and want desperately to reduce the number of decisions they must make."[14]

Toffler took a new look at some situations that had been studied and found that the idea of future shock could help us better understand them. Ever since World War I, there had been studies of soldiers in battle and the psychological damage that occurred when they experienced the stresses of war. Toffler focused on the fact that the environments, in addition to being dangerous, were constantly changing. He felt that a good deal of the emotional breakdown that many men experienced could be understood as their inability to cope with so many different changes in such a short period of time.

As you read Toffler's description of soldiers who broke down under the pressures of combat, think of men you know who might be suffering from the Irritable Male Syndrome. "Mental deterioration often began with fatigue. This was followed by confusion and nervous irritability. The man became hypersensitive to the slightest stimuli around him. He became tense, anxious, and heatedly irascible. His comrades never knew when he would flail out in anger, even violence, in response to minor inconveniences."[15]

IRRITABLE MALES IN AN AGE OF RAGE

Increasingly, we all are reacting more like soldiers in battle. "A steady escalation of stress has progressively but nearly imperceptibly turned up the heat to such an extent that our frustration simmers close to the boiling point a huge amount of the time," says Melinda Davis, author of *The New Culture of Desire: Five Radical New Strategies That Will Change Your Business and Your Life*.[16] Irritability and anger have become such an integral part of our lives that they are coming to feel natural.

Many of our relationships suffer from the irritability and anger that are so much a part of life today. Even our physical health can be damaged as a result of irritation and anger. A study reported in the *Journal of the American Medical Association* found that one of the best predictors of future heart disease was hostility. Being hostile predicted future heart disease even better than did high cholesterol, cigarette smoking, or being overweight.[17]

Worldwide, more and more individuals are reacting to the stresses of living by using anger as a standard negotiating tactic. In the past decade, acts of unquestionably intended driver-to-driver violence increased 51 percent, according to the American Automobile Association (AAA).[18] In an online Driver Personality Survey, 70 percent of polled drivers agreed with the following statement: "It's important to prevent aggressive drivers from pushing you and other drivers around, by blocking their way or giving them a scare."[19] These are pretty scary statistics. No wonder the American Psychiatric Association is considering including road rage as a new type of psychiatric disorder.

Men seem to be more susceptible than women to expressing their irritability through violent forms of road rage. In a major study on road rage, it was found that of the 10,037 cases studied, only 413 of the perpetrators were female.[20] Men's hypersensitivity to insult on the highways may be related to our ancestral need to defend territory. "Human beings are territorial," says Matthew Joint, head of behavioral analysis for the group policy road safety unit at the AAA Foundation for Traffic Safety. "As individuals, we have a personal space, or territory, which evolved essentially as a defensive mechanism. Anyone who invades this territory is potentially an aggressor. The car is an extension of this territory."[21]

IMAGINAL STRESS
AND THE IRRITABLE MALE SYNDROME

As we continue to deal with the stresses of living in the real world, we are also subjected to a new kind of stress. Just as Toffler's work on future shock helped us understand the kinds of stresses that affected us in the last half of the 20th century, Davis helps us understand and survive the stresses of the first half of the 21st century.

"Sometime in or around the winter of 1993, the world as we knew it ceased to be," says Davis. "It was then that we finally succeeded in shifting the tender balance we have always maintained between our two separate levels of reality: The world we can see and experience outside of ourselves, and the world we can only experience inside our own heads."[22] She calls this new experience the world of the *imaginal.* This is by no means an imaginary world but rather one that takes place in the very real world of our minds.

Think for a moment about the place of computer communication in your life. How often do you send and receive e-mails, get information from a Web site, or use a search engine to explore the world? For most of us, the computer has become indispensable. Our minds' travels on the World Wide Web seem endless. "Without doubt, the Internet can be cited as the number one cultural phenomenon of our age," say Jennifer Schneider, M.D., Ph.D., and Robert Weiss, M.S.W., authors of *Cybersex Exposed: Simple Fantasy or Obsession?* "It is rapidly becoming the most important instrument of social change in the developed world."[23]

As we spend more time in the world of computers, the very basis for our reality begins to shift. Reality is no longer something we can touch and feel in the outer world but something we think of in our minds. As Davis says, "There is very little 'let's lift the hood and take a look' appraisal possible in this new order of things." This shift has a particularly devastating effect on men. How do those of us raised on the model of men as "doers" understand ourselves when we do less and less and think more and more?

Our primal fear is losing our minds. "Now we are fighting for our lives inside," says Davis. "Now when we feel the deep craving for primal safety, it is increasingly for inner balance and sanity."[24] The irritability, hypersensitivity, and anxiety so many of us feel result from the assault on our psyches. We are increasingly unnerved as life continues to speed up and our brains become overwhelmed.

"As a result of increasing demands on our attention and focus, our brains try to adapt by rapidly shifting attention from one activity to another—a strategy that is now almost a requirement for survival," says Richard Restak, M.D., a neurologist, neuropsychiatrist, and clinical professor of neurology at George Washington University Medical Center in Washington, D.C. "As a consequence, attention deficit disorder is becoming epidemic in both children and adults."[25]

In fact, some believe that attention deficit disorder is becoming the norm in our society. "With so many distracted people running around, we could become the first society with attention deficit disorder," writes cyberspace critic Evan Schartz in *Wired* magazine. In his opinion, attention deficit disorder may be "the official brain syndrome of the information age."[26]

IMAGINAL STRESS AND THE WORLD OF WORK

Nowhere is stress more visible than in the ways we make our livings. "Your new ideas or your life!" Davis calls out, expressing the new bottom line of the marketplace. "The new nature of work exhorts us to innovate or die—because ideas are the new ch'i of Western civilization. Or, to use historic metaphor, ideas are the new steel."[27] The result is that millions of men who made their livings by making things now have to learn to create ideas.

In the entire flow of human history, men have never had to adapt to a change of this magnitude. "It's the biggest change since the caveman started bartering," says Arnold Baker, head economist for Sandia Laboratories, a facility that develops technologies that support our national security.[28] It is a change that contributes to the development of the Irritable Male Syndrome in millions of men.

When men made things, the threats to our survival and well-being came from our physical vulnerabilities. As we got older, we wondered whether we would have the strength to do the job. We were concerned about injuries and illness because they might keep us from being able to work and support our families. We worried about whether we would be able to carry our own weight as we competed with younger men.

As more of us make our livings as decision makers, the threats to our survival and well-being come from our mental vulnerabilities. We wonder about whether we have the mental agility to keep up with younger men. We are concerned about our ability to remember and integrate new and ever-changing information. We worry that memory will fail us completely and that one day we will just "lose it."

And more of us seem to be losing it at work. According to the Department of Justice, 2 million people are victims of workplace violence every year—1,000 of whom are murdered. "That's 20 murder victims at work a week," says Davis.[29]

The link between irritability and rage and the kind of stress we experience in the imaginal age is unmistakable. The workplace environment with the greatest violence is not manufacturing, where sweaty, macho men make big, heavy objects. Rather, it is the service sector, where we are all trying to keep our heads above water.

SEX AND THE IMAGINAL:
THE LOSS OF SLOW HANDS AND AN EASY TOUCH

For an increasing number of us, even sex is becoming increasingly imaginal. What we could not even imagine doing in a lifetime of sexual experience is available in living color on the Internet. Where once our sexual experience was limited to what we practiced with our sexual partners, increasingly, the world of sex takes place inside our minds.

Pornography has found a perfect home on the Internet. Some studies estimate that 60 percent of Web sites, our imaginal window on the world, are sexual in nature, and that some 28 million Americans alone visit those sex sites every week.[30] One Fortune 500 company discovered that 62 percent of men's computer use at work was spent engaged in cybersex. That company was by no means unique.[31] And men aren't the only ones who use the Internet for sexual stimulation. Millions of women use chat rooms and other corners of cyberspace to meet and share experiences with cyberlovers.

In the imaginal world, we can have whatever we want, whenever we want it. In the world of cybersex, we can find a partner or partners who will do anything we want, day or night, for as long as we want. We never have to worry about getting a communicable disease. If the "relationship" doesn't work out, we leave with a tap of the mouse and move on to someone else.

It has been said that the brain is the most important sex organ. We can fantasize just about anything. The Internet allows us to give in to a world of fantasy where we don't ever have to touch a real human being. The feelings can be very intense, but they don't really satisfy our needs for intimacy and passion.

It's no wonder that many people become addicted to the experience. Since it's so available without being truly satisfying, it is easy to keep going on to the next sexual image and the next one after that. An MSNBC study found that 1 in 10 adult Internet users admitted to being addicted to online sex.[32] "A significant minority of men and women, however, for whom the ease of access, anonymity, and velocity of the online sexual material is problematic, getting hooked on cybersex can lead to loss of jobs and relationships, as well as health, legal, or other concerns [sic]," say Dr. Schneider and Robert Weiss.[33]

Men who experience the Irritable Male Syndrome are particularly vulnerable to getting hooked on cybersex. At first, it seems to be a harmless distraction offering a relaxing interlude in a stressed-out day. Later, it can take over more and more of a person's life.

A negative cycle can develop. We use cybersex to deal with the stresses of work or home life. The more deeply we get involved with cybersex, the more we withdraw from other people. As a result, we often experience more stress in our personal lives. A study conducted at Stanford University showed that "the nation's obsession with the Internet is causing many Americans to spend less time with friends and family, less time shopping in stores, and more time working at home after hours." The study's principal investigator, Norman Nie, a political scientist at Stanford, said, "When you spend your time on the Internet, you don't hear a human voice and you never get a hug. There are going to be millions of people with very minimal human interaction."[34]

Men often turn to the Internet to tune out the stresses in our lives. Cybersex seems like a good way to "get away from it all." It seems a lot less dangerous than having an affair with a young secretary at the office. It seems a lot less disruptive to our relationships than leaving.

The problem is that the stresses don't go away. They are still waiting there when we log off. We haven't learned any long-term ways of alleviating stress.

Here's how Jeff, a 41-year-old married executive with two children, described his experiences with cybersex.

I just said to myself, look how hard I am working. I am giving to the family and the company, working nights and some weekends, too. There really is no time left for me. There is no time when I can just do what I want to do without interruption or obligation to others. I deserve a little pleasure in life, too! If I spend a few hours here and there online, getting off on a little fantasy, it is my only reward for all the work that I do and all that I give to others.[35]

I think most of us can empathize with Jeff. The problem is that men often become oblivious to the negative effect their behavior may be having. Jeff was finally fired after receiving three written warnings advising him that his job would be in danger if he continued to look at Internet porn sites at work.

As Jeff and countless other men have learned, we've seen monumental changes in the world. The amount of change and the speed with which we must deal with novel situations is truly mind boggling. These changes contribute to the stress that is one of the core causes of the Irritable Male Syndrome. As if that weren't enough to deal with, our male hormones and biochemistry also work against us, as we will see in the next chapter.

CHAPTER 8

THE IRRITABLE MALE BODY

Genes, Brain, Biochemistry, and Hormones

The Irritable Male Syndrome has roots in the very core of men's beings. Irritability, hypersensitivity, anxiety, frustration, and anger are experienced in the deepest recesses of our bodies, minds, and spirits. We now know that all parts of our beings are connected and all interact to produce problems as well as create solutions.

This is a time when things we thought were separate—mind and brain, physical and mental, genes and environment, psychotherapy and drugs—are being recognized as not really separate at all but ultimately connected at the deepest levels. When I was in school, emotional problems were seen as arising from *either* traumatic life experiences *or* physical trauma such as head injury. If the problem was the former, the person was seen by a "psychotherapist" who would delve into the person's past life to look for the origin of the trauma. If it was the latter, the patient would be seen by a "physical therapist," or doctor, who would likely prescribe medications.

Now we know that emotions have a physical basis and can be influenced by changes in the brain and the biochemistry of the body. We also know that emotions can actually change the structure of the brain. "The body is not a mindless machine," says Deepak Chopra, M.D., one of the pioneers of mind/body medicine. "The body and mind are one."[1]

THE INTEGRATION OF BODY, MIND, AND SPIRIT

As we have seen in previous chapters, the Irritable Male Syndrome is caused by a complex interaction between the mind, the body, the environ-

ment, the culture, and the times we live in. In order to heal, we must understand the ways these all connect.

The way in which stress affects men's bodies, minds, and spirits is clearly
explained by J. Douglas Bremner, M.D., director of mental health research
at the Atlanta Veterans Administration Medical Center and editor of *Stress
Disorder.* "Stressors, acting through a depression or disruption of mental
processes, can translate directly into an increased risk for poor health out-
comes, including heart disease, cancer, and infectious disease, in addition to
the increased risk for psychiatric disorders."[2] So we can see there is a feedback loop in which stressors interact with the mind and body to cause problems, including the Irritable Male Syndrome. When you are under stress,
chemicals released in the brain increase your levels of hypersensitivity, irritability, and anger. Eventually, these mental processes can cause you to
develop problems such as sexual dysfunction, heart disease, or ulcers.
These, in turn, can cause you to become more irritable and depressed.

Nancy C. Andreasen, M.D., Ph.D., author of *Brave New Brain: Conquering Mental Illness in the Era of the Genome,* is one of the scientists
who recognizes the interrelationship between genetics; the brain, mind, and
body; and personal experience and family heritage. She suggests that a
number of interacting factors determine whether a man experiences the Irritable Male Syndrome or other mood disturbances: **Multiple interacting factors** such as genes, viruses, toxins, nutrition, birth injury, and personal
experiences interact to influence **brain structure and function.** Changes in
the brain including brain development and degeneration, plastic changes in
response to experience, brain chemistry, changes in response to medications, and changes in response to psychotherapy influence and are influenced by **mind functions.** Mind functions such as memory, emotion,
language, attention, arousal, and consciousness influence and are influenced by **the unique person in a specific social world.**[3] The interactions of
all these factors then lead to the expression of a particular problem, such
as the Irritable Male Syndrome.

IT ALL BEGINS IN OUR GENES

"The Secret of Life: Cracking the DNA code has changed how we live,
heal, eat, and imagine the future," says *Time* magazine in its special issue
on DNA on February 17, 2003. We all know that our genes are critically

important for understanding what makes us who we are, yet most of us have only a vague understanding of exactly what that means. So to begin, I'd like to offer a very simplified view of what genes are and how they might affect our well-being.

Each gene is a different packet of information necessary for your body to grow and work. Your genes also contain the information for how you look: the color of your eyes, your height, the shape of your nose. Just as genes have an impact on who you are physically, they also have an influence on your temperament and emotional state.

We often think of something that's "genetic" as being "inevitable." If you have the gene for "X," you will have problems with "Y." As with most things in life, the ways your genes express themselves are more complicated than that.

Robert M. Sapolsky, Ph.D., a professor of biological sciences and neuroscience at Stanford University, says that many ways our emotions express themselves are based on "if-then" logic. That is, *if*, for instance, you are exposed to a stressful life event, *then* your risk of depression increases. In more complex cases, we might have the scenario: *If* you are exposed to a stressful life event *and* you have a low sense of self-efficacy, *then* your risk of depression increases. The genome "represents an informational system of if-then clauses," says Dr. Sapolsky.[4]

"ACTING IN" IMS AND OUR GENETIC HERITAGE

So far, researchers haven't isolated genes for the Irritable Male Syndrome. They are finding genes, however, that make some of us more vulnerable to developing IMS. In November 1996, the *New York Times* reported on a study published in the journal *Science* that linked a certain gene to individuals who are prone to anxiety, pessimism, and negative thinking.[5] In the July 19, 2002, issue of *Science,* researchers from the National Institute of Mental Health reported that the amygdala, the brain structure known as the hub of fear, responds differently to pictures of scary faces depending on which version of a gene one has inherited.

The gene's effect on the amygdala's response to emotional stimuli may help shape a dimension of temperament, suggest Ahmad Hariri, Ph.D., and Daniel Weinberger, M.D., two of the lead researchers. "How biologically reactive we are to a signal of danger, which is partly inheritable, can place us at risk for an anxiety disorder or it may be an adaptive, positive attribute, such as increased vigilance, depending on the circumstances," says Dr. Weinberger.[6]

Researchers call the general trait that determines how we respond to danger "harm avoidance." "Harm avoidance is a blanket trait that includes anxiety, fear, inhibition, shyness, depression, tiredness, and hostility," says Dean Hamer, Ph.D., chief of the section on gene structure and regulation in the laboratory of biochemistry of the National Cancer Institute. Clearly, these traits don't always go together. We can be anxious without being tired, fearful without being depressed. "Nevertheless, many studies have shown that people who experience one of these negative moods are more likely to experience one or more of the others," says Dr. Hamer.[7]

There is a key to all these feelings that is directly related to our understanding of the Irritable Male Syndrome. Remember that one of the core elements of IMS is hypersensitivity, or how easily our feelings are triggered by events in the outside world as well as by our own thoughts.

Dr. Hamer found that people who scored high on harm avoidance tests often had hair-trigger reactions. It is as though they walk around armed, ready to react at the least disturbance. "The common feature of all harm avoidance is emotional sensitivity, a kind of emotional sunburn that is easily inflamed," says Dr. Hamer. "Every little thing makes a high scorer feel bad, pushing out any positive emotions. They are very sensitive to punishment, always waiting for the other shoe to drop.[8]

"A high level of harm avoidance often is accompanied by an inability to control cravings and urges for food, cigarettes, or possessions," says Dr. Hamer. "Desires are perceived as irresistible, even if they later produce remorse."[9] This is why men experiencing IMS have such difficulty when their needs are frustrated. I remember going into an immediate funk or rage if my wife didn't have dinner ready when I expected it or was not as affectionate as I wanted her to be.

IMS, OTHER MOOD DISORDERS, AND HEREDITY

Increasing evidence points to harm avoidance as being a human trait that has a strong hereditary component. One of the hallmarks of genetically influenced traits is that they run in families. This is certainly true in my own case. As I discussed earlier, my father as well as many of his brothers and sisters suffered from depression, manic-depression, and other mood disorders. My mother came from a long line of worriers.

There are many famous examples of these traits running in families. The Hemingway family was devastated by the destructiveness of these traits. Author Ernest Hemingway, who committed suicide at age 61, is thought to have used the same shotgun that his father used to end his own life 33 years earlier. His father, physician Clarence Hemingway, suffered from violent mood swings and erratic behavior. Hemingway's brother and sister also committed suicide. Actress Margaux Hemingway, one of Ernest's granddaughters, struggled with bulimia and alcoholism. She committed suicide during the summer of 1996, at the age of 41.

It isn't coincidence that so many creative people suffer from mood disorders. The same emotional sensitivity that allows us to have a special sensitivity to the human condition also causes us much pain when we react strongly to even minute changes in our internal and external environments. "We of the craft are all crazy," remarked Lord Byron about himself and his fellow poets. "Some are affected by gaiety, others by melancholy, but all are more or less touched."[10]

Research has found that disorders that were once seen as totally separate entities may have an underlying genetic association. A study at McLean Hospital in Belmont, Massachusetts, showed that depression, anxiety disorders, eating disorders, irritable bowel syndrome, and several other psychiatric and medical conditions might all be traceable to a common but still unknown genetic abnormality.[11]

James Hudson, M.D., Sc.D., associate chief of the biological psychiatry laboratory at McLean, and his colleagues interviewed 64 individuals with depression and 58 others without depression, and then interviewed more than 300 members of the immediate families of both groups of individuals. The interviews covered not only depression but also a large group of additional psychiatric and medical disorders, called affective spectrum disorders (ASDs), that the investigators theorized to be related to depression. The research demonstrated not only that depression clusters in family trees but also that all of the disorders of ASD cluster together in families as well.

"We found that relatives of an individual with a form of ASD had 2.5 times the risk of developing some form of ASD themselves, in comparison to the relatives of individuals with no forms of ASD," says Dr. Hudson. The researchers are conducting genetic studies using a broader range of subjects in hopes of finding the specific common gene or genes that link depression and the other forms of ASD.

After reviewing evidence on how heredity affects mood, Dr. Hamer concludes, "Even in adulthood, after all the life events that would seem to make a person more inhibited or less so, harm avoidance is still largely influenced by genes."[12] This does not mean that we are victims of our genes. Rather, we must recognize that many of us may have strong tendencies to be very sensitive to emotional ups and downs. As we will see in later chapters, this can be an asset if we learn to understand our genetic influences.

"ACTING OUT" IMS AND OUR GENES

The same emotional hypersensitivity that can cause us to "act in" our emotions and contribute to anxiety, worry, and depression can also cause us to "act out" with anger, hostility, and violence. "Harm avoidance, neuroticism, and anxiety are about feeling bad," says Dr. Hamer. "Hostility means feeling bad about other people. This is not the type of harm avoidance that makes people shy, but rather the type that makes them see everything— including other people—in a negative light."[13] So blaming others and blaming ourselves are opposite sides of the same coin, and both have their origins in hypersensitivity to emotional stimulation.

Looking at the ways our genes affect patterns of anger and violence shows the interplay between our genetic heritage and the environments we live in. One way of assessing the contributions of genetics and environment is by studying twins who were raised apart. One of the most comprehensive experiments was conducted by Remi Cadoret, Ph.D., a psychiatry researcher at the University of Iowa College of Medicine in Iowa City, and his colleagues, who have studied more than 1,000 Iowa families during the past 20 years.[14] In this research, the biological children of parents in trouble with the law, with alcohol and drugs, or with other people were compared to the children of parents without such problems. All the children had been separated from their biological parents at birth and had been adopted by families with no blood ties. The researchers wanted to determine whether the children were more like their biological parents—who contributed the genes—or the parents who raised them—who contributed the environment. What they found was surprising. For the children who had nonproblem genes—that is, those whose biological parents didn't "act out"—the home environment made little difference. Even if the adoptive parents had all kinds of problems—if they abused alcohol or drugs, had fights, got arrested—the children turned out the same as kids raised in good homes. In other words, when the kids had good genes to start with, a bad social environment did not matter much.

Kids with problem genes *and* a problem environment got a double whammy. Their levels of childhood and adolescent aggression were dramatically increased. Measures of bad behavior such as lying, stealing, truancy, and school expulsions increased by as much as 500 percent. Some of the kids with bad genes and bad environments turned out fine, but the majority had serious "acting out" problems.[15]

In summarizing these findings, Dr. Hamer makes clear how genes impact behavior. "Aggressive and antisocial behavior increased dramatically only in children with both 'bad genes' and bad homes. That shows that what is being inherited is not bad behavior or aggression but rather a genetic sensitivity to the environment. The genes didn't make them antisocial; the genes made them vulnerable."

He concludes with an analogy that can help us all understand the contribution of genes and environment and give us hope that we can help those who have "bad genes." "A bad seed planted in good soil had a decent chance. A bad seed planted in bad soil withered. Humans by nature respond well to nurture, but they also respond to its absence."[16]

Nature and nurture work together to make us who we are. Our genetic heritage lays a certain foundation. Though the foundation acts as a constraint on what can be built, there is still a lot of leeway in what the final building will look like.

THE MALE BRAIN
AND THE MASCULINE MODE OF FEELING

The interaction between our genes and environment manifests itself in the ways our brains are structured and function. Though the basic structures and functions are the same, there are significant differences between male and female brains that help us understand who we are and what kinds of things make us irritable. I purposely use the terms *male brain* and *female brain* rather than *men's brains* and *women's brains,* because not all men have the typical male brain and not all women have the typical female brain.

As I discussed in chapter 5, while the female brain is predominantly hard-wired for empathy, the male brain is predominantly hard-wired for systemizing. "Systemizing is the drive to analyze, explore, and construct a system," says Simon Baron-Cohen, Ph.D., a professor of psychology and psychiatry at Cambridge University and author of *The Essential Difference: The Truth about the Male and Female Brain*. "The systematizer intuitively figures out how things work, or extracts the underlying rules that govern the behavior of a system. This is done in order to understand and predict the system, or to invent a new one."[17]

So the difference in brain structure and functioning can be seen in the different ways men and women experience and express emotions. "Recent studies have shown that men can take up to 7 hours longer than women to process complex emotions," says psychologist Michael Gurian, Ph.D., author of *What Could He Be Thinking?: How a Man's Mind Really Works*.[18] That's one of the reasons a man becomes so irritable when a woman wants him to tell her how he feels.

When a man becomes emotional, he is more likely to express it physically. A woman is more comfortable expressing her feelings verbally. He wants to go out and pound something. She wants to talk it out.

"Given the different brain structures of men and women," Dr. Gurian concludes, "it will come as no surprise that men inherently distrust feelings and women inherently trust them. Certainly this is a generalization, yet your personal experience has probably confirmed it."[19]

THE IRRITABLE MALE BRAIN

As we have seen, the Irritable Male Syndrome, like other syndromes, is produced by a mixture of factors including personal experience and genetic susceptibility. Whether prompted by genes or life experiences, IMS is expressed through the workings of the brain. Internal experiences of such things as irritability, hypersensitivity, frustration, anxiety, depression, and anger are created as neurotransmitters send messages back and forth between regions of the brain. The subjective experience of irritability is a result of the interplay between brain regions that store and interpret current emotional experiences in light of one's past. If you've had repeated experiences of feeling judged by your partner, for instance, you will more easily react emotionally when you have a similar experience.

The communication between the various parts of the brain is conducted via chemical couriers called neurotransmitters. One cell communicates with another by sending chemical messengers into the gap, or synapse, between the two. After these messengers activate the next cell, any excess neurotransmitters leave the synapse and return to their original cell. The neurotransmitter serotonin is possibly the most well-known because anti-depressant medications such as Prozac (fluoxetine) block the reuptake of serotonin, prolonging the neurotransmitter's mood-enhancing activity. Prozac is one of a number of medications aptly called selective serotonin reuptake inhibitors (SSRIs). Others include Seroxat (paroxetine), Lustral (sertraline), Faverin (fluvoxamine), and Cipramil (citalopram).

Although the specific mechanisms are still being worked out, it seems likely that such problems as the Irritable Male Syndrome, depression, anxiety, and even excessive worry result from imbalances in brain chemistry. As we will see in part 3, medications that help restore balance in the brain are one of the many treatment options for people who suffer from IMS.

Only a few years ago, scientists thought that brain structure and function became fixed shortly after adolescence. Now we know that the brain continues to change throughout life. "The brain never loses the power to transform itself on the basis of experience, and this transformation can occur over very short intervals of time," says Richard Restak, M.D., a neurologist, neuropsychiatrist, and clinical professor of neurology at George Washington University Medical Center in Washington, D.C. "For instance, your brain is different today than it was yesterday. This difference results from the effect on your brain of yesterday's and today's experiences, as well as the thoughts and feelings you've entertained over the past 24 hours."[20]

Although we have known for some time that stress can cause damage to the heart, the gastrointestinal tract, and other parts of the body, we have recently learned that it can actually damage the brain. "Research in only the past decade or so has shown that extreme stress has effects on the brain that last throughout the lifespan," says Dr. Bremner.[21] This means that many of the emotional distresses that we have, in the past, viewed as purely psychological may be the result of physical damage to the brain. "A group of psychiatric disorders related to stress, what I call *trauma-spectrum disorders,* could share in common a basis in brain abnormalities that are caused by stress," says Dr. Bremner.[22]

"Trauma-spectrum disorders are those that are known to be linked to stress, including post-traumatic stress disorder (PTSD), dissociative disorders, borderline personality disorders, adjustment disorder, depression, and anxiety," says Dr. Bremner.[23] I would include the Irritable Male Syndrome as another one of these trauma-spectrum disorders.

CHILDHOOD TRAUMA
AND ITS IMPACT ON THE BODY/MIND/SPIRIT

"My dad was a policeman, and I loved him with blind devotion," said William as we began one of our sessions. William was a big man, his hands callused from construction work. We had been working together for many months, but he had been unwilling to talk about his early family experiences except to say they were "okay."

William continued: "I didn't see my father a lot as a child. When I did, I would run to him and throw my arms around his neck. I remember a game we played when I was maybe 2 or 3 years old. I would climb up on a chair and yell, 'Catch me,' as I would jump into his arms, squealing with delight."

William hesitated. His breathing became shallow, and he stared off into the distance as though seeing something he didn't want to see. He continued in a voice that was flat and emotionally void. Only something in his eyes revealed a hint of what he felt. "I yelled out, 'Daddy, Daddy,' as I jumped off the kitchen chair and flew through the air with my arms outstretched. Just as I reached out to him, he turned away. I hit my head on the table as I fell to the floor. I don't remember much after that except Dad yelling at me to be quiet as we drove to the hospital. Days later, Dad took me on his lap and said, 'Baby boy, you have to learn: You can't trust anyone in this life, not even your own father.'" William's gaze was steady as he remembered his father's words. I couldn't hold back the tears that ran down my own cheeks.

William breathed a sigh. "I've never really remembered that scene, and I've never told anyone until now. I just know that I never again reached out for him. Something died in me that day, or got buried, I don't know." William paused for a long time. "There were other lessons along the way to 'make me tough.' I never resented them at the time. I just thought that's what it was like to be a boy and grow up to be a man. But I still miss jumping into my father's arms."

It took William a long while to express his rage, pain, and fear that went with the experience. It took him a long time to express the guilt he felt for not being a good enough son to his father. For most of his life, he had idealized his father and felt ashamed that he had not done better. It was only since starting therapy that the anger and rage had come out. He had sworn he would never be like his dad. Now he found that he was repeating many of the same violent behaviors. Finally being able to let out all the feelings he felt toward his father and finally forgiving him began to free William to love himself and his family.

We can only speculate on what it must have been like for William's father to watch his son screaming, his face bloody, as he taught the lessons he thought the boy needed to learn. How did he perceive the world? Why would he hurt his son in order to make him a better person? What had *his* father been like, and where will the cycle of violence end?

Charles L. Whitfield, M.D., is an expert on the effect of childhood abuse on a person's body, mind, and spirit. In his book *The Truth about Depression,* he offers extensive documentation to show the strong and perhaps causal relationship between trauma and depression. He found 209 studies that linked depression with a history of childhood trauma. "These reports found that among those with a history of childhood trauma, depression was from 1.6 to 12.2 times more common than was found among the controls, who said they had no such trauma history, and with whom they were compared," he says.[24]

In another book, *The Truth Will Set You Free: Overcoming Emotional Blindness and Finding Your True Adult Self,* psychoanalyst Alice Miller, Ph.D., draws on the most recent research relating childhood trauma to actual changes in brain function. "A number of researchers have established that neglect and traumatization of baby animals invariably leads to both functional and structural deficiencies in their brains," says Dr. Miller. "Gradually this discovery is being found true for human babies as well."[25]

Researchers at McLean Hospital in Belmont, Massachusetts, have identified four types of brain abnormalities linked to child abuse and neglect, providing the first comprehensive review of the multiple ways in which abuse can damage the developing brain. In the journal *Cerebrum,* the researchers also review evidence that suggests this early damage to the developing brain may subsequently cause disorders such as anxiety and depression in adulthood.[26]

"The science shows that childhood maltreatment may produce changes in both brain function and structure," says Martin Teicher, M.D., Ph.D., director of the developmental biopsychiatry research program at McLean and author of the paper presented in the journal. "These changes are permanent," he says. "This is not something people can just get over and get on with their lives."[27]

The McLean team theorized that the stress caused by child abuse and neglect may trigger the release of some hormones and neurotransmitters while inhibiting others, in effect remolding the brain so that the individual is "wired" to respond to a hostile environment. "We know that an animal exposed to stress and neglect early in life develops a brain that is wired to experience fear, anxiety, and stress," says Dr. Teicher. "We think the same is true of people."[28]

Research provides a good example of the ways social environment and genes interact, demonstrating that some abused children become violent or criminal because of genetic susceptibility factors. "In essence, some potential future criminals may harbor a gene or genes that remain dormant unless 'turned on' by abuse," says Dr. Restak.[29]

Despite all the obviously harmful effects of childhood trauma, one type of damage is so prevalent among males that people tend to condone it. Perhaps the most common childhood pain boys endure is circumcision. While most people agree that cutting the genitals of girls is brutal and emotionally scarring, cutting boys' penises is ironically dismissed as minor or even medically beneficial. This is despite the fact that every national medical society in the world that has reviewed circumcision has not recommended it.

TRAUMA-SPECTRUM DISORDERS AND GENDER: WOMEN CRY AND MEN RUN AWAY

One of Dr. Bremner's experiments helps us understand the difference between the way men and women experience trauma-spectrum disorders. He gave a group of former depression patients a beverage spiked with an amino acid that blocks the brain's ability to absorb serotonin, the neurotransmitter that allows us to feel upbeat and happy. Using new brain-scan techniques, he took pictures of the subjects' brains to see if he could pinpoint the areas that were associated with depression. If we knew the areas of the brain associated with depression, he reasoned, we could come up with better medications and treatment approaches. In looking at the color brain scans, he was able to show that a loss of serotonin affects all three major areas of the brain.

What I find even more fascinating are the gender-specific differences in the way men and women reacted to the potion that blocked the effects of serotonin. Typical of the males was John, a middle-aged businessman who had fully recovered from a bout of depression thanks to a combination of psychotherapy and Prozac. Within minutes of drinking the brew, "he wanted to escape to a bar across the street," recalls Dr. Bremner. "He didn't express sadness . . . he didn't really express anything. He just wanted to go to Larry's Lounge."

Contrast John's response with that of female subjects like Sue, a mother of two in her mid-thirties. After taking the cocktail, "she began to cry and express her sadness over the loss of her father 2 years ago," recalls Dr. Bremner. "She was overwhelmed by her emotions."[30]

So we see a very real contrast in the ways men and women respond to a loss of the brain chemicals that keep our emotions in a healthy balance. Women tend to share their emotions with others. Men tend to withdraw and go for alcohol to prevent us from feeling our pain. I have found that chronic irritability is one of the principal ways men withdraw.

BRAIN COMMUNICATION
AND THE MOLECULES OF EMOTION

Whether you are happy or sad, irritable or calm, anxious or relaxed is determined by how mind molecules communicate with each other. The first players in this game of emotional communication are receptor molecules. Receptor molecules are often described as keyholes that are always ready for the right chemical key to swim by and enter, a process known as *binding*. Binding is sex on a molecular level, says Candace B. Pert, Ph.D., author of *Molecules of Emotion: Why You Feel the Way You Feel*. A chemical key is technically known as a *ligand*, a word that comes from the Latin *ligare*, meaning "that which binds." Ligands are generally much smaller molecules than the receptors they bind to, and they are divided into three chemical types.

The first type of ligands comprises the classic neurotransmitters, such as acetylcholine, monoamines, amino acids, gamma-aminobutyric acid

(GABA), glutamate, epinephrine, norepinephrine, dopamine, and sero-tonin. The second category consists of steroids, which include the sex hor-mones testosterone, progesterone, and estrogen. The third category contains peptides, such as oxytocin and vasopressin. All three categories are related since they have a common function as informational substances. They are all messenger molecules distributing information throughout an organism, says Dr. Pert.

"If the cell is the engine that drives all life," she says, "then receptors are the buttons on the control panel of that engine, and a specific peptide (or other kind of ligand) is the finger that gets things started."[31] One of Dr. Pert's major findings is that, although receptors are particularly influential within the brain, they actually make their presence felt throughout the entire body. The implication is that emotion—whether joy and happiness or irritability and anxiety—is generated not only by the brain but by cells everywhere in the body, from the intestines to the muscles. So when you feel irritable, frustrated, anxious, angry, and depressed, you are not just feeling it in your nervous system. The experience occurs in your blood, organs, muscles, tissues, and bones at the same time as it registers in your brain.

Dr. Pert's work offers scientific credence to what many people subjec-tively feel: When we experience the Irritable Male Syndrome, it feels like we experience it everywhere in our beings, not just in our minds. The truth is it isn't only our minds that are irritable. Our blood, bones, and muscles are also irritable.

This may help us understand the reality of the "subconscious" mind that Sigmund Freud, the father of psychoanalysis, spent so much time exploring without ever being able to define it biologically. The subconscious mind may well be in the very cells of our bodies. This lends yet more evidence to the reality of the integration of mind and body. The mind is in the body and the body is an extension of the mind.

HORMONES AND HEALTH

For most men, hormones are a mystery. In my high school biology class, I learned that hormones were important, though exactly how I wasn't sure. I was pretty sure that they had more to do with females and their myste-rious cycles than they had to do with me. In fact, hormones do have a tremendous effect on male health and well-being. They're involved in just about every biological process: immune function, reproduction, growth, even controlling other hormones.

"Hormones are dictators," says Theresa L. Crenshaw, M.D., one of the foremost experts on sexual medicine; past president of the American Association of Sex Educators, Counselors and Therapists; and author of *The Alchemy of Love and Lust.* "Their job is to tell other substances, including each other, what to do and how to behave. Some of them can be bullies, wreaking havoc with our moods and behavior. But these molecular rascals can operate with abandon only to the extent that they are not recognized, respected, and understood."[32]

Dr. Crenshaw says that a number of hormones are particularly important in their influence on our emotional lives. These include DHEA, oxytocin, PEA (phenylethylamine), estrogen, and testosterone. She also includes the neurotransmitters dopamine and serotonin in this list of hormones, validating Dr. Pert's observation that hormones and neurotransmitters are related.

TESTOSTERONE:
THE "YOUNG MARLON BRANDO" HORMONE

In order to understand the Irritable Male Syndrome, we have to pay particular attention to the role of testosterone in males. In her popular book on hormones, Dr. Crenshaw describes testosterone this way: "Testosterone is the young Marlon Brando—sexual, sensual, alluring, dark, with a dangerous undertone." She goes on to say that "it is also our 'warmone,' triggering aggression, competitiveness, and even violence. *Testy* is a fitting term. Testosterone doubles as an antidepressant but also makes us (men, especially) angry and irritable when it spikes."[33]

The emotional roller coaster that we see in men may be from the continual fluctuations in testosterone levels that males experience, believes James McBride Dabbs, Ph.D., professor of psychology and head of the social/cognitive psychology program at Georgia State University in Atlanta, who has been studying the effects of testosterone for the past 20 years and is one of the world's experts in the field. "Our average testosterone level is inherited from our parents, but physical and social conditions produce changes around this average level," he says. "Testosterone falls with ill health and physical exhaustion. It rises when we win important contests and falls when we lose. It changes with our status in life."[34]

"Testosterone levels oscillate every 15 to 20 minutes in men and also follow daily, seasonal, and annual rhythms," says Dr. Crenshaw. We often think of hormones wreaking havoc on the emotional lives of women. They may have an even more powerful impact on men.

Since men do have hormonal cycles, why don't we recognize them or talk about them? Estelle Ramey, M.D., a professor of endocrinology at Georgetown University School of Medicine in Washington, D.C., believes this is because men respond to their cycles in a way that is a function of their "culturally acquired self-image. They deny them." This denial is, she feels, the main reason the largely male scientific and medical communities have taken so long to study changes such as male menopause and IMS. Men who are out of touch with their body rhythms, afraid that "cycles" are feminine and hence to be avoided at all costs, are unlikely to be aware of the whisperings within until they get very loud.

Testosterone fluctuations do have a powerful impact on mood, and there are many things that can cause these hormonal shifts. "Testosterone levels seem to be influenced by just about everything," says Dr. Crenshaw. "The seasons, the environment, competition, the military, stress, a D cup, just to name a few." Based on her extensive research, Dr. Crenshaw has no doubt that men are affected in major ways. "The morning highs, daily fluctuations, and seasonal cycles whip men around. Think about the moment-to-moment impact of testosterone levels firing and spiking all over the place during the day, and what this must be doing to a man's temperament. Men who so strongly need to feel in control are in fact in much less control than they realize. No wonder they can be, well, testy!"[35]

HORMONAL CYCLES: MEN HAVE THEM, TOO

Winnifred B. Cutler, Ph.D., author of six books on hormones and health, is a researcher who has found a significant relationship between men's moods and their hormonal cycles.[36] "Now it is known that men show a hormonal rhythm," says Dr. Cutler, "a rhythm I call the hormonal symphony of men."[37]

A cycle might last a few minutes, a day, a week, a month, a season, a year, or a lifetime. There are also cycles within cycles. If a man, for instance, has blood taken from his arm six times a day starting in the early morning and continuing every 4 hours thereafter, lab results show a rhythmic rise and fall of testosterone throughout the day:

• When a man goes to sleep, his hormone levels start rising hour by hour until, by the time he wakes, his testosterone levels are at their highest. This is part of the reason why men experience morning erections.

• By late morning, his levels are likely to level off and begin to decline.

• By late afternoon, his testosterone will usually be at its lowest ebb.[38] Though I know of no research in this area, this low testosterone may be another reason why men tend to be more irritable when they come home from work.

Men's hormones also cycle throughout the year. In studies conducted in the United States, France, and Australia, it was found that men secrete their highest levels of sex hormones in October and their lowest levels in April. There was a 16 percent increase in testosterone levels from April to October and a 22 percent decline from October to April. Interestingly, though Australia is in its springtime when France and the United States are in their autumn, men in all three parts of the world showed a similar pattern of peaks and valleys.[39]

I have noticed a seasonal aspect of the Irritable Male Syndrome. Men tend to be more irritable as the days shorten and there is less light. Perhaps the decline in testosterone between October and April may contribute to this irritability (at least in the northern hemisphere).

Despite these commonalities, men's cycles seem to be relatively unpredictable and individual. A study of 20 young men showed that the majority had a discernible cycle of testosterone with regularly repeating rises and falls, but each man who did show a cycle had a cycle unique to himself and different from the others.[40] "In other words, men emerged as cyclic but with unique individuality to their cycles," says Dr. Cutler, who reported on the study. "This pattern of individual cycles is very different from the pattern in women, where the 29.5-day cycle is the universal optimum for fertility. . . . Thus, males are hormonally individualistic creatures, whereas females are hormonally harmonic with one another."[41] This may contribute to the unexpected way in which the Irritable Male Syndrome expresses itself. Many women tell me that the angry moods they see in the men they live with seem to occur spontaneously, often exploding out of the blue.

Perhaps the least understood and most problematic of men's hormonal cycles is the rapid oscillation of testosterone that occurs three or four times every hour. Testosterone levels cycle in males every 15 to 20 minutes. The extent of the highs and lows is influenced by a whole host of factors, including age, stress level, presence of male competitors, and the proximity of a desirable sexual partner. We don't really know the degree to which each of these factors influences testosterone levels. Nor do we know how the testosterone levels affect irritability. Are men more irritable when their testosterone levels are very high or very low, when they are increasing or decreasing?

Some research findings are helping us understand these complex issues. Could men go through a kind of "PMS" every 15 to 20 minutes as their testosterone levels fluctuate? A number of researchers, including Dr. Crenshaw, feel they do. "The speed or rate at which your blood hormone levels change can be as important or more important than the amount of change," says Dr. Crenshaw. "For example, the man's rapid quarter-hourly surges of testosterone can have more emotional and physical impact than the greater but more gradual changes of some of the hormones that fluctuate during the menstrual cycle."[42]

This is an extremely important finding from one of the world's leading researchers studying the relationship between hormones and moods and helps us gain a greater understanding of the hormonal basis of the Irritable Male Syndrome. PMS, long associated with women, may be a fact of life for men as well. "One of the most misleading consequences of the popular focus on premenstrual syndrome is that it omits men as a comparison group," says psychologist Carol Tavris, author of *The Mismeasure of Women: Why Women Are Not the Better Sex, the Inferior Sex, or the Opposite Sex.*[43]

In a study in which men were given a checklist of symptoms from a typical PMS questionnaire, including items such as reduced or increased energy, irritability and other negative moods, back pain, sleeplessness, headaches, and confusion, and omitting female-specific symptoms, such as breast tenderness, men reported having as many "premenstrual symptoms" as women do.[44]

We also need to recognize the shifts in testosterone levels that occur as a result of continuous stress and assaults on a man's self-esteem and how they contribute to the Irritable Male Syndrome. The research findings of Dr. Dabbs shed some light on these issues.

• The major social effect of testosterone is to orient us toward issues of sex and power.[45]

• It appears likely that testosterone is a factor in stubbornness and persistence.[46]

• Testosterone may be a useful biological marker for children at risk for disruptive behavior disorders. Testosterone is associated with withdrawal and aggression in boys.[47]

• Men have higher testosterone levels when they are competing for mates as adolescents and young adults. (Women have higher testosterone levels when they ovulate.)[48]

• When testosterone levels are too low, men have lowered energy and reduced interest in sex.

• A general restlessness and dissatisfaction with marriage goes along with high testosterone. Individuals in the top 2 percent of the testosterone distribution were twice as likely to have extramarital affairs as men in the bottom 2 percent. The top 2 percent were twice as likely to be physically abusive, hitting or throwing things at their wives. High-testosterone men are also psychologically remote from their wives.[49]

• The high-testosterone drive for domination can translate into the desire to control a wife or girlfriend, with the result that when a woman leaves a man, she not only insults him but also makes him feel as though he has lost control. Men are most likely to attack women they think have belittled or insulted them, as happens with women who leave them or threaten to leave.[50]

• When males compete, testosterone levels rise in the winner and drop in the loser.[51]

• Some men try to increase the effect of testosterone by taking steroids to make themselves stronger or more competitive. Most of them experience little emotional effect; but for some, increased steroid use can lead to uncontrollable rage—what the press calls 'roid rage.

So, we see that there is a rather complex relationship between testosterone, stress, and IMS. When testosterone is very high, men experience more stress in interpersonal relationships and are more aggressive. When it is too low, we have decreased energy and reduced interest in sex. When we win in a competition, whether for a woman or in a sport, testosterone goes up, along with feelings of well-being and power. When we lose, testosterone drops and we feel frustrated.

It seems a lot depends on the individual man. Someone with naturally high levels of testosterone may have difficulties in interpersonal relations and may feel particularly frustrated when testosterone diminishes. A guy with naturally low levels may be more easygoing but may become irritable if his levels become too low.

Although fluctuations in testosterone levels occur throughout life, the cycles are more chaotic and the emotional fluctuations are more intense during adolescence, when testosterone and other hormones are beginning to come online. "When a boy hits puberty, the influence of testosterone on his body and brain increases many-fold," says Dr. Gurian. "His testosterone level itself will increase in quantities 10 to 20 times more than girls'. . . . You can expect him to masturbate continually, bump into things a lot, be moody and aggressive, require a great deal of sleep, lose his temper, want sex as soon as he gets up the emotional guts to propose to a partner, have a massive sexual fantasy life, and so on."[52]

Another hormonal cycle that males must deal with, and one which is influenced by all the other shifts, is the drop in hormone levels that occurs in midlife. This cycle is part of the change of life known as andropause, or male menopause. It usually begins around age 40 and lasts until around age 55, though it can begin as early as 35 and may last until age 60. In my research on andropause, I found that irritability occurred in approximately 80 percent of the midlife men.[53]

In summary, we can say that men experience seven types of testosterone cycles:

1. Rhythmic fluctuations three or four times an hour
2. Daily changes, with hormone levels higher in the morning and lower in the afternoon
3. Monthly fluctuations that are rhythmic but that are different for each individual man
4. Fluctuations throughout the year, with levels highest in October and lowest in April

5. Testosterone changes associated with adolescence

6. Fluctuations that are part of the Irritable Male Syndrome and occur as a result of stress, loss of self-esteem, and changes in brain neurochemistry that can occur at any time in a man's life

7. Decreasing hormone levels associated with andropause or male menopause

Research on male hormonal cycles is still in its infancy. Yet it is clear that men as well as women have hormonal cycles that profoundly affect personality, mood, sexual interest, and sense of well-being. Perhaps the proverbial battle of the sexes would produce fewer casualties if men and women recognized how similar we are and how much our emotions fluctuate with the rhythms of our hormones.

The more we delve into the underlying causes of the Irritable Male Syndrome, the more we see how interrelated the various aspects truly are. Our genes, our brains, and our hormones all interrelate to contribute to our emotional life experience. Work by researchers such as Dr. Pert shows that what we have thought of as the "mind" is much more complex than we ever believed. Based on research on neurotransmitters and other "molecules of emotion," Dr. Pert demonstrated that what we know is not just a product of activity in the brain but also is contained in the cells of our body. "I had a gut feeling about that" turns out to be not just a figure of speech but a biochemical reality. With this integrated knowledge about our mind/body/spirit, we can now move forward to see how we can best treat and prevent the Irritable Male Syndrome.

PART 3

HELP IS HERE

"The body can and must be healed through the mind, and the mind can and must be healed through the body."
—neuroscientist Candace Pert, Ph.D.

CHAPTER 9

DEALING WITH DENIAL

What to Do When the Irritable Male Says,
"I'm Not Irritable.
It's *You* Who Has the Problem."

If you're this far in the book, you fall into one of five categories.

1. You're a man who has recognized that you have been suffering from the Irritable Male Syndrome, and you're ready to take some steps to do something about it.
2. You're a man who suspects that IMS is a problem, but you figure you don't need your wife to make you read some book to tell you how to fix it.
3. You're a man whose family or friends think you have a problem, but you believe the problem isn't you, it's *them*.
4. You're a woman living with a man who recognizes he has a problem, and you are both anxious to get help.
5. You're a woman living with a man suffering from the Irritable Male Syndrome—but he doesn't recognize he has a problem. You're probably suffering from the Why-Does-He-Lash-Out-at-Me-for-the-Least-Little-Thing Syndrome.

If I'm making this sound a bit humorous, it isn't because I don't recognize the pain that IMS causes men or their partners. I simply know from my own experience that sometimes humor is the only way we can survive the pain.

On the surface, IMS can be seen as a syndrome characterized by *others'* suffering. One of the primary symptoms of the Irritable Male Syndrome is that a man doesn't think he has a problem. It seems obvious to him that the problem is caused by someone else and that things would improve if only that other person would change. So, as I've mentioned time and again, most of the people who initially come to see me are women. They live with very irritable men, and they are in pain. Sometimes, they think something must be wrong with them. Why else would their men be so upset with them? Other times, they know that they aren't the problem, but they can't understand why he has a problem. They are perplexed that he can't see that he is not acting like himself, that something is dreadfully, painfully wrong.

That's why, in this chapter, I emphasize the relationship between irritable males and their partners. But I don't want to neglect other important relationships. Irritable Male Syndrome can be a problem for men who are not in romantic relationships and for young men still living at home. It can cause tremendous conflict and strain within families as well as with friends and co-workers. In younger men, irritability seems to be such a significant part of adolescence and early adulthood that it is difficult to distinguish between Irritable Male Syndrome and the normal difficulties of growing up. But the irritability, hypersensitivity, anxiety, frustration, and anger are excessive in those dealing with IMS. And just like older men, younger men also tend to see their problems as being caused by something or someone else. The attitude of denial is the same with males of any age: "Things would be okay if my ____ (dad, mom, sister, brother, teacher, girlfriend, wife, lover, partner, boss, co-worker, whomever) would just get off my back."

If you're living with an IMS male of any age who thus far refuses to recognize the problem or do anything to make things better for himself and for you, don't despair. The rest of this chapter is for you.

WHY MEN HAVE DIFFICULTY SAYING, "I'M SORRY," ASKING FOR DIRECTIONS, AND ACKNOWLEDGING THEY ARE SUFFERING FROM THE IRRITABLE MALE SYNDROME

Do you remember when boys first learned to ask girls to dance? If you're female, do you remember sitting and waiting to be asked?

Guys learn that we must take that long walk across the room and ask the girl of our dreams to dance. It feels like every eye in the room is on us.

Our hearts pound, our hands are clammy, and our mouths are dry. Unless we are the dream guy that every girl wants (in my time, it was the sports star), more often than not, we will be turned down.

We then have to make a choice. Do we ask someone else or slink back to the other side of the room, knowing that everyone is aware that we've been shot down? If we ask someone else, we risk being turned down because she, too, is waiting for a better offer or because she doesn't want to dance with someone who didn't pick her first. If we make the long walk back, we feel devastated and ashamed. We want to sink into the floor and disappear.

We learn two things pretty quickly. The first is that if we are not the football star who can have any girl he wants, we better come across as if we are super confident and sure of ourselves. We have to pretend that we are so sure of ourselves that no one would turn us down. If we are turned down, we have to pretend we don't really care. So the second thing we learn is that we'd better hide our pain. If we show our true feelings, no one will feel that we are confident. Feeling our true feelings may so wound us that we won't want to reach out ever again.

The result is that most of us act like we have it all together, all the time. We pretend that nothing bothers us. At the next dance, we act like we are impervious to pain. We repeat the same process when we go out on dates and when we make mistakes. By the time we pass the age of 21, we are very good at acting like we have all the answers and are impervious to pain.

Soon we forget why we made these choices in the first place. It just feels like who we are. Do you see the problem we create for ourselves and for those who love us? In order to say, "I'm sorry," we have to acknowledge we are wrong. Being wrong often makes us feel small, inadequate, and vulnerable and rekindles feelings of shame.

We've long forgotten the pain of the many times we were turned down or the defenses we learned to employ to keep up a strong front in the face of rejection. All we know is that saying, "I'm sorry" feels worse than driving a stake through our hearts. We don't remember the long walk across and back, or the many other times we had to be the initiators, but the shame of feeling "inadequate, ineffectual, and unwanted" is lodged in our hearts and souls.

Feeling sorry is even worse. Have you ever noticed that when a guy finally admits that he is sorry (usually only after he has done something so outrageously off the wall that he can't deny it), the apology doesn't have any feelings attached? His partner may be devastated, tears running down her cheeks in rivers. "Okay, I'm sorry," he says in a voice as dry as sand. We learned as children that boys should always perform well and not make mistakes. We learned to keep our feelings of sorrow so deeply buried that we lost connection with them.

Ask for directions? Easy for a woman to say. For men, it means making ourselves more vulnerable at the very time we feel the weakest. We learned long ago that real men don't eat quiche, real men don't complain, and real men don't get lost. Asking directions isn't usually as bad as saying, "I'm sorry." It only hurts about as much as having your top lip pulled up over the top of your head.

Here's the dilemma: We already feel foolish for getting lost. We feel worse knowing our women think we're foolish for not asking for directions sooner. If we overcome our resistance and go into a petrol station or ask a passerby, there are only two possibilities. One is that we will have to ask directions from a woman, which will recall the shame from the past when we stood in front of a girl and felt like a total klutz. The other possibility is that we will have to ask directions from another man, which will lead us to re-experience the feelings of pain and shame when life was all about competing with other guys for access to the most treasured young ladies.

Many women have a difficult time understanding why asking directions can be so threatening. Most guys have blocked out those uncomfortable past memories and have no idea why they have such difficulty reaching out for help. Our denial can be so strong that we can be totally lost, driving in circles for an hour, and say with a straight face, "Don't worry—I know what I'm doing. We're almost there." Our female companions roll their eyes and mumble, "Yeah, right."

If it feels like pulling out fingernails or having a stake through the heart to say, "I'm sorry," or "Excuse me, could you help me find this address?" you can imagine what it feels like to say, "I'm suffering from the Irritable Male Syndrome." We would have to admit we have a problem, we are hurting the ones we care about the most, we can't make the problem go away, and we need help from someone else. Let's just say it's something like having your fingernails pulled out at the same time that someone is pounding a stake through your chest. The surprise isn't that men are reluctant to reach out for help. The surprise is that we do it at all.

Points of Understanding

• Younger men and teens, who are just beginning to establish a sense of what it means to be men, are particularly vulnerable. As they become more irritable and angry, they deny that there is a problem. The problem gets worse and they must deny even more strongly that anything is wrong. It quickly becomes a vicious cycle.

• Older men in these situations don't recognize that they have a problem. Why treat a problem that doesn't exist?

• Even when we recognize there is a problem in our relationships, we're sure the problem is with our partners. "If there's a problem in the relationship, *you* get help," we may think. "It's your problem."

• If we begin to recognize that we may be contributing to the problem, we are sure we can work it out ourselves.

• Everyone knows people who went to a counselor and then ended their marriages. Most guys are more likely to believe that the counseling was the cause of the breakup than to realize that the problem may have been the couple waiting too long before seeking help.

• Counseling or therapy is expensive. We often have to take time off from work in order to see a counselor. Whether rich, poor, or in between, most men have money worries. Spending money on counseling and losing money when we don't work seem crazy to us. It seems a lot easier to hope things will work out on their own.

• Finally, there are the unconscious reasons. We may not even be aware of them, but they are highly influential. I have found the following three to be the most significant. First, even in our more enlightened view of "mental health," many people, particularly men, carry deeply embedded images of "crazy people" in "nuthouses" getting "shock treatments" and "sitting in wheelchairs talking to themselves." We think of movies like *One Flew Over the Cuckoo's Nest* and are afraid that maybe we will end up like that. For teens and young men, seeing a "shrink" may be viewed as totally uncool and unmanly.

Second, most of us already feel bad about ourselves, even if we don't show it. We believe that seeing a counselor will make us feel even worse. We are sure the counselor will take the side of our partners. (Why not? Deep down inside, we sense we are the cause of the problem.) If we don't have a partner, we often feel we will be told, directly or indirectly, that what we are doing is wrong, that there is something bad about us.

Third, most of us have a shaky hold on our feelings of manhood. We interpret going to see a "shrink" as a mark of failure as men. ("What kind of man am I if I can't take care of my family? What's the matter with me that I can't make things work?") Teens and young men may view seeing a therapist as an indication that they are different from their peers, deeply inadequate, and in need of "nurturing." It can cause them to feel they are becoming children again, just at the time they are trying to establish themselves as men.

WONDERING WHAT TO DO
WHEN HE WON'T SEE HE HAS A PROBLEM

Melissa called me after hearing an interview in which I described the Irritable Male Syndrome. "When I heard you talk, I just about broke down in tears. You were describing my husband, Jeff. You must have been living in our house for the past 5 years." She sounded desperate. I saw her in my office the next day.

Melissa told me that she had just turned 40 and Jeff was 45. They had been married for 21 years and had three children—a 19-year-old girl, a 15-year-old girl, and a 9-year-old boy. They had the usual ups and downs of being a couple and raising three children, but she described their life together as very happy and said she looked forward to spending the rest of their lives together.

> *Jeff is the executive director of a statewide program for people with mental health problems. He's a natural helper, happiest when he is doing things for others.*
>
> *Lately, he seems to care about everyone else but us. He's got super busy at work. When he comes home, he's like a different person than the old Jeff. At first, he'd get angry at the least little thing. When he saw how hurt I was, he'd apologize. We'd hug and make up, and everything would seem to be okay. Later, he'd just get a certain look in his eye as if to say, "Can't you do anything right?" He wouldn't actually say anything. He'd just withdraw.*
>
> *God, I'm not even sure when it started, but it's got to be 4 or 5 years ago. He had just been promoted and had taken on additional responsibilities. I thought he was just feeling the stress of*

more work and being responsible for more people. He's always liked big challenges, so I was sure things would settle down. When they didn't, I'd ask him what was wrong. He'd say, "Nothing" or "Just stresses at work."

Jeff has always been a wonderful father. He played ball with our son, went to his practices, and was a coach for many years. Our younger daughter also loves sports. She plays basketball and volleyball. She's tall, like her dad. In the past 6 months, Jeff seems to have forgotten he has children. They want to tell him about their day, share their ups and downs. He used to listen and always understood. Now he buries himself in his books, or he reads the newspaper and grumbles about the state of the world, or he gets lost in his computer.

I've tried to give him his space, hoping he'd snap out of it. I've got mad and demanded that we talk. I've asked him if he loves me. He tells me he does. I've asked him if there's another woman. He insists that there isn't. I've pleaded with him to go to counseling with me. He just snaps back that I should leave him alone, that there's nothing wrong with him.

Well, I can't just leave him alone. . . . I love him. I can see that he's in pain. I know that something's wrong with him, that he needs help.

Things are getting worse, and I don't know what to do. I'll do anything to save our marriage. I just want to help him. If it's me, I can change. If it's his job, I'll support us while he finds out what he wants to do. I alternate between anger and despair. I just want my husband back.

15 ACTIONS YOU CAN TAKE TO HELP AN IMS MAN IN DENIAL

1. Recognize that he is hurting but feels stuck. Remember that his irritability and anger are covering over his hurt and fear.

2. Take a step back. You can't push him to change. He can make changes only when he is ready. You can step back only if you can keep yourself from panicking. This is a good time to tell someone you trust about what is going on.

3. Recognize your own feelings and fears about the situation. What are his actions triggering in you? Are you feeling angry? Do you want to fight back? Do you feel inadequate? Are you wondering what you did wrong? Are you afraid that he's going to leave—or that you will?

4. Slow down. Take care of yourself. Don't make any decisions while you are in a panic. Remind yourself that no matter how important your relationship is, it is not the only aspect of your life. There are other people who are important to you, and there are other things that give you pride and pleasure.

5. Find your own place of emotional safety so you don't let yourself feel battered by his stormy moods. Tell yourself over and over again, "I am not the target. These are his feelings of pain and powerlessness." What he is saying or doing, no matter how hurtful, is not a statement about you or your adequacy.

6. Never listen to what he thinks about you. Listen for how he *feels*. Judgment and blame are only cover-ups for his feelings and unmet needs. Words can be deeply wounding. When men experience the Irritable Male Syndrome, they may say things that can be very hurtful. For instance, an IMS male may say, "Damn it, can't you ever do anything right? Are you really that stupid?" You can think, "I must be a lousy wife" or "He's a vicious, mean bastard." Or you can say to yourself, "I wonder if he's feeling enraged because he needs support or comfort or understanding."

7. Let him know you are aware that he is in pain and you are open to listening to what is on his mind, when he is ready. Irritable males seem to be doing everything they can to push people away, yet they want more than anything to be understood. Like angry children, they want to know that you are there, that you won't be driven away, and that you will listen when they are ready.

8. Suggest walking and talking. Men often open up more easily when they are communicating "side by side" rather than "face to face." Sitting down and talking about what is going on might not be the best way to reach them. Men tend to be "doers," not "discussers." They often find it easier to talk when they are doing something (throwing a ball, fixing a car, taking a walk) and when they are not looking into someone's eyes. To women, eye contact provides a feeling of nurturing and a sense of support. It often makes men feel that they have been put on the spot, so they then become defensive and withdrawn.

9. Let him know that you care about him and that you know he cares about you. Ask him if he'd be willing to listen, without responding, for 5 minutes while you tell him how his irritability and blame make you feel. Share your own needs for safety, self-esteem, intimacy, and love.

10. Get help and support from friends and family. Don't try to solve the situation by yourself. You may feel ashamed to ask for help. You may want others to know the man in your life is acting the way he is. He may be telling you, directly or indirectly, not to tell anyone about what is going on. Don't give in to the fear; reach out to people. Be good to yourself.

11. Seek out a counselor, if necessary, who can help you work with your feelings and suggest ways to work with the IMS man. Sometimes you need more than the support of friends and family. Professional help may be necessary. Many times, people hold back, thinking, "If he won't go for help, what's the use?" Getting help for yourself may be the first step in breaking destructive cycles and getting help for him.

12. If you are seeing a counselor, request that he call the IMS man and ask him to come in to help you and the family. Often, a man has trouble asking for help for himself but will go in to help a woman and children. Even teens and young men will often go if they think their thoughts will be heard and they can help others. It helps a man's self-esteem to know that he is doing something good, even if he feels confused and angry inside.

13. Tell him, and remind yourself, that you are both on the same side. The problem isn't you or him. The problem is his irritability and anger that are caused by his unmet needs. Let him know that you are committed to working with him to find out what those needs are and to help him meet them.

14. Don't give up. Create an atmosphere of safety. Invite him to join you in finding ways to create a better relationship for you both. If he doesn't respond, pull back. Approach again at another time.

15. Be firm. Let him know you love him but you aren't going to give up on your own happiness. Tell him things need to change and you want him to join with you in making a life that works for both of you.

WONDERING WHAT TO DO
WHEN YOU'RE THINKING ABOUT LEAVING HIM

For many couples, the tension and pain in the relationship reach a point where it seems the only way to survive is to split up. Judy, a 45-year-old woman, came to see me on the advice of her lawyer.

I'm tired of being blamed for all his problems. Nothing I do seems good enough for him, and he's become emotionally abusive. I don't think he'd actually hit me. Even so, I'm tired of being treated like I'm worthless. I'm just not going to put up with it anymore.

I've begged him to get help, but he just tells me it's my problem. I've gone to see a counselor. He refuses to go with me. I don't want a divorce, but I decided to go see a lawyer, just in case. I guess I can live with things for a while longer, but I'm really running out of patience. He's just oblivious to what he's doing to me and the kids. What do I do?

SIX KEY QUESTIONS YOU MUST ASK YOURSELF WHEN YOU'RE THINKING OF LEAVING

1. Have you given up on the relationship, or do you still feel there is some chance that things can change? Be honest with yourself. You need to look deeply within your heart but also take inventory with your mind. Is there enough left in the relationship to build on? Do you really want to put in the time and energy to make the changes?

2. Are you willing to get help and confront your own fears about leaving and about staying? You can't change him, but you can change you. Many people stay too long or leave too soon. Often, they are in such emotional pain they are unable to think clearly. It's useful to consult a good therapist who will help you sort things out.

3. What are the pros and cons of staying? Of leaving? In the midst of confusion, it is difficult to take a clear look at your situation. I recommend asking and answering the following questions:

A. What are the benefits of staying?
B. What are the benefits of leaving?
C. What are the drawbacks to staying?
D. What are the drawbacks to leaving?

Think of A and D as being on one side of a scale with B and C on the other side. Many people have told me that this has been very helpful in making decisions they can live with.

4. Is it worth staying and giving it a try? If you decide that it is, it isn't likely that there will be a significant change unless something new is added to the mix. Will you get counseling? Are you reading this book together? Are you getting help from your church or friends? If you're willing to stay while you work on making changes, be clear about how long you can stay. No one wants to remain in an abusive relationship forever. Yet change won't occur overnight. How much time are you willing to give it? Setting a time limit will allow you to work for change while reminding you that if positive change does not occur, the situation won't continue indefinitely.

5. Are you overwhelmed by the bad times or can you still remember when things were good? Don't close your mind or your heart to love. Remember what your relationship was like at its best. Stay focused on how you would like things to be, not on how bad they have become.

6. Are you putting energy into making the rest of your life wonderful? Be sure you do things you enjoy. See friends, enjoy family, and involve yourself in what you love. Take the attitude that your life will be fine, with him or without him.

WHAT TO DO WHEN HE IS ABOUT TO LEAVE OR ALREADY OUT THE DOOR

Jennifer is a 50-year-old mother of three who contacted me when it looked like her marriage was coming apart. She and her husband, Jerry, had been married for 25 years.

> *We seemed to have a wonderful relationship. He has been an attentive father and a good husband, but a few months ago, things began to change. All of a sudden, he became irritable, angry, and sullen. He told me he had never been happy in the relationship and was thinking of leaving.*
>
> *I was totally shocked. This was so completely unlike him. I didn't know what to do. I finally convinced him to come with me to see a counselor. He was able to talk about some of his frustrations with work and some of the anger that he'd never spoken about. Things seemed to be improving. That is, until the day everything fell apart.*
>
> *I was looking for some tax information on his computer.*

In the course of finding it, I also found an e-mail from a woman describing times they had been together. I was totally devastated. Once I could stop crying, I confronted him. He finally told me that he had been seeing this woman, who it turned out was 34. He is 53. He insists that he loves her but doesn't want to leave our family. He says the affair has ended, but I don't know if I can trust him. He tells me he's trying to make our marriage work, but that he can't stop thinking about her.

I don't want our marriage to end. I think I can get over the affair and forgive him, but I need to know he wants to be with me. Am I just being a fool or is there really hope for a relationship when a man has strayed?

Here is what I told Jennifer and what many other women have told me has been helpful.

1. Recognize that you haven't done anything wrong. When a man wants to leave, sometimes his partner blames herself. This is not your fault.

2. Remind yourself that his leaving has nothing to do with your desirability as a woman. This is his problem, not yours. You haven't become less desirable because he is experiencing problems associated with IMS.

3. Take time to improve your own self-esteem. After the initial shock, you may find you have been living your life in fear of his leaving. You may feel bad about yourself, but you can change that. Begin doing things that give you a sense of accomplishment.

4. Use your anger to make positive changes in your own life. Often a crisis in the marriage can be the impetus to do things you have wanted to do but have neglected. One woman began a serious exercise program. Another decided to go back to school. Any changes have to be ones you want to make for yourself, not simply to hold on to him.

5. Break the "I'll be perfect/You're a shit" pattern. Many women try to be "good." They revert to a childhood practice: "If I'm good enough, maybe Daddy will love me." When that doesn't work, they sometimes become angry and blaming.

6. Confront your own fear of abandonment. What experiences have you had in the past where you were afraid of being left? Were there times growing up when you had to deal with these kinds of insecurities? Have there been other times you've been left?

7. Make it your business to make your life so great that, whether he leaves or stays, you will feel fulfilled. I'm not talking about being a Pollyanna and pretending that everything is fine when it isn't. I'm suggesting that you make it your goal to feel so good about yourself and your life that his leaving won't wreck it.

8. Let him know his needs can be met in the relationship and you are willing to do whatever it takes to help that be so. Also let him know that your own needs can be met as well, and challenge him to work with you to bring about the changes necessary for mutual growth and happiness.

9. Suggest that his unhappiness, and maybe your own, may stem from the call of something deep inside. Sometimes, we think the problem is with our partners or families, when it is really about dealing with the larger issue of finding expression for our authentic selves. Midlife is often a time when major changes need to occur to give our lives meaning. So are other times of major change, such as adolescence and young adulthood. A teenager's rage at his parents may really be about his need to be more independent. A young man's anger at his boss may be an expression of his need to find work that is meaningful.

10. Open a discussion of what psychologist James Hillman describes as the *soul's calling*. Often, a man's restlessness and irritability come from the pull of his inner world, not a pull from outside. He may think he needs to leave his family, have an affair, change jobs, run away from home, leave the country. The real longing may be to fulfill his soul's calling. Recognize that this may cause a man to want to escape from his old life. He knows he has to break away, but he's not sure what he must break away from or where he is headed. Your support for his need to be free may be exactly what is needed for a man to choose to stay close.

Men need to understand that our irritability is real but the cause isn't "out there"—it's "in here." There is a need to "get away," but it usually isn't from our partners and families. It's from the fears that hold us back from going after our souls' desire. We need to know we don't have to give up our dreams, no matter how unclear or "unrealistic," in order to stay in our relationships.

We want to know that our partners and families will be with us as we explore who we are at this stage of our lives. Once they understand our need to "escape," they often can be supportive. When they think we are trying to get away from them, they become more frightened. Realizing that we are fighting our own inner demons allows them to be much more supportive.

HOW TO DEAL WITH
THE RESISTANT IMS YOUNG MAN

Jimmy is a 16-year-old boy who wrote to me after taking the Irritable Male Syndrome Questionnaire on the *Men's Health* magazine Web site. His score put him in the "extremely irritable" category. In his letter to me he said:

> *My irritability has caused a 10-month relationship with my girl-friend to crumble. I really loved her and the relationship was important to me. She said I started to be snappy with her and she said I had changed from when we first met.*
>
> *I'm also very angry at home. My younger brother and I fight constantly. My father works long hours; when he's home, it just seems like he's yelling at me all the time. My mother tries to cool things out and is super nice to me when my father is gone. I've become more moody and angry at little things that shouldn't bother someone.*
>
> *I've even started getting angry at work. I don't know why. The job is simple. My duties are to make sure all the items on shelves are moved to the front of the shelves, to make them look neat, and to help out with customers. The job gives me a little extra money, but it sure doesn't interest me much.*

POINTS OF UNDERSTANDING

• It's important for parents to understand the difference between normal adolescence (which of course can range from not-too-chaotic to very, very chaotic) and IMS. A number of indicators differentiate between the two. First is a high score on the Irritable Male Syndrome Questionnaire. The scoring range is from 0 to 150. A score above 76 indicates that a person definitely is suffering from IMS. Jimmy, for instance, scored 130. A second sign of IMS is that irritability affects many important aspects of a boy's life—family, girlfriend, school, job. Third, irritability causes serious problems in his life, as when Jimmy's girlfriend left him, telling him that his irritability was a major factor. Fourth, others recognize that the irritability is getting worse. Finally, the young man may recognize that he has a problem, as Jimmy did.

• Once parents do recognize IMS, there is a real need to reach out to their son and find out what unfilled needs are being covered by his anger. Clearly, Jimmy had a need to express his sadness and hurt at the loss of his girlfriend. He seemed to be concerned about the fighting with his brother and his father's anger toward him. There were strong implications that he missed his father's positive presence and felt wounded by his anger. Mom's attempts to "cool things out," though welcome, didn't fully compensate for Jimmy's need to have a good relationship with his father.

• There may be a need for outside support. The concept that it takes a village to raise a child is very true. Boys (and girls) need some kind of initiation into adulthood. They need support from men and women outside their families. A father often is too hard on his son and a mother is often too soft. Our society suffers from a lack of initiation for our young men. In chapter 12, I will discuss this need in more depth and talk about a number of programs that initiate young men and help families understand and deal with these testosterone-driven bundles of passion and potential.

• Adolescence is a time when young people are passionate about making the world a better place. If encouraged, they will get involved in activities that have real meaning. There was a time when a young person could apprentice to a master and not only learn a trade but also learn something about what it meant to be a man. We have now come to accept "work" for teens as make-work, rather than a meaningful undertaking. It is not surprising that Jimmy was concerned about the lack of meaning in his work.

• Teens are often more comfortable learning about issues and asking for help through the computer. The online world is familiar to them and offers an anonymity that allows them to feel safe. This is one of the reasons why Jimmy was able to open up in responding to the Irritable Male Syndrome Questionnaire on the Internet.

THE COURAGE TO CONFRONT IMS: RALPH'S STORY

There's just no way around it: It takes a whole lot of courage to deal with IMS in our lives. What is required of men when our tendency is to believe the problem is "theirs" not "ours"? How do we break through the fears that keep us locked into old, destructive patterns? How do we recapture the joy that we all want in our relationships and in our lives?

Ralph was able to begin dealing with IMS after reading what I had written about it on my Web site.

I am 51 and have noticed a change over the past 6 months in my mental and emotional attitude. I thought that I had outgrown my wife of 22 years and that it was time to move on. Luckily, I came across your writings and now can relax into what I am going through. I can put a name on my feelings, and it is Irritable Male Syndrome rather than I've-Got-to-Get-Out-of-This-Marriage Syndrome. I am still experiencing emotional highs and lows, but I am not reacting so strongly to them now.

Some of my main symptoms were restlessness, irritability, anxiousness, and feeling I was missing out on life. I could not put my finger on what was the matter. Until reading about it on your site, I had never heard of the Irritable Male Syndrome.

My wife and I had known each other for some time and had lived together for 2 years before we decided to get married. Although, like all couples, we'd had our ups and downs, I felt we had a good marriage. When our two children came along, it added some stress but also a great deal of joy to our marriage.

Over the past 6 months, I found I wasn't having as much fun. We seemed to be drifting apart emotionally, and we began arguing more. It seemed my wife was less supportive of me and more involved with the children and her other activities. When we were together, it seemed like she was always criticizing me about something. "Why don't you put your dishes in the sink when you are done?" "Can't you call when you're going to be late?" "Turn out the lights; you're wasting electricity." Give me a break, I don't need this kind of shit.

For several reasons such as lack of time, I was no longer doing activities that I found fun. I was also starting to question my work, wondering if I shouldn't be doing something that would benefit society more than just selling software. I was starting to consider working for nonprofits. I knew that, due to financial commitments to older family members as well as cur-rent home renovation projects, this was not realistic. I con-tinued to resent and blame my wife for this. I guess I knew that it wasn't really her fault. But she never seemed to listen to me, never seemed to understand the stresses I was feeling.

It seemed like my whole life was about someone else—first my parents, then my wife and children. I began to wonder when it was going to be my turn. "How about me?" I wanted to scream. "Don't I get a chance to live?" I felt trapped and often had dreams about getting in my car, driving off, and starting a new life somewhere else.

I even started to think about future partners, including a 25-year-old, very cute medical student who is the daughter of one of our neighbors. The more distance there was between my wife and me, the more this young girl seemed to occupy my thoughts. I even found I was making excuses to go by the neigh-bors just so I could see her. She did seem to genuinely like me, and we even had a few meaningful conversations. These all fed my fantasies that she might really want to be with me. Part of me knew it was silly. What would a 25-year-old, attractive med student want with a 51-year-old computer geek? But oh, did I want her. If I hadn't come across your writing, I might have done something really stupid.

At first, it seemed like it was always my wife causing fights. Finally, with all this going on in my head, I realized I was starting to pick on my wife. I wanted to cause a fight where I would finally say that I was not happy and that I wanted a divorce. After a weekend about 3 weeks ago when I called my wife names and told her she was a lousy wife and mother, I could see that this all couldn't be her fault. I must be con-tributing to our problems in some way.

I came across your book Male Menopause. There was a lot about what you said that made sense and that led me to your Web site. You described some of the same feelings that I was going through and you talked about how these changes are related to hormones, brain chemistry, stress, marital conflict, pain from the past, and hopes for the future. That same evening, my wife confronted me about my actions and unhappiness. We talked about it. For the first time, I was able to hear her unhappiness and fear that our relationship was drifting apart. I didn't feel blamed or judged. I could also hear how much she loved me and wanted us to work things out.

Once we began talking about what was underlying our unhappiness, a lot of my restlessness, anxiety, and irritability began to go away. It was so helpful to know what I was going through. Being able to talk about Irritable Male Syndrome gave us some ways to be on the same side, rather than be adversaries. We didn't need to fight each other. Now we could fight IMS.

On good days, I feel that I am like a snake shedding an old skin (my first half of life) and emerging with a new one. I am also trying to take a more detached view of my experiences and am not reacting emotionally to the ups and downs. Finally, I am talking to my wife about my experiences. I feel that I am on the right track now. I am very grateful that I did not actually "do" anything stupid or drastic to ruin my marriage. I know I would have regretted it later.

POINTS OF UNDERSTANDING

• There are men who find the courage to deal with the Irritable Male Syndrome. Being aware that IMS exists and learning how to recognize it are critical.

• Timing is important. Getting the information at the proper moment can make the difference between resistance and openness.

• Unfortunately, a man rarely wears a sign saying, "I know I've been irritable as hell for years, but now I'm ready to hear about IMS." Information can be shared, but only the man can decide when he's ready to hear it. Trying to convince him he has a problem only makes him more resistant to the truth.

• It isn't easy hearing a man's unhappiness and pain underneath his irritability, accusations, and blame. His anger often pushes others away. Underneath his irritability, he's telling you about his feelings and needs. What would it be like if you could say to him, "Are you angry because you want greater emotional connection, more appreciation for what you do for us, and more support for your efforts? Are you feeling frustrated because you want to do more of the things you used to love, do work that makes a difference in the world, and feel free to take time for yourself? Are you hungry for the passion you associate with youth, because you want to stay desirable and attractive as you age?" Having a caring partner who can listen without judgment can help a man recognize and deal with IMS.

• Sometimes, the irritability has to become extreme before a man recognizes that, even if his partner *is* contributing to it, his overreaction means there is something going on inside him. One type of extreme irritability is physical violence. At that point, most men know they have gone too far and need to make some changes. Other extreme reactions can also wake a man up. One man told me he realized he was overreacting when he found himself yelling at his 3-year-old daughter. Another said it happened when he told a friend he never wanted to see him again. Each man has his own experience that says, "Wow, this isn't right. Something's wrong here. I better find out what it is."

Once there is at least some recognition that "I have the problem," a whole lot of energy is freed up to solve it. As long as we continue to blame others, our irritability feeds on itself and we remain stuck. As soon as we let go of our view that someone else must do something if we're going to be happy, we are ready to take charge of our own recovery and healing. The rest of this book will provide some additional guidance for the process.

CHAPTER 10

STRENGTHENING THE BODY

Healing the Sprained Brain, Exercising and Eating for Health, and Restoring Hormonal Balance

When we think about irritability and what can help us deal with it, we often forget that all this is taking place inside a brain that can be damaged by life events. Brain injury does not result only from too much time in the boxing ring, from pounding our heads against someone else's helmet playing football, or from concussions sustained at work. Life can damage the brain in ways that affect how we perceive reality, how we feel, think, and interact.

Just as a fall while skiing may cause a back sprain in one person and no injury in another, a life stress like a divorce or a job loss may cause irritability or depression in some, though others endure it without incident. While back sprain may signal its presence through pain and stiffness, IMS causes pain of its own, typically manifesting as grumpiness, anger, gloominess, and frustration.

STOP BANGING YOUR BRAIN AGAINST THE WALL

Despite the parallels between the pain of irritability and types of physical pain, in the Western world most people react to mental injuries very differently than to physical ones. While people generally avoid activities that cause physical pain, we often respond to symptoms of irritability and depression by pushing ourselves back into the very situations that are most stressful to us. Not surprisingly, this often worsens our emotional state.

For a back injury, proper treatment combines an adjustment of physical activity to avoid further strain and exercises to strengthen supporting muscles. It may also include medication or a homeopathic remedy to reduce pain and inflammation. Similarly, effective treatment for an irritable or depressed brain may combine the physical and emotional nurturing of our growing boys, good physical activity to reduce stress, a healthy diet, mainstream and alternative medications to balance the neurochemistry of the brain, and hormonal restoration to replenish hormones that are lost as a result of stress or aging.

KEEP OUR CHILDREN INTACT: DON'T CIRCUMCISE

Until I began gathering information for my book *The Warrior's Journey Home: Healing Men, Healing the Planet,* I hadn't thought much about circumcision. As a Jewish male, I had been circumcised as an infant. I had had my own son circumcised as a newborn, before he left the hospital nursery. But the more I read and talked to experts in the field, the more I came to believe that circumcision is not good for baby boys.

I now believe that this practice is one of the physical factors that contribute to IMS. Although there haven't been studies linking circumcision to IMS, there is enough evidence of the effects of early childhood trauma that I believe it's wise for parents to carefully consider the subject before making a decision.

Circumcision is a touchy subject, with medical, legal, cultural, and religious aspects. It triggers an emotional reaction for many, and there are strong feelings on both sides of the issue. "Many people cannot even discuss the subject of circumcision without guilt, denial, or other strong emotions," says Christiane Northrup, M.D., author of *Women's Bodies, Women's Wisdom: Creating Physical and Emotional Health and Healing.* Dr. Northrup concludes that circumcision "has profound implications for male sexuality and is a form of sexual abuse."[1]

Two physicians who have studied circumcision in depth are Thomas J. Ritter, M.D., who has practiced general surgery for over 3 decades, and George C. Denniston, M.D., M.P.H., a graduate of the University of Pennsylvania School of Medicine and the Harvard School of Public Health. Among their many conclusions in their book *Doctors Re-Examine Circumcision* are the following:

1. Circumcision is really foreskin amputation and is abusive.

2. Circumcision is very painful and traumatizing.

3. When unaroused, the glans of the penis is meant to be an internal organ, like the clitoris under its hood.

4. The foreskin enhances sexual pleasure.

5. It makes as much sense to circumcise baby boys as it does to circumcise baby girls.[2]

This last point came home to me when I attended an international conference on female and male circumcision. One of the women activists was from Africa, where female circumcision is still practiced in a brutal procedure in which some or all of the clitoris is removed. She said she had never even considered that male circumcision could be anything like what females experience. "That changed for me when I heard the babies cry when they were cut," she told me. "The scream of outrage and pain I heard from boy babies was the same that I had heard from little girls."

TOUCH BABY BOYS MORE OFTEN

The fact that we live in a touch-deprived world is such a given that we don't even notice it. Anthropologist Jean Liedloff spent 2½ years living with indigenous tribes in the South American jungle. She was struck by how charming the children were. The way the boys interacted was particularly noteworthy. "The children were uniformly well-behaved: never fought, were never punished, always obeyed happily and instantly," she said. "The deprecation 'Boys will be boys' did not apply to them."[3]

It took Liedloff a while living with the tribes to understand the underlying reasons for the children's amiability. She discovered that babies were held nearly continuously from the moment of birth. Liedloff concluded that this physical contact is a practice that was part of our species development but had become less often practiced in many countries in our modern world. "Every nerve ending under his newly exposed skin craves the expected embrace, all his being, the character of all he is, leads to his being held in arms," Liedloff says of baby boys.[4]

Those societies that give their infants the greatest amount of physical affection have less theft and violence among adults, according to a study of anthropological data done by research neuropsychologist James W.

Prescott, Ph.D., while he was at the National Institute of Child Health and Development. This supports the theory that deprivation of bodily touch and pleasure during infancy is significantly linked to a high rate of crime and violence.[5]

KEEP FATHERS CONNECTED TO THEIR CHILDREN

Research findings, in addition to common sense, demonstrate that children do need active, literally hands-on involvement of their fathers as well as their mothers. Dads matter simply because "fathers do not mother," says Kyle Pruett, M.D., in his book *Fatherneed: Why Father Care Is as Essential as Mother Care for Your Child.*[6]

Father love and mother love are qualitatively different kinds of love, agrees the influential psychoanalyst Erik Erikson. Fathers "love more dangerously" because their love is more "expectant, more instrumental" than a mother's, says Erikson.[7] Fathers tend to play with children, and mothers tend to care for them. While both mothers and fathers are physical, fathers are physical in different ways.

Fathers tickle more, they wrestle, and they throw their children in the air. Fathers chase their kids, sometimes as playful, scary "monsters." Fathers are louder at play, while mothers are quieter. Mothers cuddle babies, and fathers bounce them. Fathers roughhouse while mothers are gentle. One study found that 70 percent of father-infant games were physical and action oriented. Only 4 percent of mother-infant play was like this.[8] Fathers encourage competition; mothers encourage equity. One style encourages independence while the other encourages security. We need both of these styles for children to grow up to be healthy adults.

Some have assumed that the roughhousing that goes on between males leads to irritability and violence when sons become adults. It seems that the opposite is true. Children who roughhouse with their fathers learn that biting, kicking, and other forms of physical violence are not acceptable, says fathering expert John Snarey. They learn self-control by being told when enough is enough and when to settle down.[9] Both boys and girls learn a healthy balance between timidity and aggression.

So children need Dad's roughhousing as well as Mom's softness. Both provide security and confidence in their own ways, by communicating love and physical intimacy.

RECOGNIZE THAT YOU MUST EXERCISE
OR YOU WILL DIE

I sat in my doctor's office asking that my allergy medications be refilled. I had had allergies and asthma since I was a kid and had been taking medications on and off since I was 8 or 9 years old. This was a new doctor whom I hadn't seen before. "How old are you?" he wanted to know. I told him I was 28. "How much exercise do you get?"

"I joined the YMCA a while back, but I haven't had a chance to use it much," I told him. "Work keeps me pretty busy, and when I'm home, there's my wife and young son to deal with. I do as much as I can."

He nodded and continued. "Are you under a good deal of stress at work?"

"I sure am," I told him, shaking my head. "All day, I deal with one project after another. I supervise others' work and have to deal with many different agencies, none of which can agree on what is needed. I'm irritable most of the time. Some days, it's all I can do to keep from exploding.

"When I get home, I'm so tired that all I want is to be left alone. My wife wants to talk, but I know if I do, I'm just going to blow up at her. I don't want to do that. It isn't her fault. So I just try to stay away from her until I calm down. She acts like I don't care about her. I really do care—that's why I stay away. I don't want to dump my anger on her."

I waited for the look of understanding to express itself and for sympathetic words to be spoken. I got neither. Instead, the doctor looked me in the eye and said, "Do you know what's going to happen to a man of your age, with the kind of stressful job you have and your lack of serious exercise?" I shook my head from side to side. I still had a smile on my face.

"You're going to die," he told me seriously.

I felt like I'd been slapped. My smile vanished instantly. "Get in a regular exercise program, at least three times a week," he said. "Come see me in 3 months. I suspect that you're going to feel a whole lot better and less stressed. But if you're still having problems with allergies then, we'll see what else we can do."

"You're not going to give me any medication?" I asked timidly.

"No," he said. "You need exercise a lot more than you need medications. Medications will treat the symptoms. Exercise will treat the core of the problem." He finally smiled as he got up and shook my hand. "Good luck," he told me. "I know you'll do the right thing."

I felt stunned as I walked out of his office. No doctor had ever talked to me like that before. I didn't know whether to be infuriated or grateful. Somewhere deep inside, I knew he was absolutely right. That day, I went to the YMCA and signed up for an exercise class that met Mondays, Wednesdays, and Fridays. It meant taking off a half hour from work on those days. When I caught myself saying, "I can't do that," I remembered the doctor's warning.

I started exercising and jogging three times a week. The first weeks were painful. I wheezed around the track, stopping often to walk. After a month, I began to feel better. At the end of 3 months, I felt wonderful, for the first time in a long time. Not only did I feel better physically but I found I wasn't as irritable. I no longer felt as if I were on the verge of exploding most of the time. When I got home after work, I looked forward to interacting with my wife and young son. I wasn't so tired, and I felt more involved. Even my sex life improved greatly. My wife found I was much easier to live with after I had spent time exercising. I didn't need to withdraw when I got home, because I had "run" my irritability away on the track.

I called the doctor to thank him. "I don't think I need the medications," I told him. "Good," was his only reply.

My doctor isn't the only health professional who tells us we must exercise or die. In 1996, the World Health Organization (WHO) and the World Association of Sports passed a resolution saying that inactive people are putting their lives on the line. "Adults should engage in moderate physical activity for at least 30 minutes every day, e.g., by walking at a fast pace, hiking, or climbing stairs," WHO wrote in its recommendations.[10]

LEARN THE EXERCISES
THAT HUMANS WERE MADE FOR

Exercise has been a part of our lives since humans first walked the savannas of Africa hunting and gathering the necessities required for life. In their book, *The Paleolithic Prescription,* authors S. Boyd Eaton, M.D.; Marjorie Shostak, Ph.D.; and Melvin Konner, M.D., Ph.D., tell us about the importance of exercise in maintaining a happy and healthy lifestyle. "Our genetic constitution has been selected to operate within a milieu of vigorous, daily, and lifelong physical exertion," they say. "The exercise boom is not just a fad; it is a return to 'natural' activity—the kind for which our bodies are engineered and which facilitates the proper function of our biochemistry and physiology."[11]

In our Paleolithic past, humans got all the exercise they needed just going about their daily lives. Today, in a world where exercise involves hitting keys on the computer, lifting cell phones to our ears, thumbing the remote for the TV, and walking to the refrigerator for a snack and a beer, we need to go out of our way to build exercise into our lives. I have found that a complete program for physical fitness involves three main components: cardiorespiratory (aerobic) endurance, muscular strength, and flexibility.

One of the prime problems men have as we age is with our backs. This seems to be one of the side effects of having only recently, in evolutionary time, begun to walk upright, as well as the amount of time we sit in chairs. Anyone who has ever had his back go out—and that seems to be most of us over 40—knows it's difficult not to feel irritable when that happens. It hurts to move, and it hurts not to move. We are grumpy all the time, even when we try to ignore our discomfort. It also makes us mad to find that we are passing up opportunities for sex because we don't feel like it.

I have found daily yoga stretches (which my wife, Carlin, taught me) to be very helpful. Yoga is not only good for your sex life but also a great stress reliever that does a lot to combat IMS. Men are finally catching on. A 2003 *Newsweek* magazine issue on men's health featured an article titled "Real Men Do Yoga." Men seem to have discovered this ancient art and are adapting it to their modern routines. All over the country, men are hitting the mats. In Nashville, yoga teacher Hilary Lindsay says her early morning classes are often two-thirds to three-quarters male. "And almost all of my private clients are men," she says.[12]

Here are some other exercise tips that I've learned over the years.

Realize it's never too late. Whether you have never exercised in your life or were a world-class athlete who hasn't done anything for years, you can begin wherever you are.

Take the first step. That first step is the hardest, but once you get going you will find good reasons to continue.

Make the early steps small ones. The key to developing an exercise program is to see it as a lifelong practice. Too often, we resolve to make a big exercise commitment only to see it fade away because we couldn't keep it up in a life that probably feels too full already. Remember the saying "It's hard by the yard but a cinch by the inch." Walking for 5 minutes in the evening is a start. Swimming once a week is a start. Doing 10 pushups in the morning is a start.

Gradually build up to the basic health level. What is that level? Like the WHO and the World Association of Sports, I have found that a half hour per day is best. It's better to stay at the basic level longer than to alternate spurts of excessive exercise with breaks where you do nothing.

Find a balance between aerobic exercise, strength training, and flexibility. Most of us tend to be drawn more toward one type of exercise. Some love to lift weights. Others like the quiet feelings of long-distance runs. More men are finding that flexibility is necessary for a complete workout. Gradually add in what you've been missing, and strive to keep all three in your life.

Be sure to warm up. Many of us feel time driven. Once we begin an exercise program, we want to get through it as quickly as possible. Take your time. Give your muscles a chance to get ready. You will find your patience will pay off in fewer injuries.

When you're tired, exercise. Many of us don't exercise because we just feel too tired. We've worked hard and exercising feels like the last thing we want to do. I've found that's just the time I need to exercise the most. Even if I cut back the duration of my workout, doing something is always better than nothing. Here are some things you can do when you're still telling yourself you're too tired or busy to exercise.

- Do knee bends while brushing your teeth in the morning and evening.
- Don't use elevators; take the stairs.
- Find reasons to walk instead of driving short distances.
- Do stretches while you're waiting for your computer to do its thing.
- Alternate abdominal crunches and pushups during TV commercials.
- When walking in the office, the shops, the market, or to the bus stop, take the long way around.

When you feel irritable, depressed, anxious, or frustrated, think exercise. You'll find it's like taking a magic pill. You will feel refreshed and ready to deal with the things that have been bugging you. As I play racquetball and handball, swim, and lift weights, I feel better in many different ways. Physical activity not only helps my body feel better but also exercises my brain. After an hour or two at the gym, my brain seems to operate at a higher level of ability. I feel less stressed, more relaxed. I walk into the gym feeling irritable and nasty and walk out feeling calm and happy. These days, I joke with my friends about going to the gym so I can work out the kinks in my brain.

YOU ARE WHAT YOU EAT, SO EAT AN ANTI-IMS DIET

Many nutrition experts offer advice on eating well. My colleague Larrian Gillespie, M.D., is the only one I know who has developed a way of eating specifically to help men prevent and treat the Irritable Male Syndrome. The key to helping irritable males, Dr. Gillespie believes, is to eat in a way that keeps our hormones in balance. She recommends men eat a diet that's 40 percent protein (watch those hormone-laced steaks and chickens), 35 percent low-glycemic carbohydrates (think squash and green veggies instead of cream cakes), and 25 percent fat. Of the latter, only 10 percent should be saturated fat.[13]

As discussed in chapter 8, a key factor for men experiencing IMS is their testosterone level. If levels are too low or too high, men have problems. Here are the dietary guidelines Dr. Gillespie recommends to maximize healthy testosterone levels.

Be sure you have enough zinc in your diet. "Even short-term losses of zinc can reduce a guy's semen volume, sperm count, and testosterone," says Dr. Gillespie.[14] For men ages 30 to 50, the Recommended Dietary Allowance of zinc is 15 milligrams. The foods that contain the highest amounts of zinc are protein-rich ones including beef, poultry, oysters, legumes, and nuts.

Watch your alcohol consumption. Alcohol slows down and even damages important enzyme systems in the liver, lowers zinc levels, and raises estrogen. "Alcohol has a direct toxic effect on the testicles and can lower testosterone concentrations in men even if they don't drink chronically," says Dr. Gillespie.[15]

Drinking alcohol can cause a significant rise in estrogen in both women and men. A woman's estrogen level can triple after just one drink, says Eugene Shippen, M.D., coauthor of *The Testosterone Syndrome*. "The rise in men is less dramatic but very significant nonetheless," he says.[16] Dr. Gillespie says that young men have a testosterone-to-estrogen ratio of

50 to 1. As men get older, the ratio can drop to 20 to 1 or less.[17] If our estrogen levels go up as our testosterone levels go down, we experience the Irritable Male Syndrome. Dr. Shippen agrees that alcohol contributes to the increasing imbalance in the testosterone/estrogen ratio as men get older.[18]

Beware of licorice and stevia. Just 7 grams of licorice (less than an ounce, the amount found in a few cough drops or breath mints) can slice testosterone levels more than 34 percent. Studies have shown that stevia, a herb that some people use as a sweetener, also cuts testosterone levels.

Keep track of your weight. Being as little as 10 pounds (4.5 kg) overweight will increase the estrogen in your system, says Dr. Gillespie.[19] This occurs because fat cells have a lot of aromatase, an enzyme that converts some of a man's testosterone to estrogen. (The reverse is not possible—estrogen cannot be made into testosterone.) So the more weight we put on, the more we become "estrogenized" and the more irritable we're likely to feel.

"Obesity has been clearly associated with lower testosterone levels at all ages," says Dr. Shippen. It's not surprising, therefore, that overweight men invariably show signs of an unfavorable testosterone-to-estrogen ratio.[20]

A number of researchers believe that we must eat in a way that maintains not only a normal testosterone level but also a high serotonin level. The neurotransmitter serotonin is vital if men want to reduce irritability and depression, says Siegfried Meryn, M.D., professor of medicine at the University of Vienna, chairman and president of the World Congress on Men's Health, and author of *Men's Health and the Hormone Revolution*. "Serotonin is the male hormone of bliss," he says. "The more serotonin the body produces the happier, more positive and more euphoric we are. It plays an essential role in psychological stability and affects eating behavior, the circadian rhythm, mood, sexual behavior, and the perception of pain. Low serotonin can contribute to a man's irritability and aggression."[21]

Diet can also affect serotonin levels and the Irritable Male Syndrome. For instance, research has shown that protein, if consumed in excessive quantity, suppresses central nervous system (CNS) serotonin levels.[22] And when we stop eating carbs, our brains stop producing serotonin, say Judith Wurtman, Ph.D., and her colleagues at the Massachusetts Institute of Technology. So a high-protein, low-carbohydrate diet may cause increased irritability. Eating protein when we need carbohydrates will make us grumpy, irritable, or restless, says Dr. Wurtman.[23]

Alcohol consumption increases serotonin levels initially. Chronic use, however, dramatically lowers CNS serotonin, resulting in depression, carbohydrate cravings, sleep disturbances, and proneness to argumentative behavior and irritability.

TAKE PILLS TO HELP WITH IMS

I'm probably like most men who have been reluctant to "take something" to relieve their symptoms of aggression and depression. As I've said earlier in the book, I finally saw a doctor (after my wife gave me a good shove), got a complete evaluation and diagnosis, and began taking medications. It has made all the difference in the world for me. My life is more stable and joyous than I could ever have imagined.

If you, or someone who cares about you, is concerned that you may be suffering from the Irritable Male Syndrome, I recommend you see a doctor and explore the options. There are four classes of antidepressant medication currently available that seem to help treat IMS.

1. SSRIs (selective serotonin reuptake inhibitors) bring about higher brain levels of serotonin. Prozac (fluoxetine), Faverin (fluvoxamine), Seroxat (paroxetine), Lustral (sertraline), and Cipramil (citalopram) are all SSRIs.

2. Tricyclics affect serotonin and dopamine (another neurotransmitter). Tryptizol (amitriptyline), and Tofranil (imipramine) are examples of this class of medications.

3. MAOIs (monoamine oxidase inhibitors) inhibit the breakdown of serotonin, dopamine, and norepinephrine. Nardil (phenelzine) and tranylcypromine are both MAOIs.

4. Atypical antidepressants include medications that work on multiple neurotransmitter systems. Wellbutrin (bupropion), Dutonin (nefazodone), and Efexor (venlafaxine) are all atypical antidepressants.

There are many other medications available and more coming out all the time, so consult your physician. Many people have found that they have to be patient and work closely with a doctor they trust in order to find the right medication or combination of medications that will work for them. The same kind of sensitivity that makes us more likely to suffer from the

Irritable Male Syndrome also makes us sensitive to the side effects of medications. It may take awhile, but finding the right medications is well worth the effort.

No medication is without side effects. Sexual side effects are some of the most troubling for men (and women) taking antidepressants. Not everyone experiences them, but many people do. It's discouraging to find that a medication that helps IMS can create problems with erections and sexual desire. Fortunately, medications such as Viagra (sildenafil), Cialis (tadalafil), and Levitra (vardenafil) can help restore sexual function.

Be aware, too, that there are more natural, "alternative" medications that you can consider. Although there is a lot of hype and misinformation, I have found the following to have good, scientific grounding for their efficacy.

B vitamins. Even marginal deficiencies of B vitamins—thiamin, riboflavin, B_6, B_{12}, and folic acid—can cause or aggravate depression, according to Melvyn R. Werbach, M.D., assistant clinical professor at the University of California, Los Angeles.[24] People are often low in B vitamins if they tend to eat refined grains rather than whole grains. Refined grains have had all of their B vitamins removed during milling.

If you think that you're low in B vitamins, take a 50- to 300-milligram B-complex supplement every day, suggests clinical nutritionist Shari Lieberman, Ph.D. Be sure that any supplement you take contains 25 to 300 micrograms each of B_{12} and folic acid.[25]

L-tryptophan. I wrote earlier about the way irritability and depression are treated with medications that regulate serotonin levels. Some researchers believe that some people can get similar benefits by taking L-tryptophan, an amino acid that boosts the production of serotonin. "Several studies have shown that L-tryptophan helps relieve depression," says Alan Gaby, M.D., professor of nutrition at Bastyr University in Seattle.[26] A typical dose of L-tryptophan is 1 to 2 grams three times a day with meals, says Dr. Gaby.

Until 1989, L-tryptophan could be purchased over the counter (OTC) at most heath food stores. A contaminated batch caused the FDA to order that OTC L-tryptophan be discontinued. Now, the supplement can be obtained only by prescription.

Ginkgo biloba. This natural medicinal tonic is derived from the leaf of the common ginkgo tree. More than 200 scientifically sound, double-blind experiments on ginkgo biloba show that it helps improve cognitive function, says Dharma Singh Khalsa, M.D., author of *Brain Longevity*.[27]

"Ginkgo improves bloodflow through the brain, which is why it's used in the treatment of strokes and Alzheimer's disease," says Michael Castleman, author of *Blended Medicine: The Best Choices in Healing*. "The herb also normalizes levels of certain brain chemicals and, as a result, can help treat depression."[28]

"I strongly recommend ginkgo to virtually all of my patients," says Dr. Khalsa. For people in midlife who have no apparent cognitive dysfunction, Dr. Khalsa believes a daily dosage of 90 milligrams is often sufficient. If cognitive decline has begun, increasing dosages to 120 to 160 milligrams can be helpful. If significant problems with brain function are occurring, he suggests increasing the dose to 200 to 320 milligrams daily.[29]

St. John's wort. This mild to moderate antidepressant is taken from the yellow-flowered plant *Hypericum,* says Kay Redfield Jamison, Ph.D., a psychiatry professor at the Johns Hopkins University School of Medicine in Baltimore. It is widely used throughout Europe; in Germany, it is prescribed for depression more often than Prozac or other antidepressant medications. In recent years, it has become increasingly popular in the United States.[30]

In 2001, Duke University undertook a major study to see how effective St. John's wort is in treating depression. The conclusion, published in the April 10, 2002, issue of the *Journal of the American Medical Association,* was that "an extract of the herb St. John's wort was no more effective for treating major depression of moderate severity than a placebo." The study also found that both St. John's wort and the placebo were less effective than the antidepressant Lustral. Further research is expected to test the efficacy of St. John's wort with milder forms of depression.[31]

It's important to remember a number of things if you are considering taking herbal or natural alternatives to traditional medications. First, they should never be taken without consulting a health care practitioner who understands their use. Just because a substance is "natural" doesn't mean it is safe—arsenic is a natural substance. Second, many herbal remedies can interact with medications. If you use both, be sure your practitioners know about them. Third, if remedies are to have an effect at all, they must change the body chemistry. Even though a herb, such as St. John's wort, may be popular and recommended by health care practitioners, that doesn't mean studies have shown that it works. Fourth, since there is little reason for drug companies to test natural substances, good studies are rare. Fifth, when dealing with symptoms of serious depression, most clinicians still recommend traditional medications first. Herbal remedies usually take longer to have an effect, and a seriously depressed person needs relief quickly.

SEE WHETHER YOU ARE A HIGH-T GUY OR A LOW-T GUY

Testosterone isn't the only important hormone, but it is the most central in treating the Irritable Male Syndrome. It is credited with making men strong, shrinking their bellies, and protecting their hearts, as well as with boosting sexual desire in both men and women. It also helps with irritability and depression, particularly in older men.

It is testosterone that helps men stay "forever strong, forever young," according to Dr. Gillespie. She calls it the "Holy Grail of manhood."[32] As is true in all aspects of life, quantity is important. "The average male pumps out 260 to 1,000 nanograms (ng) of testosterone per deciliter (dl) of blood plasma," says Dr. Gillespie.[33]

Given the praise heaped on testosterone by many advocates, we might think that having a high testosterone level is always positive. If we associate testosterone with manhood, it seems logical that the more testosterone we have, the greater our feeling of manhood and the lower our irritability. If high T is good, well, higher T must be even better. And why not go for the highest T possible? In fact, this seemed to be the attitude of many men in a study conducted by Robert S. Tan, M.D., author of *The Andropause Mystery: Unraveling Truths about the Male Menopause*. He asked the men this question: "If the doctor told you that your testosterone levels were normal, would you still want a testosterone shot?" Dr. Tan said he was surprised by their responses. "Almost half (48 percent) said yes, implying that there is never too much of a good thing!"[34] As with so many other things we have discussed in this book, however, things are more complex and interesting than that.

Those who study testosterone have discovered some interesting facts. There are two kinds of people who differ in their normal levels of testosterone, says James McBride Dabbs, Ph.D., professor of psychology and head of the social/cognitive psychology program at Georgia State University in Atlanta.

In his book *Heroes, Rogues, and Lovers: Testosterone and Behavior,* Dr. Dabbs says that although too much or too little testosterone can be harmful to men within the normal range, there are men who are naturally at the high end or the low end of the testosterone spectrum. He likens these two kinds of men to male archetypes from the world of music. "Frank Sinatra sang, 'I did it my way,' and the Beatles sang, 'I get by with a little help from my friends,'" Dr. Dabbs reminds us. "These are the ways in which high- and low-testosterone people approach the world. Sinatra's song is the self-congratulatory, high-testosterone way. They are opposing strategies, one based on dominance and the other on cooperation."[35]

When I think of higher T and lower T, I think of the Beatles and the Rolling Stones. The two bands started at about the same time, dominated the music world, and will leave a lasting legacy. In contrasting them, writer Tom Wolfe says, "The Beatles want to hold your hand. But the Stones want to burn your town." Can you guess which one might be the higher-T group?

But Frank Sinatra isn't a better singer than John Lennon, and the Beatles aren't a better band than the Rolling Stones. They are just different. And Dr. Dabbs in fact found a number of interesting differences between higher-T and lower-T people. In one experiment, he had researchers check out 12 fraternities on two university campuses. The study showed the relationship between the physical aspects of the Irritable Male Syndrome and the psychological ones, with revealing results. "Fraternities with lower mean testosterone levels had a calm and polite atmosphere, responded quickly to the visitor, and made her feel at home," says Dr. Dabbs. Things were quite different in fraternities with higher mean testosterone levels. "They were rambunctious. They had more chaotic surroundings, were less gracious toward the visitor, left her standing alone, and were interested in getting the money, not in discussing the experiment."[36]

Dr. Dabbs found that "high-testosterone people seem to be unhappy when they are alone and happy when they are with people. . . . Low-testosterone people, on the other hand, seem to be less compulsively social."[37] We can see this in the testosterone levels of various professions. Dr. Dabbs and his researchers measured the testosterone levels of physicians, firemen, football players, salesmen, professors, ministers, and actors. They found that ministers, as a group, had the lowest testosterone levels, actors had the highest, and the other groups were in between. "Actors want to be stars," Dr. Dabbs says, "while ministers want to help."[38] My father was an actor, and in the early years of his career, he was ambitious, highly sexual, very social, and often irritable. I chose not to follow in his footsteps and went into a helping profession. (I must say, though, that when I went on a book tour and did my first major TV show, I enjoyed the rush of being onstage.)

Even though high-T people are very social, they can also be more irritable and confrontational. "On the average, high-testosterone individuals are tougher, and low-testosterone individuals are friendlier," says Dr. Dabbs.[39] So it may not be an accident that young men often have testosterone levels exceeding 1,000 ng/dl while men in their eighties average 200 ng/dl. Look at it from an evolutionary perspective: Young men need all that testosterone to compete with other testosterone-driven males for the right to mate with the most attractive females. Higher testosterone may be important in securing a mate, but lower testosterone may be better for being a good parent and caregiver. Dr. Dabbs found that married men are lower in testosterone than single men and that testosterone levels drop when men get married and go up when they get divorced. He also found that men have lower levels of testosterone immediately after they become fathers. "Perhaps these hormonal changes set them up for the gentler activities of parenthood," Dr. Dabbs concludes.[40]

It probably wouldn't occur to a young man to wonder how to lower his testosterone levels, but there may be some good reasons to consider doing so. I've talked to many young men who find that they are more irritable and aggressive than they would like to be. They would like to have the characteristics of a high-T male when it is appropriate— for instance, when they are on the football field competing for the championship. On the other hand, they might like to have a more low-T profile when they are with young women who want kindness and gentleness.

What's a young man to do? I've found that one of the most helpful things a young man can do is spend some time with young children and older adults. The kind of nurturing required to hold an infant and the kind of care it takes to be with an older person can help trigger the low-T feelings that can be very valuable for males at any age.

Testosterone levels fall naturally as men age. For some men, that is terri-fying. Others may welcome it. We may not want to admit it, but many men are glad to be driven less by our one-eyed friends. "It's nice not to be led around by my cock," one 60-year-old man told me. "It seems that my whole life has been driven by my need to succeed so that I could get an attractive woman to pay attention to me. Once I had one, I felt I had to keep driving myself to prove to her I was worthy of her attention. Meanwhile, I was always being drawn like a magnet to younger and prettier women. I know it may seem unmanly to say it, but I'm happy to feel less sexually driven. I can finally think about what I really want to do with my life."

FIND OUT WHETHER
YOU HAVE LOW TESTOSTERONE

We see that there is a range of testosterone that is healthy. Within that range, some men are at the higher end and some are at the lower end. How-ever, as we've seen in chapter 8, just as very high testosterone levels can contribute to the Irritable Male Syndrome, so too can abnormally low testosterone levels, especially in midlife men.

How do we know if we are outside the normal range, if our testosterone levels are too low? One simple way is to take the testosterone test devel-oped by John E. Morley, M.D., chairman of the department of geriatric medicine at St. Louis University School of Medicine:

LOW-T SELF-TEST

1. Do you have a decrease in libido (sex drive)?
2. Do you have a lack of energy?
3. Do you have a decrease in strength and/or endurance?
4. Have you lost height?
5. Have you noticed a decreased "enjoyment of life"?
6. Are you sad and/or grumpy?
7. Are your erections less strong?
8. Have you noticed a recent deterioration in your ability to play sports?
9. Do you fall asleep after dinner?
10. Has there been a recent deterioration in your work performance?

If you answer yes to questions 1 or 7 or to any three questions, you may be suffering from testosterone deficiency, says Dr. Morley.[41] In that case, I suggest you get a blood test to get a more definitive answer.

When you see your doctor to get a blood test, be prepared for the fact that he may not be familiar with the subtleties of testosterone or the test to see if it is low. Most physicians may recommend a blood test that will determine total testosterone, but that may not be the most useful measure.

"Total testosterone does not in any sense accurately represent the hormone's activity," says Dr. Shippen. Most of a man's testosterone is bound by a protein aptly called sex hormone–binding globulin (SHBG). "Free testosterone—the unbound remainder—typically constitutes 2 to 3 percent of the whole," says Dr. Shippen. "That 2 to 3 percent is hormonal gold, able to penetrate the cells of the body and command performance: strength in the muscles, potency in the gonads, energy in the mind, activity in all the cells and tissues where testosterone plays a role."[42]

In a study of men over 55, conducted by Lisa Tenover, M.D., Ph.D., chief of medicine at Wesley Woods Center at Emory University in Atlanta and an international expert on testosterone in aging men, only 20 percent were deficient in testosterone. When the study looked at free testosterone, 50 percent of this same group of men were testosterone deficient.[43]

A study by Malcolm Carruthers, M.D., author of *The Testosterone Revolution,* found that only 13 percent of men showing symptoms of andropause had abnormally low levels of total testosterone, but 75 percent showed low levels of free testosterone.[44]

So it's important to know both your total testosterone levels and your free testosterone levels. How much of each is "just right?" For most men, Dr. Gillespie recommends a total testosterone level of 400 to 600 ng/dl or a free testosterone level of 25 to 30 picograms per milliliter. Some clinicians will also suggest measuring levels of SHBG, estrogen, and other hormones. If they are low, you may want to consider testosterone restoration therapy.

TESTOSTERONE RESTORATION

I'll tell you at the start that testosterone restoration, also called testosterone replacement therapy (TRT) or hormone replacement therapy (HRT), is a controversial issue. The larger question about health programs such as hormone restoration is whether we should mess with Mother Nature. Some believe that changes associated with aging should be accepted. They believe that preoccupation with the latest technologies to stay young keeps us from recognizing and appreciating the benefits and joys of mature living in the second half of life.

Others believe that aging, and the losses associated with it, is not necessary. They support the concept of antiaging medicine, where a great deal of attention is paid to eliminating some aspects of aging and slowing down what can't be eliminated fully. They argue that we don't believe that poor eyesight should be accepted as we age. Why then, they ask, should we accept the effects of hormone loss?

The other controversy has to do with the specific effects of testosterone. Unlike reading glasses, testosterone has potential physiological drawbacks as well as benefits. Many are concerned about its effects on the heart and prostate. They would like to see more long-term studies before recommending that men replace lost testosterone with supplements.

An expert panel assembled by the Institute of Medicine, part of the National Academy of Sciences, issued a report calling for more study on the long-term effects of testosterone restoration. "There are people out there who say testosterone replacement therapy is just wonderful, and others who say it doesn't do any good at all. What we're saying is we just don't know," says Dan Blazer, M.D., Ph.D., a geriatric psychiatrist at Duke University Medical Center in Durham, North Carolina, who headed the institute probe calling for careful study to begin in 2005.[45]

Many men don't want to wait for the definitive results to be in before deciding whether to give testosterone restoration a try. This was shown by statistics quoted in the Academy report. More than 1.75 million prescriptions for testosterone therapy products were written in 2002, a jump of approximately 30 percent from the number written in 2001 and a 170 percent increase from 1999.[46]

Clearly, a lot of men believe testosterone restoration can be helpful. Since 1982, Jonathan V. Wright, M.D., medical director of the Tahoma Clinic in Kent, Washington, has used testosterone replacement to treat over 2,000 patients. Based on his findings, he feels that restoring testosterone levels can achieve the following:

- Enhance sex drive (libido)
- Restore the ability to achieve and sustain erections
- Protect against heart disease and stroke
- Increase energy

- Build stronger bones and muscles
- Reduce weight
- Prevent age-related losses in mental acuity
- Relieve depression[47]

Based on everything I have read, all the patients I have seen, the programs I have visited, and my own experience, I believe that properly administered hormone restoration can be of great value to men in treating Irritable Male Syndrome as well as problems such as andropause. (For a more complete discussion of these issues, I refer readers to my books *Male Menopause, Surviving Male Menopause: A Guide for Women and Men,* and *The Whole Man Program: Reinvigorating Your Body, Mind, and Spirit after 40.*) Each man must review the pros and cons with his doctor and decide what is best for him.

The field is still a new one, and the knowledge we have is not generally available to the medical community. Of the few experts in the field, most are researchers and don't offer treatment for the general public. The doctors in your local area may not know what you are talking about when you ask about the Irritable Male Syndrome, andropause, or testosterone deficiency. Others have heard about it but are not willing to treat it. It seems that most are taking a conservative approach to offering testosterone replacement for men. The concerns that have arisen as a result of the studies of hormone replacement for women have added to their beliefs that they should wait until the results of longer-term studies are available.

Whatever you decide about testosterone restoration, I hope you can see that there are many other physical options for preventing and treating IMS.

In the next chapter, I will explore the more psychologically oriented aspects of IMS prevention and treatment.

CHAPTER 11

EXPANDING THE MIND

Emotional Longevity
and the Pursuit of Happiness

In 1965, world-renowned psychologist and author Martin Seligman, Ph.D., who describes himself as a born pessimist, stumbled onto a field of study that would change his life and the lives of all of us who suffer from irritability and depression. In doing experiments with dogs, he found something completely unexpected. He gave dogs a mild shock paired with a tone, expecting that the animals would become conditioned to associate the tone with the shock and would therefore feel fear and run away. Instead, he found that the conditioned dogs just pathetically laid back and took the shocks. Apparently, the dogs learned that trying to escape from the shocks was futile. They learned to be helpless.

A new field of study was born, one perfectly fitted to a born pessimist. The theory of learned helplessness was extended to human behavior, providing a model for explaining worry, irritability, and depression. Depressed people became that way, Dr. Seligman felt, because they learned to be helpless. They learned that whatever they did, it was futile. Depressed people apparently came to believe that they had no control over important aspects of their lives.

On a summer's day in 1998, Dr. Seligman had another critical insight that once again shifted his personal and professional life. "It took place in my garden while I was weeding with my 5-year-old daughter," he remembers. "I am goal-oriented and time-urgent and when I'm weeding in the garden, I'm actually trying to get the weeding done. Nikki, however, was throwing weeds into the air and dancing around. I yelled at her. She walked away, came back, and said, 'Daddy, I want to talk to you.'

"'Yes, Nikki?'

"'Daddy, do you remember before my fifth birthday? From the time I was 3 to the time I was 5, I was a whiner. I whined every day. When I turned 5, I decided not to whine anymore. That was the hardest thing I've ever done. And if I can stop whining, you can stop being such a grouch.'

"This was an epiphany for me. As for my own life, Nikki hit the nail right on the head. I was a grouch. I had spent 50 years mostly enduring wet weather in my soul, and the last 10 years being a nimbus cloud in a household of sunshine. Any good fortune I had was probably not due to my grouchiness, but in spite of it. In that moment, I resolved to change."[1]

I had an awakening similar to Dr. Seligman's one evening when my wife and I were fighting. I had felt irritable and had low energy for weeks. I said something and she said something—I don't even remember the words. I do remember that I stormed out of the house feeling angrier and more hopeless than I'd felt before. Once outside, I became caught up in the sounds of the night. I calmed down and said to myself, "I don't like feeling this way. Life's too short to be this irritable, this often. I've had enough."

I walked back into the house. Everything looked different. I smiled. She smiled. It was like awakening from a bad dream. What struck me was that "nothing" had changed. I still had the same money worries. My wife and I still had different views on what we did and how we lived. My job hadn't changed, and the same stresses were likely to be present.

Yet, it felt like nothing was the same. A stifling cloud had blown away and I could breathe again. I was astounded to realize that the only thing that had changed was something in my mind. It was as if a switch had been turned off and my irritability had vanished. Another one had been turned on and I felt peaceful and cheerful.

I won't pretend that life has been all uphill from there. There have been many ups and downs. But the key thing that I discovered, and that Dr. Seligman discovered, is that transformation can occur—and that it can occur when we change some things in our own minds.

SHADOWS OF THE PAST: WHAT CAN WE DO TO HEAL FROM OUR PARENTAL HERITAGE?

Like Dr. Seligman, I see myself as a born pessimist. I suspect I inherited this trait from my family. My mother constantly worried about the usual things most people worry about: "Will we have enough money to pay the bills?

Will I keep my job in bad economic times? Will my son remember to remember my birthday? Will he earn a good living? Will we ever have a government that represents people who aren't rich?" She also worried about things most people *don't* worry about: "Will I be alive to see my son graduate from college?" (She was in her thirties and healthy.) "Will he find a good woman to spend his life with?" (I was about 8 years old when she began worrying about that.) "Will his family be able to survive when he dies?" (I was 9 when she bought me my first life insurance policy.)

My father never worried. He was just convinced that the world was against him. He seemed to be perpetually irritated about something. He was only rarely angry, but when he was, he was explosive. It seemed that no matter what he did, it didn't work. He couldn't find work in the field he loved, and he wouldn't learn to do something he wasn't happy doing. When he looked for work, he was sure he was being discriminated against because of his religion (Judaism), his age (over 35), his marital status (married), his parental status (father of one son), or something else. It never occurred to him—at least not until he was over 80—that the problem might be in the way he looked at the world.

So are we stuck with what we inherited from our parents? If we received "unhappy genes," are we doomed to lives of irritability, worry, and depression? If we grew up with unhappy parents, will we pass this on to our own children? Well, as you might expect, things are not as bad as the extreme pessimists among us might think, nor are they as positive as the extreme optimists would have us believe.

Dr. Seligman believes that a set range determines how happy or unhappy you are. "Roughly half of your score on happiness tests is accounted for by the score your biological parents would have got had they taken the test," he says. "This may mean that we inherit a 'steersman' who urges us toward a specific level of happiness or sadness."[2]

Dr. Seligman and others have learned about set range by studying people who had such positive experiences that most of us would expect them to be happy, as well as studying people who had such negative experiences that we would believe they'd become sad. Most of us would be overjoyed to win the lottery. We imagine all the ways it would make our lives better, all the joy it would bring. We also imagine that we would be devastated if we had some catastrophic medical problem.

The reality is quite interesting. People who win the lottery are overjoyed in the short run, but the joy doesn't last. "A systematic study of 22 people who won major lotteries found that they reverted to their baseline level of happiness over time, winding up no happier than 22 matched controls," says Dr. Seligman.[3]

How about those experiencing a major catastrophe? It seems to work the same way. After feeling devastated in the short run, they return to their former level of happiness fairly quickly. "Even individuals who become paraplegic as a result of spinal cord accidents quickly begin to adapt to their greatly limited capacities, and within 8 weeks they report more net positive emotion than negative emotion," says Dr. Seligman.[4]

"Each of us has our own personal set range for happiness, a fixed and largely inherited level to which we invariably revert," concludes Dr. Seligman.[5] So when good fortune comes our way and takes us above our normal level, we soon go down again. And when something brings us down, we pop back to the surface like a cork pushed under the water.

Two points about Dr. Seligman's findings can help heal IMS. First, everyone has a set "range" not a set "point." That means you have some room within your range where you can make things either better or worse for yourself. So, yes, you are unlikely to go from a Mr. Moody personality to the life of Brother Sunshine. On the other hand, coming from pessimistic stock does not doom you to misery. You can improve your level of happiness and change your irritable personality within your set range.

Second, a lot of irritability comes from feeling frustrated and angry at yourself for becoming so irritable. I often blamed myself or my wife when I would blow up. Once I accepted that my irritable mood was not totally within my control, I began to relax. The result? The more I accepted my irritability, the less irritable I became.

CHANGE YOUR MIND, CHANGE YOUR EMOTIONS, CHANGE YOUR HEART

When I began my own counseling to treat the anger and depression that went with the Irritable Male Syndrome, my doctor told me to buy the book *Mind over Mood: Change How You Feel by Changing the Way You Think* by Dennis Greenberger, Ph.D., and Christine A. Padesky, Ph.D. I saw that there was a foreword by Aaron Beck, M.D., who is known as the father of cognitive therapy, the fastest-growing and most rigorously researched talk therapy in the world. Cognitive therapy is the subject of at least 325 clinical trials evaluating its efficacy in treating everything from depression to schizophrenia.[6] It is akin to the Rational-Emotive Behavior Therapy (REBT) developed by Albert Ellis, Ph.D., in 1955.[7] I remembered Dr. Ellis's ABC approach from my graduate training in the 1960s—A stands for action, B for belief, and C for consequences. Though I had used ABC with my clients, I still had trouble applying it in my own life.

Like most people, I often felt that consequences were caused by actions. For instance, I believed that my irritability was caused by the way my boss treated me, the stresses of raising children, or the way my wife behaved. Drs. Ellis and Beck demonstrated that there is actually an intervening step between actions and how we feel. We always have beliefs (the B in the formula) that actually create our experiences of the actions. "Whenever we experience a mood, there is a thought connected to it that helps define the mood," say Drs. Greenberger and Padesky.[8] "Once a mood is present, it is accompanied by additional thoughts that support and strengthen the mood. For example, angry people think about ways they have been hurt, depressed people think about how unfortunate life has become, and anxious people see danger everywhere."[9]

I could relate to that. It did seem that the more irritable I became, the more I thought about the ways Carlin had hurt me. And the more I thought about the hurts, the more irritable I became.

But even when I saw what I was doing, I didn't know how to change it.

The first thing my doctor wanted me to do was fill out a "Thought Record."[10] There was a clear description of the process in Drs. Greenberger and Padesky's book. I was skeptical that going through the steps would change my irritable, dark moods. Since I was paying the doctor for her expertise, I went through the steps and answered the questions despite my cynicism.

THOUGHT RECORD

1. Situation
Write down the details: Who? What? When? Where?

---

2. Moods and Feelings and Their Intensities
What did you feel? Rate each mood (0 to 100 percent).

_____

_____

_____

_____

3. Automatic Thoughts (Images)
What was going through your mind just before you started to feel this way? Any other thoughts or images? Then, circle the "hot" thought—the one that seems most powerfully connected to the feeling that is most intense.

_____

_____

_____

_____

4. Evidence That Supports the Hot Thought

_____

_____

_____

_____

5. Evidence That Does Not Support the Hot Thought

_____

_____

_____

_____

6. Alternative/Balanced Thoughts and How Much You Believe in Each
Write an alternative or balanced thought. Rate how much you believe in each alternative or balanced thought (0 to 100 percent).

_____

_____

_____

_____

7. Rate Moods Now
Re-rate moods listed in step 2 as well as any new moods listed here (0 to 100 percent).

_____

_____

_____

_____

Here is one of the first Thought Records I filled out.

1. Situation

It's 8:00 A.M. and I come downstairs and reach out to give Carlin a hug and kiss. She seems stiff and seems to hold back and turn away.

2. Moods and Feelings and Their Intensities

Irritated (70 percent)

Angry (60 percent)

Hurt (40 percent)

Confused (30 percent)

3. Automatic Thoughts (Images)

Here we go again.

She's angry with me about something.

She never wants to be intimate.

She doesn't love me.

4. Evidence That Supports the Hot Thought

Carlin seems to have more interest in the children than she does in me.

She is so busy we don't have a lot of time to be close.

I'm the one who most often initiates sex.

5. Evidence That Does Not Support the Hot Thought

Carlin is often more withdrawn in the morning. Unlike me, she likes to quietly get into her day.

Just the other night, she snuggled very closely when we were watching TV.

I remember that she said her back hurt. Maybe she is in some pain.

There are times when she isn't busy or preoccupied and she is very passionate.

6. Alternative/Balanced Thoughts and How Much You Believe in Each

Even though she didn't respond the way I had hoped, she still loves me (90 percent).

Maybe I caught her at a bad time and she wasn't feeling very loving (80 percent).

She was feeling some pain and didn't want to be held too closely (30 percent).

Sometimes I'm too aggressive in my desire for intimacy and that can put her off (70 percent).

We are often intimate when we both feel relaxed and rested (80 percent).

7. Rate Moods Now

Irritated (30 percent; initially it was 70 percent)

Angry (20 percent; initially it was 60 percent)

Hurt (30 percent; initially it was 40 percent)

Confused (20 percent; initially it was 30 percent)

There were two new moods that hadn't been present initially.

Calm (50 percent)

Loving (70 percent)

Trying to describe this process is a bit like trying to write directions for someone you want to teach to dance. To get the benefit of the Thought Record, you really have to keep one. I can still remember how absolutely amazed I was that a 20-minute process of examining my thoughts could actually change the way I felt. It seemed almost like magic. One minute, my irritability was making me crazy; the next, it had died down to a manageable level. One minute, I was ready to blow my stack; the next, my anger had nearly gone away. And lo and behold, as I completed the Thought Record, I found I had new feelings that were totally absent when I began. I felt loving and calm.

When I was suffering most intensely from IMS, I filled out Thought Records nearly every day. Sometimes I did a number of them in one day. They never failed to take away some of the venom that seemed to be poisoning me and my marriage. Sometimes the negative feelings nearly went away and were replaced by positive ones. Sometimes there was only a small change in how I felt. Always there was some movement in a positive direction.

Knowing that my feelings didn't just "happen" was freeing. Knowing that I could do something about how I felt gave me a sense of power. For the first time, I felt like the irritability, blame, and sadness that had been so much a part of my intimate relationships had a chance to be healed.

WHAT YOU CAN DO NOW TO BECOME LESS IRRITABLE AND MORE OPTIMISTIC

I have found that the Thought Record is a wonderful tool for changing the way we see ourselves, others, and the world. Using it on a regular basis can help you reverse the cycle of irritability, anger, and depression that can be so debilitating. What follows are some additional strategies you can employ to change the way you think and feel about the world.

Recognize that you may be looking at the world through "irritable male lenses." As I have said a number of times, one of the difficult things about treating the Irritable Male Syndrome is that a man doesn't know he has it. What's more, it seems absolutely clear to him that the problem is not with him but with others. Getting help makes about as much sense to him as it would if his wife broke her leg and both she and the doctor insisted that he come in for treatment.

When I can get an IMS male to talk to me, one of the things I say to him is something like this: "I know it seems absolutely clear to you that the whole problem is with your partner. That's certainly the way I saw things. Would you be willing to entertain the possibility that you may be seeing through distorted lenses? When we wear these lenses for a long time, as I know I did, we are not even aware that we have them on. We are convinced that what we see is the way things are. Would you be willing to take a little time to see if there may be more to your situation than meets the eye?"

On some level, most guys know that something isn't quite right about the way we're seeing things. We know that our partners can't be the cause of all our problems. We suspect that we contribute somehow; we just don't know how. We fear that if the problem isn't all hers, it must be all ours. I try to assure guys that is not the case. "What you'll see if you take off those old, dirty lenses is that no one is to blame for your unhappiness. And there are things you and your wife can both do to make things better."

Make new choices. It should be clear by now that IMS doesn't come on overnight, though it can seem like that sometimes. Our attitudes and beliefs about ourselves and the world develop over many years. By the time people recognize their health or relationships are being affected, their minds have often developed rigid ways of seeing the world.

Most of us get locked into the belief that the only way we can be happy is to get everyone around us to recognize that we are right. We're like a lab monkey that reaches inside a box to grab a banana. The box is built so the monkey can't get his hand out while he's holding the banana. He can see more bananas waiting on another table, but he won't let go of the first banana, pull out his hand, and get the ones that are waiting. He keeps pulling harder, trying to force the banana and his hand through the hole in the box. He just won't let go, even when what he is doing isn't working, even when there is a better choice available.

I tell guys that even when our old ways of seeing things are keeping us stuck, it isn't easy to let go of them. Sometimes we have to recognize that things boil down to a simple choice. Would we rather be right (about ourselves, our partners, our children, the world), or would we rather be happy? When it gets down to it, most of us choose happiness.

Keep it in and transform it. When I was going to school, the prevailing view of therapy was still Freudian-based "psychodynamic psychotherapy." The idea was that our emotions exist within a closed system and if not let out, will cause problems in the form of symptoms. I always pictured a pressure cooker: If the steam wasn't released, the whole thing would explode. One strategy, called the *Vesuvius,* prescribed letting go and spewing out anger. I tried it, and sometimes I did feel better—though the person on the receiving end of the lava flow usually wasn't overjoyed. When the anger returned, I figured I just needed to let it out more often. It took me a long time to realize that expressing my anger actually created more anger.

I found a similar thing with depression. We were taught to help our clients get in touch with their feelings and learn to express their irritability and unhappiness. When the symptoms came back, we assumed they just needed more therapy sessions. Our therapies were perpetuating the very problems they were intended to remedy. No wonder psychoanalysis could go on three to five times a week for 5 years.

Using psychodynamics to treat depression didn't seem to be effective for Dr. Beck. This is what led him to develop cognitive therapy, which teaches us how to take some time before expressing strong emotions, change the way we think, and experience the way our emotions can be transformed as we change our thoughts. We used to think that letting out our anger would keep it from coming out in even more destructive ways, such as heart disease. Now we know the opposite is true. Dwelling on past hurts and letting out all our anger produces more cardiac disease and more irritability and anger.

Heal the irritable male brain through meditation. We've known for years that meditation can help us relax and quiet the mind. But many people have been reluctant to try meditation because it seems too esoteric and unscientific. A study published in the July/August 2003 issue of the prestigious journal *Psychosomatic Medicine* offers the first scientific rationale for why meditation works. People who are generally happy and calm typically show greater activity in the left side of the brain's frontal area as compared to the right side. In contrast, those who are more prone to sadness, anxiety, irritability, and worry tend to show more activity on the right side of the frontal area and less on the left side. Meditation can shift the emotional balance in a more positive direction. The study discovered that a group who had been taught meditation had a significant increase in activity in the left side of the brain's frontal area. The meditation subjects also reported feeling more positive emotions in daily life. A control group didn't show these changes.[11] So it seems that meditation can actually change one's usual range of emotions, helping Mr. Moody move closer to feeling like Brother Sunshine.

Let others in. One of the most difficult aspects of the Irritable Male Syndrome is that we push others away just when we need them the most. At the core of our irritability is the pain we feel because our needs aren't being met. One of the strongest needs we have is for intimacy and closeness. We are hungry to be accepted, held, nurtured, and loved. Yet we push away the people we love the most.

When I was recovering from IMS, I felt cut off and alone. When I could reach out and admit I needed help, I could begin the healing process.

Forgive the past. Once a man and the people around him begin to directly address IMS, all of those involved often feel a lot of anger about past behaviors and a lot of guilt about the parts they have played in someone else's unhappiness. I remind people that they did the best they could, given what they knew at the time. To IMS males and those around them, irritability and blame made sense, given how the men saw the world. Learning there is a different way allows for a new future. We need not hold resentment and anger about what was done in the past. Nor do we need to feel guilty about the things we said or did that contributed to others' pain.

We do need to make amends, as 12-step recovery programs like Alcoholics Anonymous recommend. Often that involves acknowledgment of our actions and a willingness to genuinely say, "I'm sorry." I know this was the most difficult thing I had to do with my wife, Carlin. Many times, I wanted to say, "Look, I know that my irritability, blame, and anger contributed to your pain. I'm truly sorry." I just could never do it. For a long time, I didn't really know why I couldn't. I thought maybe it was because I had nothing to feel sorry about. It was only later that I came to see that what was keeping me from acknowledging my hurtful words and actions was my overwhelming guilt. I felt terrible about what I had done, and I was ashamed to admit I had done it.

Forgiveness is a circular drive. We must forgive ourselves in order to acknowledge what we've done. Also, acknowledging what we've done allows us to forgive ourselves. As we get the poison created by the Irritable Male Syndrome out in the open, we are able to heal. "Love truth, but pardon error," Voltaire reminds us. We are all human. We all make mistakes. Even irritable males must be forgiven, most especially by ourselves.

Appreciate the present. We are told that when we are caught in a riptide, we should resist the urge to fight against it. We should relax, stay calm, and swim parallel to the shore rather than try to swim directly back. Once we are free of the current, we can make it safely to shore. Likewise, when caught by the Irritable Male Syndrome, we must relax into the present moment. Rather than fighting to change our moods or fighting to get other people to change so we'll feel better, we need to breathe and ask, "How am I feeling now?" When I do that, I find answers that surprise me. "I feel really angry. I'm enraged. She always does this. No, no, stick with your feelings. Okay. I'm hurt. I'm afraid. I'm lonely."

The more we stay in the present moment, the more we stay with our feelings rather than our judgments, the better able we are to keep up our strength. It's like swimming parallel to the shore. We may not make any progress in getting our needs met, but we don't exhaust ourselves and make things worse.

Most of our irritations, angers, fears, and worries exist in the past or the future. I keep asking myself, "How are things now?" Every time I ask, I find that in the present moment, things aren't nearly as bad as I imagined them to be.

Enjoy the future. The way we see the future determines whether we are consumed by the Irritable Male Syndrome or whether we free ourselves. We all know the saying "Shit happens." The cognitive therapy approach to health notes that guys who are susceptible to IMS believe that each negative event is *personal, permanent,* and *pervasive.*

One of the recurrent events that would trigger my irritability would be the way Carlin and I interacted when she returned from being away. I would immediately want to hug and kiss. She'd often act less than enthusiastic. I would usually take this personally. I would think to myself things like, "She isn't glad to see me. Maybe she doesn't like coming home. She knows I want to be close. She's being cold just to annoy me." When I had worked myself up into a really irritable frenzy, I would think, "She's probably been with someone else—or she's thinking about being with someone else and she's trying to hide it."

I believed that her behavior was permanent. I would think, "That's always the way she is. She never wants to be close. She always keeps herself distant from me." I was sure that things had always been this way and would always be this way.

These events and thoughts were pervasive and seeped into every aspect of my life. I would chew on our interactions over and over again. I would let them grow like a mind cancer and take over my internal life. "I must be repulsive. No one cares about me. Women are all like that. They suck you in, then push you away."

The future doesn't need to be this way. I learned that not everything is personal. I don't need to assume that everything Carlin does is about me. She may come home tired and need a rest before she wants to hug. She may be preoccupied with concerns about a client. I learned that one event does not predict all future events. Today, Carlin might not feel like a full body hug when she comes home. Tomorrow, she might very much enjoy one.

I found that a single event is not an indicator that everything in life is negative. The fact that Carlin doesn't feel like giving me the kind of hug I want today does not mean I'm a failure as a man, doomed to live the rest of my life as a sexual celibate. And it certainly doesn't mean that all women are out to make my life miserable.

If you are one of the many millions of men who have the kinds of negative thoughts that I did, called "stinkin' thinkin'" in 12-step recovery circles, just know that you aren't alone and that you can enjoy the future without driving yourself and those around you bonkers.

Cultivate positive emotions. People often think that irritability and calm are polar opposites. If you are unhappy and irritable, they assume, you can't be happy and relaxed. It turns out that this isn't true. Even when caught in irritability, we can still seek out experiences that bring us joy.

One of the most distressing aspects of the Irritable Male Syndrome is the belief that we will never get better. When we are caught in the cloud of darkness, it seems like we have always been in it and always will be. Our efforts to stop being so irritable often fail, and we lose hope. Since we are convinced that we can never have any joy in our lives until our irritability lifts, we can sink into despair. Knowing that we can still create our own positive feelings, in spite of our unhappiness and irritability, can be freeing.

This reality came home to me when I was having a particularly difficult time with my wife. We weren't fighting. We weren't talking about what we didn't like. We weren't blaming each other. We were pleasant with each other, but we weren't happy. We were both emotionally exhausted. We were living together and feeling like we were roommates rather than lovers. When we made love, which was rarely, it was more tension release than emotional bonding. My feelings ranged from unhappy to numb. If I had put them on a scale of 0 to 100 for positive emotions and 0 to −100 for negative emotions, they would have ranged from −50 to 0. I was convinced that no joy or happiness could come until I was consistently in the positive range, which seemed impossible at the time. I felt hopeless and helpless and could see nothing that I could do to make things better.

Then a wonderful thing happened. A friend called and suggested we go for a walk in one of my favorite spots, along the edge of San Francisco Bay. As we walked, I could let in the beauty of the light on the water, the sound of our feet crunching on the pebbles of the path, and the warmth of the sunshine. Though my down mood and the thoughts about my wife hadn't changed a bit, I began to feel better. I felt at ease and calm, for the first time in a long while.

Coming home, the good feelings remained. Even being with my wife, still feeling sadness at our state of unhappiness, I felt better. Somehow things felt more hopeful. If I could feel good even when things felt bad, maybe things could change. It was an important insight for me that has served me well through the years.

DECREASING IRRITABILITY BY MAINTAINING AND DEEPENING INTIMATE RELATIONSHIPS

Nearly every adult male going through the Irritable Male Syndrome has fantasies of getting away from it all. Such a man often feels an intense pull to leave his partner and start over with someone else. Sometimes he thinks he has lost that loving feeling and will never get it back. Sometimes he thinks he's fallen in love with someone else. Sometimes he thinks he just needs to get away.

I suggest that men think long and hard before they end long-term relationships. They might be much more likely to find the peace and passion they seek by revitalizing their marriages rather than looking elsewhere. Happiness, in the jargon of research scientists, is "robustly related to marriage." In a survey of 35,000 Americans over the past 30 years, the National Opinion Research Center found that 40 percent of married people said they were "very happy," while only 24 percent of unmarried, divorced, separated, and widowed people said this.[12]

Men can also receive the benefits of marriage without formalizing the process. For many people, marriage is defined not by the official ceremony and piece of paper but by their commitment to each other. In their study of very happy people, Dr. Seligman and his research associate Ed Diener found that the happiest 10 percent of those people studied were involved in romantic relationships.[13]

Maintaining and deepening friendships is also important. As men become more involved with career and family, we often neglect our friendships. Those men who are the happiest and least irritable have put time and energy into keeping the connections with buddies from the past. Happy guys also find time to develop new friendships that deepen as they age.

One day when I was feeling particularly low, I saw a notice on the bulletin board at our local church about an upcoming men's group. At first, I passed it by and laughed it off. "I don't need some wimpy men's group," I thought. "I see guys at work. I enjoy having a beer with the guys I play ball with. I belong to a number of business clubs where I see guys." Passing the notice each week, I became more intrigued. I finally called the number and was invited to a group meeting. It was like nothing else I had ever attended. The men didn't talk about business or sports or women. They talked about feelings and fears and hopes for the future. They talked about health concerns and problems they were having in their relationships with wives and children.

I have been in the group for nearly 25 years now and expect I will be with them until all of the members have passed on. The men have become like the brothers I never had and the friends I always wanted. They've been there for me when I felt totally alone. They've celebrated my triumphs. They've enriched all aspects of my life.

There are a number of specific ways that being with men helps with the Irritable Male Syndrome. We know that adolescent males who are raised without the involvement of their fathers tend to be more violent than those whose fathers remain close. It seems that without consistent male contact, the boys are constantly trying to prove they are men. "Studies of delinquent boys have convinced many sociologists that boys raised by mothers alone are particularly prone to violence because of their susceptibility to 'hypermasculinity,'" says Myriam Miedzian, Ph.D., author of *Boys Will Be Boys: Breaking the Link between Masculinity and Violence*.[14]

I have also found that midlife men, who find their testosterone levels dropping, often react to a fear of losing their manhood by becoming hypermasculine. They may become demanding, controlling, and aggressive.

Being with other men, particularly in a men's group where they can open up and be vulnerable without fear of appearing weak in the eyes of a woman, can help a man feel more accepting of his changes. Men can understand each other's concerns and fears and can support each other's expression of feelings. The result, I have found, is that men who are involved in men's groups are much less irritable than those who are not.

DANGER!! SEEING A THERAPIST
MAY BE DETRIMENTAL TO YOUR HEALTH

As I've suggested, there is much you can do on your own to temper an irritable mindset. More people are choosing to seek out professional help. We do need to be cautious, however, because not all help is helpful. The truth is that many kinds of therapy have never been scientifically tested to see if they actually work. Though well-meaning, many therapists *do* in fact contribute to patients' problems.

George and his wife, Marion, came to see me after having spent 4 months doing counseling with another therapist. When they sat down, I introduced myself and asked them, "What would you like in coming to see me today?" They both seemed a bit confused and slightly stunned by the question.

"What do you mean?" George asked in a low, rumbling voice.

"What would you like?" I asked. "If you could leave this session feeling like you had got something of real value, what would you like?"

"We need help communicating," Marion said, her voice tiny and tentative. Then she took a deep breath and continued. "We've had a very wonderful marriage, or at least I thought we did, until about 5 years ago. George began to change. He became much more withdrawn and unaffectionate. When I would try to ask him what was wrong, he'd just say, 'Nothing.' If I pressed him, he would explode and tell me to just leave him alone. Even when we weren't interacting, he seemed irritable and unhappy and. . . . "

"Tell him how you always nag at me," George interrupted, his voice getting louder and more cutting. "'George do this. George do that.' You never leave me alone. I just got tired of your constant whining and complaining."

I could see that Marion felt hurt and was starting to cry. "Why did you decide to see the other therapist? What did you want?" I asked.

"I wanted to save our marriage," Marion said with a voice that seemed to be choking out the words.

"Yeah, and look what happened," George jumped in. "When we started therapy, I admit, things weren't the best between us, but we were getting by. All couples have some problems along the way. But you insisted we go, and like a fool, I agreed to see this guy. What a joke. We got to the bottom of our problems all right, but we never were able to get back up again. If anything, the therapy made the problem worse."

This is a complaint I hear over and over again from clients, particularly those who are having difficulty with their relationships. The problem, I've found, is that most therapy is still tied to the disease concept of treatment. Usually, the first question the therapist asks is "What is your problem?" The idea is that if we can understand the problem, we will be better able to find the solution. That's the kind of approach I was taught in school. Learn about the problem, go back into the person's past to see where it began, bring it to the light, and hopefully things will improve. Over the years, I've found that talking about problems doesn't always lead to solutions. In fact, it often leads to more problems.

Many years ago, in my own work, I began with a simple shift of focus. Instead of asking about the problem, I ask about the solution. "What would you like?" Most people are thrown off balance. They are so used to talking with therapists who are problem oriented that they don't know how to respond to someone who wants to talk about the solution, who asks to look into the future instead of the past, who believes that healing can happen in an instant, not after years of psychotherapy.

When I explained this to George and Marion, they brightened noticeably. "I just had a gut feeling that talking about our problems didn't help," George said. "It was strange—just taking time to drive to our session, sit together, and then be together coming home seemed to be therapeutic. Actually talking about all the things that were going wrong in our marriage didn't really help at all."

"All I know is that I love George more than anything and want our marriage to work," Marion said with tears in her eyes. "I'm not willing to give up. That's why I decided to keep trying and find someone with a different approach to helping people. I came feeling desperate and hopeless. I feel a little lighter and more hopeful."

Once again, I asked each of them to tell me what they would like. "If we could wave a magic wand and you could leave here having your needs met, what would they be?"

"Well, I guess I want Marion to understand the pressures I'm under," George began tentatively. "I want her to know that I love her, but I feel it's a different kind of love now. I want to be close, but I also want to be free."

"I want the same things," Marion began, her voice upbeat and almost cheery. She reached out to hold George's hand. "I want this kind of gentleness and tenderness between us. I want to know what George is feeling and what he needs. And I guess I want something different from what we've had. I've been afraid to hope for more, afraid that I'd lose what I had."

I've found that the Irritable Male Syndrome, as well as other psycho-biosocial problems, cannot be solved as long as we focus only on the problems. When a woman comes to see me and says, "My husband has become so irritable lately; I can't stand it," I ask her what she would like instead. When a man complains about his wife's nagging or her loss of sexual desire, I want to know, "How would you like things to be?" Remember that old saying "Birds of a feather flock together"? I think it applies to healing. The more we talk about problems, the more problems we attract. The more we talk about love and intimacy, the more love and intimacy we attract.

It really *is* that simple. Yes, simple—not easy. Changing old patterns of thought, feelings, and behavior takes a willingness to make our lives the way we want them to be. Would you like to continue being or living with someone who is irritable, or would you like to be calm, content, and joyful?

In the next, final chapter, I will show you why the Irritable Male Syndrome may actually be a sign of your soul's recognition that you need to change old patterns.

CHAPTER 12

DEEPENING THE SPIRIT
Healing the Irritable Male Syndrome
in Ourselves, Our Relationships, and Our World

In earlier parts of the book, I've suggested that there are hormonal, nutritional, psychological, economic, and social aspects of IMS. In this last chapter, I want to suggest that there is another aspect that transcends those. Some call it the spirit, others call it the soul or inner self. Whatever name we give it, it is an aspect of our beings that must be satisfied if we are to live meaningful lives. When we are not acting in integrity with that part of us, we become uncomfortable, restless, and irritable. We can try to satisfy this inner need by altering our hormones, our brain chemistry, our stress levels, and our interpersonal relationships. But we still feel unfulfilled until we come to grips with this inner calling.

What is this nonmaterial, inner self that seems to call us to something larger and grander than our day-to-day existence? The Romans named it *genius*; the Greeks, *daimon*; and the Christians, *guardian angel*. Romantics, like Keats, felt that the call came from the heart. The Neoplatonists saw an imaginal body, the *ochema,* that carried us like a vehicle. For indigenous people, such as Native Americans, it is *spirit, free-soul, animal-soul,* or *breath-soul.*[1]

"The soul of each of us is given a unique daimon before we are born," says psychologist James Hillman, author of *The Soul's Code: In Search of Character and Calling,* "and it has selected an image or pattern that we live on earth. This soul-companion, the daimon, guides us here; in the process of arrival, however, we forget all that took place and believe we come empty into this world. The daimon remembers what is in your image and belongs to your pattern, and therefore your daimon is the carrier of your destiny."[2]

WHY ARE WE HERE?

There is a story of a man getting ready to come into existence on the earth plane. An angel tells him the plan for his life. He finds out what lessons he will need to learn in order to fulfill his destiny. He learns about the kind of family he will be born into. He gets a clear picture of the kind of childhood traumas and illnesses he will experience so that he will learn certain lessons. He is told about the historical influences that he will need to deal with throughout his life. He sees his marriages and divorces, his children being born and growing up, his midlife crises, and his old age. He sees it all. His life and his death, as well as the lives and deaths of those he will interact with on the journey of this lifetime.

As you might expect, he experiences a complex mixture of feelings. He is excited, invigorated, scared, worried, irritable, expectant, and joyful. He is looking forward to the good and the bad, and he knows that he will come into the world with support and guidance. He never has to worry about doing the wrong thing or making a mistake, because it is all part of his life. Although he has a destiny, he knows that his future is not carved in stone. There are millions of choices that he will make, and these choices will determine how he goes through his life.

He is ready to go. He is chomping at the bit. Just before he comes into this life, the angel snaps a finger against the man's upper lip, causing the man to forget all that he has learned about his future. It is said that the small indentation that we all have on our upper lips is the impression that remains from the touch of the angel. But our daimons remember and draw our attention to the choices we need to make to fulfill our destinies. We are not always happy to be reminded.

GETTING IN TOUCH WITH OUR DAIMONS

There are certain times in our lives when we need to make a change but are afraid and hold on to our old ways. We may have spent a lot of time moving from place to place, searching for happiness and success. Now, we feel called upon to take an inner journey. This often makes us anxious, irritable, and depressed. We might say that our daimons are really pissed off and aren't going to take it anymore. They are calling us to our true paths, to the journeys that are ours alone to take.

Our daimons might tell us that we are on the wrong path. They may try to awaken us to the truth that we have been trying to fulfill someone else's dream, one that isn't our own. We may be trying to live up to our fathers' expectations or trying to be the men our mothers always wanted us to be. On the other hand, we may be rebelling against expectations.

Our daimons may hope we will figure things out for ourselves. If we are too thickheaded, they might get a wee bit irritable. If we still don't pay attention, they might get downright angry. Of course, we don't know why we are suddenly furious. We think our problems are being caused by our wives or our bosses, our parents or our children, the politicians or the people on the highways and byways that cut us off and make us shake our fists with rage.

If we have stopped looking for outside causes, we may think that the problem is physiological, psychological, or hormonal. As I've said in earlier chapters, these are some of the causes of the Irritable Male Syndrome. They are not the whole story, though. One cause that we don't often recognize is that our daimons may be calling to us, making us uncomfortable so that we will pay attention.

Our daimons shake things up in our lives. They remind us of why we are here. They would have asked the same question posed by God to the Jewish rabbi Sushya at the end of his life. "Why did you spend so much of your life trying to emulate Moses? Why did you not become Sushya, the man only you could become?" The Irritable Male Syndrome may be God's, or our daimons', way of calling each man back to the person only he can become.

The Roman philosopher Epictetus admonished us 2,000 years ago to be true to our personal daimons. "Now is the time to get serious about living your ideals. How long can you afford to put off being who you really want to be? Put your principles into practice—now. This is your life! You aren't a child anymore. The longer you wait, the more you will be vulnerable to mediocrity and filled with shame and regret, because you know you are capable of better. From this instant on, vow to stop disappointing yourself. Separate yourself from the mob. Decide to be extraordinary and do what you need to do—now."[3]

Hillman suggests there are three things we must do in order to fully fulfill our life's dream.

1. Recognize the call as a prime fact of human existence.
2. Align life with it.

3. Find the common sense to realize that accidents, including the heartache and the natural shocks the flesh is heir to, are the path our daimons are asking us to walk.[4]

I would add a fourth: Never give up hope. At times, we become discouraged, concerned that we may never be able to follow our souls' calling. We must not stop our efforts—not even when they don't look like they are getting us anywhere. "Hope is not the conviction that something will turn out well," says Vaclav Havel, former president of the Czech Republic, "but the certainty that something makes sense regardless of how it turns out."[5]

THE VOICE OF OUR CALLING

Early on, it is often difficult to hear the voice of our calling. Though we reach out, we're not sure what to look for. "I don't feel drawn to anything in particular," one young man told me. My response was that our true calling develops over time. The process differs from person to person. I know some people who had a clear vision of their calling when they were children. Most people don't find their true calling until later in life, after they have done some living.

Even when we have found our calling, it isn't a 24-hour high—all good, all the time. There are still times of excitement and boredom. But I've found that we know our calling when we find we must do it not as an expression of success but as an expression of who we are. "Before you can label it your calling, it has to take on personal significance and be woven into the story of your life," says Po Bronson, author of *What Should I Do with My Life?*[6]

The influential psychoanalyst Erik Erikson was one of the first to examine the stages we go through at different times of our lives and the issues we must face if we are to be successful. He suggested that there are eight stages, beginning at birth and ending when we die. At each stage, there is a conflict we must resolve and two ways of coping with each crisis, an adaptive and a maladaptive way.

After four childhood stages, we come to the fifth stage, which Erikson said generally occurred between the ages of 12 and 18. It is the time when we begin asking, "Who am I?" At this stage, there is a crisis between *identity* and *role confusion*.

In young adulthood, between 19 and 40, the most important issues revolve around our love relationships. The crisis of this stage is between *intimacy* and *isolation*. The next stage, middle adulthood, occurs between 40 and 65. It is a time to create a living legacy through mentoring. Here the crisis is between *generativity* and *stagnation*. Between 65 and the end of our lives, Erikson says, we deal with issues of late adulthood. We reflect on our lives and our role in the big scheme of things. The crisis here is between *integrity* and *despair.*

At every stage, we must confront these inner crises. If we are generally successful, developing identity, intimacy, generativity, and integrity, we feel content and satisfied. If, on the other hand, we are drawn toward role confusion, isolation, stagnation, and despair, we experience the symptoms of the Irritable Male Syndrome.

Successfully completing each stage makes it more likely that we will do well on the next. I have found that it is never too late to heal from the pain of our pasts. In fact, one of the primary opportunities we have in the second half of life is to heal old wounds that were unresolved earlier.

Some people believe that our major successes take place before we are 40. More and more people, however, are finding that our true passions may not be evident until the second half of life, perhaps after the age of 65. One of those people is James V. Gambone, Ph.D., who believes that we should "retire" the concept of retirement in favor of what he calls "refirement."

Dr. Gambone, an expert on intergenerational relationships, asks, "What if we replaced the retirement concept with a new and positive vision of basing your life and work choices on your core values, your passions, a commitment to lifelong learning, an intentional connection to all generations, and a willingness to use your legacy as a starting point for deciding how you want to live today?"[7] Often, men think they want to retire, relax, and play golf, only to find out they have a different calling. For many, retirement does not make them happy—it's more like a slow decline toward boredom.

"If somebody says to me, 'I'm not happy about the way I'm growing old,' I talk to them about shifting from aging to saging," says Rabbi Zalman Schachter-Shalomi.[8] In his book *From Age-ing to Sage-ing: A Profound New Vision of Growing Older,* Rabbi Schachter-Shalomi talks about what elders have gone through to get where they are. "Like mountain climbers who have scaled a high peak, we have achieved a vantage point in old age from which to observe the path of our ascent and to appreciate the personality that we have created with discipline and devotion."[9]

This is clearly a perspective worth honoring and sharing with others. Yet it often takes a crisis to make us realize that life does not have to go downhill as we age.

THE CALL COMES IN CRISIS

There is a story of a man sitting beside a river on a warm summer's day when he hears a faint cry. Soon, he sees a child being swept away by the river's current. The man immediately dives into the water, swims out to the terrified child, and pulls him to shore.

No sooner is the child safely on shore than the man hears another call out. Once again, he dives in and swims out to help. The same thing happens again, and the man is back in the river doing his best to help. Back on shore, he gasps for breath and hopes that the children are safe. But he soon hears more cries for help.

What can he do? What would you do? He is becoming exhausted. He doesn't know if he has enough energy to pull another child out of the water. He wonders whether he should let the next child go by, hoping he can rest himself and be ready to help others. He begins to wonder what is happening upstream that is causing so many children to be cast into the current. Should he ignore the screams of the one he hears now and race upstream to see if he can prevent the problem and save the lives of future children?

In chapter 1, I defined the Irritable Male Syndrome as a state of hypersensitivity, anxiety, frustration, and anger. I believe that a good deal of the stress we feel comes from the difficulty of dealing with three levels of problems.

1. We are called upon to continuously deal with day-to-day crises in our own lives and in the lives of those we care about.

2. We know there are larger issues at the root of our day-to-day pain. Our daimons call us to action, but it isn't clear what we are called upon to do.

3. The more frustrated we become, the less energy we have for constructive action, which leads to even more frustration, anger, anxiety, and hypersensitivity.

How do we break the impasse of immobility? Here's what the man in the story does. He swims out to deal with the most immediate crisis of another drowning child. Then, as he swims ashore, he repeatedly calls for help until a small group gathers. He instructs a few of them on rescue techniques for the children he expects will be calling out for help. He takes a few people with him to find out what is happening upstream. While he's walking there, he reaches out to one of the men to get support and help him regain his strength.

This story has many variations, but they all speak to me in a similar way. We are at a time of crisis where more and more people, particularly the young, are in danger of dying. We can't ignore their calls for help. We need to rouse ourselves from the slumber of our day-to-day lives if we are to be the kind of human beings most of us aspire to become.

If we don't get to the root causes of the problems in our culture, however, we will continue to be overwhelmed by casualties until we ourselves break down. Our only hope is to connect with other people so that we can deal with the present problems while, together, we work to change the social conditions that bring about the problems in the first place.

We also need support to meet our own needs so that we have the energy and strength to keep going for the long haul. We must follow the callings of our hearts, or the work we do will feel unfulfilling, and we will find we cannot do it. No one is served if we burn ourselves out trying to help others or if we try to solve problems in a way that conflicts with our own unique callings.

I've been doing healing work for nearly 40 years now. There are always immediate problems that need to be addressed. My self and my family are in continuous change, and I need to attend to our own healing. I know too many "helpers" who do good work in the world while their own families fall apart because they are neglected.

As a therapist, I see clients every day who need support to deal with the stresses of life. After years of working with people, I keep seeing many of the same problems. I begin to wonder what's happening "upstream" that continues to cause people to become irritable, anxious, frustrated, and depressed. I want to prevent the problems so that I don't feel like I'm pulling one child out of the water only to see three more being pushed in.

I want to keep my own hope alive. I want to keep my psychological, physical, interpersonal, and spiritual health as good as it can be. I want to reach out on all levels. I want to find ways of helping myself, helping others, and helping the world. Though I have long had the desire to do all these things, I've found I always fall short. It seems when I focus on the day-to-day problems, I don't have energy for the larger issues. When I commit myself to the larger issues, I feel like I'm letting down someone today—my wife, my children, my clients. When I take care of myself, I feel guilty that I'm not helping others.

Sometimes I feel I'd rather just be a tree and not have to worry about these things. As I get older, I find that I'll never be able to do all these things perfectly. I won't even be able to do them adequately some of the time. The best I can do is to recognize that I'm doing the best I can. The German poet Rainer Maria Rilke offers guidance in his *Letters to a Young Poet*:

> *I want to beg you, as much as I can, to be patient toward all that is unresolved in your heart and try to love* the questions themselves, *like locked rooms and like books written in a foreign tongue. Do not now seek the answers that cannot be given you because you would not be able to live them. And the point is to live everything.* Live *the questions now. Perhaps you will then gradually, without noticing it, live along some distant day into the answer.*[10]

We can listen to our inner voices, to the direction of our personal daimons. We can keep our passion for this wonderful dance of life alive and feel the joy of living at a time of great problems and also great opportunities. We can also learn from our elders, from those who are a bit farther along the path of creating identities based on healing ourselves, healing others, and healing the planet.

MARSHALL ROSENBERG, NONVIOLENCE, AND 9/11[11]

I had heard about Nonviolent Communication (NVC) as a way of preventing problems, but I had only a vague idea of what it was and of the man behind the message. That changed for me on September 11, 2001.

Like so many others, I was awash in conflicted feelings and thoughts.

A friend of mine sent me an article written by Marshall B. Rosenberg, Ph.D. entitled, "Retaliation Will Not Bring Lasting Safety and Peace." It was written September 27, 2001, and began, "After the attacks on the World Trade Center and the Pentagon, millions of people throughout the world are feeling deep pain and grief. They feel outraged, scared, power-less—and very vulnerable. Many have a deep need to feel safe again. They long for a world where they can live in peace. Others have a deep desire to get even. They long for revenge and retribution."[12]

Dr. Rosenberg seemed to understand my feelings and acknowledge both my desire to strike back and my need for peace and forgiveness. As I read further, I was impressed by the fact that this was not some armchair psychologist preaching peace from the safety of his office but someone who was at the forefront of conflict resolution in the world.

"For the last 35 years, my associates and I have worked throughout the world to help resolve conflicts between warring gangs, ethnic groups, tribes, and countries. Over and over, we have observed that actions motivated by the desire for punishment produce retaliation from the other side, and that actions motivated by a desire for peace produce acts of peace from the other side. In either case, these actions create cycles that can go on for years—generations—centuries.

"I, and others in my organization, have worked with people from the warring factions in Rwanda, Burundi, Sierra Leone, Nigeria, South Africa, Serbia, Croatia, Israel, and Palestine. Our experience has taught us that real safety and peace can be achieved, despite enormous odds, only when people are able to see the 'humanity' of those who attack them. This requires something far more difficult than turning the other cheek; it requires empathizing with the fears, hurt, rage, and unmet human needs that are behind the attacks.[13]

"If there is an answer to the enormous problem before us, it is to seek solutions that will meet the needs of all concerned. This is not utopian idealism. I have seen such solutions created—over and over again—around the world."[14]

In his peacekeeping work throughout the world, Dr. Rosenberg has found that the principles of Nonviolent Communication that he developed apply equally well to large groups and to intimate relationships. When we are frustrated, anxious, irritable, or angry, he tells us, there are three things going on.

1. We are upset because we are not getting our needs met.

2. We are blaming someone or something else for not getting what we want.

3. We are about to speak or act in such a way that will almost guarantee we will not get what we need, or that we will later regret.

In Nonviolent Communication, Dr. Rosenberg offers specific ways we can deal with difficult situations. For instance, let's consider two typical irritable male interactions. A man comes home from a hard day at work, expecting to relax and have a nice dinner. When he walks in the door, he finds that the house is a mess and his partner is nowhere to be found. He is furious and can't wait until his partner returns. Another man's supervisor tells him that he has made a mistake that is going to cost the company money. "What's the matter with you?" the boss wants to know. "Don't you give a damn about your work?"

How might these men react? The first man may confront his partner as soon as she comes in the door. "Where the hell have you been?" he wants to know. "This place looks like a pigsty. I bet you've been hanging out with those lazy friends of yours." The other man may hang his head and say nothing. He may be holding in a great deal of shame and rage.

The alternate, NVC response to such situations is to make a caring connection with the other person, focusing on needs, feelings, and requests. The first man might say something like, "I'm glad you're home. There are some things I want to say to you. Would you be willing to listen to me for the next 5 minutes?" Depending on what's going on with his wife, she may agree to talk or she might need some time to get settled first. When she is ready to listen, the man might tell her, "When I came home and saw that there were papers all over the living room and you weren't home . . . " (a nonjudgmental description of what happened). "I felt really angry. I also was kind of scared." (He shares feelings.) "I didn't know where you were. I had been looking forward to a quiet evening with you and a nice dinner." (He expresses what he needs and wants.) "Would you be willing to tell me how you feel about what I just said?" (He requests connection.)

I hope you can recognize that this guy is much more likely to get his needs met and become less hostile in the second scenario than in the first.

Without Nonviolent Communication, "stuffing" his feelings may cause the second man to develop physical problems early in his life. Or he may keep things bottled up inside until he blows up, becoming one of those guys about whom everyone says, "I don't know how he could have done that horrible thing. He seemed like such a nice, quiet man."

On the other hand, with NVC, he might say to his boss something like, "Jerry, I can see you're upset . . . " (listening to the other person's needs) " . . . because you want to be sure our company does well and remains profitable." (He guesses what needs the other man may have.) "Am I hearing you correctly, Jerry?" (He requests connection.)

The boss may correct his perception. The important thing is not to guess correctly about another's feelings and needs but simply to be interested in knowing what those needs are. The boss may need to vent more, and the employee may need to keep reminding himself, "This doesn't mean there's something wrong with me. This is about Jerry, his feelings, and his needs." The conversation may continue until the boss, feeling that he's been heard, says something like, "I'm sorry I blew up at you. It's been a hell of a day, and I'm really worried about keeping ahead of the competition." Once a person feels as if he is genuinely being heard, anger often dissipates like air released from a balloon. From that point, both men feel as if they are on the same team. They can get past the feelings of hurt and develop better ways of working together.

Learning the language and techniques of Nonviolent Communication has been a tremendous help for me in healing the Irritable Male Syndrome in my own life, in people I counsel, and in my friends. I have seen the way it can help people throughout the world. It's not easy to learn, but I have found that, with practice and support, anyone can do it.

THE GIFT OF MENTORING YOUNG MEN

I first met Mitch DeArmon in January 1992. He and a friend had heard me speak at a conference, and his friend convinced Mitch to come see me. My first impression on meeting him was, "This is a big bear of a man—kind of scary." His voice was deep, his hands were big, and he looked like someone you didn't want to meet in a dark alley. He told me he was a butcher, and I could picture him hefting sides of beef off hooks in a cold warehouse and wielding saws and large knives to cut the cow into steaks.

As we talked, I found a gentler side underneath the gruff exterior. "I want to work with people," he told me in his low, firm voice. "I feel like I have something to contribute, particularly to younger men."

I've found that as men get older many of us are drawn to mentoring younger men. In tribal cultures throughout the world, this eldering function is built into the fabric of society. Malidoma Patrice Somé, a leader in the men's movement who was born in Upper Volta (now Burkina Faso) and initiated in the ancestral traditions of his tribe, describes the importance of this process. "When a child grows into an adolescent, he or she must be initiated into adulthood. A person who doesn't get initiated will remain an adolescent for the rest of their life, and this is a frightening, dangerous, and unnatural situation."[15]

I have found that young men suffering from the Irritable Male Syndrome often become violent or depressed because they lack the guidance of older men. As more young males grow up without male mentoring, their anger explodes into our communities. "Elders and mentors have an irreplaceable function in the life of any community," Malidoma Somé reminds us. "Without them the young are lost—their overflowing energies wasted in useless pursuits. The old must live in the young like a grounding force that tames the tendency toward bold but senseless actions and shows them the path of wisdom. In the absence of elders, the impetuosity of youth becomes the slow death of the community."[16]

Mitch sees what happens when we don't have mentors. "Our society has completely failed our young men," he told me. "The rise in hazing, violence, depression, medicating, and self-medicating through alcohol and drugs is only the beginning. Our hope and our challenge lie in men reclaiming our young men and in women trusting us enough to let us."[17]

Mitch teamed up with a friend and colleague of mine, Mark Schillinger, D.C., a chiropractor and healer, to develop a weekend program for young men that draws on the best in the youngsters and the older men who mentor them. The purpose of the weekend is to provide young men incredible fun and challenges while building a foundation for confident and successful adulthoods by teaching them teamwork, fostering a sense of accomplishment, and giving them leadership skills.

The two men believe that there are significant similarities between young males between the ages of 15 and 25 and older males between 40 and 60. "Simply put, they are both experiencing changing levels of testosterone associated with their move from one stage of life to another." For the younger men, there are few opportunities in our society to express their testosterone-driven physicality and aggression in a safe and positive way. "This is an obvious formula for irritability, frustration, and violence," says

Dr. Schillinger."[18] The older men are experiencing a decrease in testosterone levels and therefore no longer view themselves as virile and strong. They don't know how to act because their mindset is "If you can't get it up and get it on in life, you can't compete; and if you can't compete, you're not a real man."[19]

"The blending of the wisdom of mature men with the vitality of young men deepens the young man's sense of belonging and self-worth while raising the testosterone levels of the mentor," says Dr. Schillinger. "It's as though the younger man shares his excess testosterone with the elder male, while the elder shares his life experience with the younger man."

"The young men," says DeArmon, "come away from the weekend with a greater sense of appreciation for who they are and a clearer sense of direction in their lives. These two qualities offer hope and encouragement for them to aspire toward manhood. This is a good starting point for a life filled with spirit and purpose. The mentors in the event come away with a sense of belonging and a feeling that they have something important to contribute to young men, simply by being themselves and listening with an open heart to the young man's feelings and needs. They also can grieve their own losses and sadness that they did not have this kind of mentoring when they were growing up."[20] When this reciprocity between youth and age breaks down, we move increasingly toward becoming what author Robert Bly calls a "sibling society." Bly describes a society in which "adults regress toward adolescence; and adolescents—seeing that—have no desire to become adults."[21]

We are each put on the planet to offer our special gifts, and what we have to offer is unique and precious. This truth has been recognized by many of our most beloved elders. Albert Schweitzer, who spent 50 years of his life serving his fellow man in the oppressive heat of the African jungle, providing medical aid to those most desperately in need, offered the following wisdom that can guide us through the Irritable Male Syndrome: "I don't know what your destiny will be, but one thing I do know; the only ones among you who will be really happy are those who have sought and found how to serve."[22]

Perhaps Martin Luther King, Jr., summed it up best when he observed, "Every man must decide whether he will walk in the light of creative altruism or in the darkness of destructive selfishness. This is the judgment. Life's most urgent question is, what are you doing for others?"[23]

DeArmon and the other mentors working with the Young Men's Ultimate Weekend have found their way to serve. Mitch told me about a brief exchange he had with one of the young men who had gone through the weekend. Mitch asked him, "What was the single greatest quality you got from the Young Men's Ultimate Weekend?" The young man's simple reply: "I treat people better." The program has become so successful that DeArmon has expanded his efforts and established LeadershipWorks, an organization that serves adolescent males and their families through mentoring programs, camps, workshops, information, and consulting—all designed to empower youth to take responsibility for their actions, communities, and futures.

ESTY MEN, TESTY WOMEN, AND WHY GUYS NEED TO BELONG TO A MEN'S GROUP

Many of us are beginning to recognize the relationship between spirituality and love. Few are aware of the powerful connection between spirituality and biology.

As men get older and our testosterone levels drop, our estrogen/testosterone ratios increase. I say that men become more "esty." As women age, their estrogen levels drop, their testosterone/estrogen ratios increase, and they become more "testy." This can be a source of tension and conflict. It can also be the basis of an expansion into a new spiritual realm for men and women.

"Now that I'm getting older, I enjoy staying home more," a 55-year-old man told me. "I'd like to cuddle more and be closer to my wife, to ponder the ultimate questions of life. When I was younger and working all the time, she used to beg me for more nonsexual touching. Now, she's always on the run. She never seems to have time to slow down and relax with me. What's going on?"

What is happening is a universal shift, a kind of gender crossing, that all men and women will go through. In evaluating cross-cultural data from around the world, David Gutmann, M.D., Ph.D., professor of psychiatry and education and the director of the Older Adult Program at Northwestern University in Chicago, says that a significant sex-role turnover takes place as men begin to live out directly, to own as part of themselves the qualities of "sensuality, affiliation, and maternal tendencies—in effect, the 'femininity' that was previously repressed in the service of productivity and lived out vicariously through the wife."[24]

"By the same token, across societies," continues Dr. Gutmann, "we see

the opposite effect in women. . . . They generally become more domi-
neering, independent, unsentimental, and self-centered."[25] These are the
exact qualities that would most often trigger my irritability when I would
experience them with Carlin.

I think this shift, which few people understand, contributes to a lot of
the confusion and pain that men and women experience during this time
of life. I have found that many guys alternate between confused irritability
and hangdog unhappiness. The women go back and forth between frustrated disappointment and catlike attacks.

So what are we to do? Are we doomed to be disappointed in love? The
short answer is no, but the solution isn't easy to come by. First, we need to
accept this shift in polarity. It's best not to fight it. Becoming more esty
allows us to simplify by cutting back on many of the trivial distractions that
grabbed us while we were so busy "making it" in the high-testosterone
world of our past. We might as well enjoy the fact that we can slow down,
turn inward, and live life more simply. This can be a time of spiritual
growth for both men and women. Men grow spiritually as we turn inward.
Women grow as they take their inner experiences and use them to bring
spirit to the outer world.

We also need to renegotiate new kinds of relationships with our partners. The sexes don't have to become angry adversaries or distant cousins.
We can learn a new way to deepen the intimacy of our relationships. For
instance, we might spend less time looking for the latest pill to keep our
erections hard or for the cute young thing who makes our hearts pound
faster and instead learn the pleasure of more sensual contact. The song
about slow hands and an easy touch might be right up our alley. We might
learn to listen better and share our feelings and needs more directly.

Finally, we need to develop closer, more intimate connections with other
men. As I mentioned in the previous chapter, nearly 25 years ago I joined
with a group of seven other men to find out more about what we had in
common as men and what we could do to deepen our relationships—with
ourselves, each other, our partners, and the world. At the time, our ages
ranged from 30 to 50. We've experienced divorces, marriages, 50th wed-
ding anniversaries, the death of a loved dog, the birth of a man's first child,
job promotions and firings, business successes and failures, problems with
teenage children, worries about adult children who still act like teenagers,
family health problems, the joys and strains of one man's retirement, the

death of parents, and a diagnosis and treatment of prostate cancer.

After we had been together about 15 years, we decided we wanted something more: an experience that would deepen our purpose and extend our ability to mentor younger men. We decided to attend the New Warrior Training Adventure, a powerful experiential weekend sponsored by the Mankind Project. Its mission is simple and powerful: "To heal the world, one man at a time." The weekend was truly a rite of passage for each of us, allowing us to more clearly understand and articulate our mission in the world and tap more clearly our spiritual essence.

There are many men's groups seeking to help us learn to become the men we were meant to be. I encourage you to find one that is right for you. We increasingly hunger for connection and intimacy. Too many men still seek the fool's gold of losing ourselves in new women when what we really need is the real substance of connecting deeply with other men.

Although we come from different backgrounds and religious traditions, being with these men has helped deepen my spiritual life. Despite having grown up in the Jewish faith, I was never really comfortable with the religious tradition. I have found that many men at midlife return to the religions of their youth, find another tradition that fits them better, or put down spiritual roots that are not linked to any particular religion. In whatever form we are drawn to, deepening our relationship with spirit can be of tremendous value in healing the Irritable Male Syndrome. Looking at the common element in all spiritual practices, it seems that they all offer hope to those who believe. "The relation of hope for the future and religious faith is probably the cornerstone of why faith so effectively fights despair and increases happiness," says psychologist Martin Seligman, Ph.D., author of *Authentic Happiness* and the primary founder of the field of positive psychology.

COMING HOME TO OUR PLACE AND TIME

My wife and I live on 22 acres of land on Shimmins Ridge, above Bloody Run Creek, in Willits, California. Early this morning, I heard coyotes calling out to each other. Their sound was at once melancholy and hopeful. We came here 12 years ago to get away from the stress of living in a big city. We had both moved around a lot in our lives and were looking for a place where we could settle. We wanted a place for our souls to rest.

It never occurred to me how important place and time were until we moved here. In the past, the place I lived was just the place I happened to be at the present time. It was the background for the important things I was doing: pursuing a career and raising a family. It didn't have any independent meaning. That began to change, little by little, during the first 3 years that we lived here. I fell in love with the wildness and beauty of the natural environment and with the helpfulness and warmth of the people on the ridge and in the town.

During my morning runs on the back roads, I began to recognize the places where I would likely see deer, the trees where hawks would perch, the areas where I could count on wildflowers in the spring. The following year, it seemed the animals noticed me as I moved along. They weren't afraid. I realized I was becoming one of them, another creature inhabiting the area.

Over the next few years, my father died and Carlin's mother passed away. We had them cremated and decided to bury their ashes beneath the branches of a beautiful madrone tree outside our living room window. I was struck by the change in me. "This is my home," I realized. "This is the place where my ancestors are buried. This is where I will spend the rest of my life."

For the first time, I understood how native people feel about their land and how devastating it has been for them to have been driven off the land where they lived for generations. I felt how attached I had become to this place after living here a few years and having our parents buried here. What must it be like to be in a place for hundreds of years and have many, many generations buried on the land?

After that, I changed my thinking about my place and my community. I realized that I had to get more involved. If the water became undrinkable, the air polluted, the traffic jammed, the town overcrowded, I couldn't simply move away. This was my place, forever. If I wanted it to be livable, I had to be part of the process of keeping it that way. I began to see that a part of the irritability, anxiety, discomfort, and depression that I felt was related to a need to put down roots, to make a stand, to plant my flag in the ground.

When Carlin and I forst moved to this place, something changed in our relationship as well. When we put down roots on this ridge, we also deepened our relationship in a way we weren't even aware of at first. Making a commitment to live here, surprisingly, created a greater feeling of joy and security in our relationship. Just as we know we will weather the storms that cause problems on the land, we also know we can weather the problems created by living together for many years. Now, I can truly identify with the words of writer Scott Russell Sanders: "For me, the effort to be grounded in family and community is inseparable from the effort to be grounded in place."[26]

I have visited my childhood home only to find it changed almost beyond recognition. I can still feel its faint resonance of life when I was a boy, but it is not a place I'd want to stay. I didn't choose the place I grew up in; my parents did. Finding a place as an adult has a different feeling. I chose to search for and find this place, and having done that makes it richer, more vital, more important for me. I can't imagine leaving.

Have you found your place yet? It doesn't need to be in the country. It just needs to be someplace that nourishes your spirit. "Loyalty to place arises from sources deeper than narcissism," says Sanders in his book *Staying Put: Making a Home in a Restless World.* "It arises from our need to be at home on the earth. We marry ourselves to the creation by knowing and cherishing a particular place, just as we join ourselves to the human family by marrying a particular man or woman."[27]

When I was younger, the Irritable Male Syndrome was in large part related to the stresses in my life. I was often overwhelmed because I had too much work. Raising children was a source of joy and pain, blessings and "stressings."

Then Carlin and I moved here, and I experienced a peace I had not known before. I hadn't realized how much the stress of city life had affected me until I was out of it. Seeing our children grow up and move away brought a sense of satisfaction and relief. "Now it is our time," I thought. "Finally, we will be able to focus our attention on what we want, what is truly satisfying to us." I pictured a free and easy lifestyle with more time for travel. When we were home, I imagined, we would enjoy more times of intimacy and a more enjoyable sex life. "Less stress, more sex" was my motto.

It didn't work out that way. As I approached 50, IMS had more to do with the hormonal and other physiological changes going on inside my body. It had never occurred to me that I might need to replace my lost testosterone, take something to restore erections, evaluate my need for antidepressants, or explore a new identity.

Neither had I anticipated how unsettling it would be for me to live without children in the home. I had been sure that seeing them grown and on their way would feel wonderful—and it did feel great. But it also meant that Carlin and I were alone with each other. Little irritations that weren't noticeable when we were busy with life became magnified when our hormones were bottoming out and we had only each other to look at.

Moving out of the city meant that I had less job stress, but it also meant a change of identity. If I wasn't a program director, who was I? I worried about whether I would have enough work to support us as we got older.

Whatever our age, men with IMS are confused and frightened. We don't know what to do. It's not surprising that so many men become withdrawn, act out, leave their families, or have affairs. We feel we have earned the right to enjoy our lives. If things are not the way we had hoped, we feel betrayed. Someone must be to blame. We often feel the fault must be with our partners or our same old way of life. Many of us drive our families to despair or simply run away.

But staying put can be the best thing we can do. Digging in can often save our lives. Firefighters learn that when you can't outrun a fire, you need to burrow down and let the fire go over you. Healing from the Irritable Male Syndrome can be like that. It can get awfully hot and the fear level goes through the roof, but if you can hang in there, the best is yet to come.

Understanding who we are is an important aspect of healing from IMS. Knowing where we belong is also crucial. I believe there is an intimate relationship between our sense of belonging to a place and our feeling of knowing ourselves. Since Carlin and I chose to live on Shimmins Ridge, putting down roots and committing to live in this place the rest of our lives, I have felt much more comfortable and relaxed in my own mind and body. Coming home to a place has enabled me to come home to myself, to feel more joy, compassion, and hope for the future.

THE FUTURE OF MEN:
FROM IRRITABILITY TO WARMHEARTEDNESS

When I was at my most irritable, I also felt the most unhappy and shut down. My heart felt heavy. My thoughts and feelings turned inward in an endless spiral of self-doubt and unhappiness. Although I would usually get through my days without any outward appearance that something was wrong, inside I felt frustrated, unhappy, and hopeless. At my worst, it seemed I was living inside a dark cloud that had no beginning or end and from which I could never escape.

Once on the other side, I felt reborn, like I'd awakened from a bad dream. Now, it's sometimes difficult to remember that things were ever that bad. My wife remembers. She still nurses the wounds. Those experiencing IMS do a great deal of damage to others, and that hurt takes time to heal. We also do damage to ourselves, though it is less obvious. Healing is slow. There are setbacks when my anger bursts forth or threatens to. But the times of joy are more frequent, and the times of irritability take up less and less space in my life.

Carlin still doesn't trust me completely. "I've had too many experiences where I opened up and felt attacked," she tells me. "I'll come around—just be patient." Though patience isn't a virtue I feel I practice easily, I find that when I am no longer in the grip of IMS, I can breathe easier and let time, and our love, heal old wounds. I see progress inside myself, in our relationship, and in my relationship with the world. My men's group is a great support.

I find it helps to know that change doesn't occur overnight. We have to be willing to be gentle with ourselves as we grow and to take care of ourselves as we age. I've always had a desire to live a long, healthy, and productive life. I think I got that from my father. I know now that he suffered from the Irritable Male Syndrome as well as from manic-depressive illness. It wasn't until late in his life that he was able to get ahold of his problems and allow the light of healing to soften his heart.

After his suicide attempt, when I was 6, he was committed to the State Mental Hospital in Camarillo, California. After being hospitalized for 8 years, he escaped when my uncle took him into town for a visit. My runaway father hid by day and walked at night. He was determined never to return to the hospital. He found his way to Santa Monica and lost himself with the beatniks and beach people who populated the area. He changed his name to Tom Roberts, headed north to San Francisco, and became a street puppeteer, creating his own stage and peopling it with his own characters—puppets he was given or made himself. You might say his daimon was keeping him true to his calling. He no longer had to worry about supporting a family or driving for success. He walked all over the city, turning up whenever there was a gathering of any kind. He would take his puppets out of one of his plastic bags he always carried, and the show would begin.

When he and I reconnected in 1981, he had been doing his puppet shows for 25 years. We never could go out together without someone coming up to him and asking for a show. Often, young women with small children told me they remembered their mothers holding their hands while they watched Tommy the Puppet Man entertain young and old.

In addition to doing his puppet shows, my father would hand out copies of his poems. One that he wrote in 1976, "Resiliency," speaks to the spirit that keeps us on our life path when the going gets tough:

> *Resiliency—One of humankind's finest graces*
> *Time and time and time without end*
> *Life bends us, twists us, knots us, stretches us*
> *Out-out-out-out*
> *'Til we're positive we're going to break*
> *But out of our pains, our agonies, our heartaches*
> *We snap back and go on*
> *That power and strength to be stretched and stretched*
> *And stretched, and then to snap back*
> *Again and again and again*
> *And go on*
> *And live on—*
> *Of all humankind's*
> *Finest graces—one of the finest*
> *Is*
> *Resiliency*

In the last 10 years of my father's life, I rarely saw the irritability, anger, and blame that had been so much a part of his earlier years. By the time he died, at age 90, he had done a lot of healing.

The headline in the *San Francisco Chronicle* read REQUIEM FOR S.F. PUPPET MAN. "The puppets were there, sitting on a small table," the article said. "There was a king, a dog, a scarecrow, and a bunch of little men. All were silent, an unusual condition for a Tommy Roberts puppet, which worked harder than any other marionettes in history."

The day room at the downtown hotel where he spent the last years of his life was packed. "The crowd jammed every seat and spilled out into the hallway. They signed the memorial book—one of the cheap scratch pads that Roberts always carried in his pocket. They snatched up free copies of Roberts's poems.

"'Because of you,' said one, 'old madness has become new meaning. Because of you, my tongue is no longer lead.'"

In his book *The Varieties of Religious Experience,* the influential psychologist and philosopher William James included a passage attributed to an anonymous patient but later revealed to be autobiographical: "Whilst in this state of philosophic pessimism and general depression of spirits about my prospects, I went one evening into a dressing-room in the twilight . . . when suddenly there fell upon me without any warning, just as if it came out of the darkness, a horrible fear of my own existence. . . . "[28]

I understand these words very well. So would my father and the millions of creative people who suffer from some form of the Irritable Male Syndrome. The poet John Berryman spoke of the way adversity can spark creative talent. In an interview, he stated, "I do strongly feel that among the greatest pieces of luck for high achievement is ordeal. . . . The artist is extremely lucky who is presented with the worst possible ordeal which will not actually kill him. At that point, he's in business."[29]

While nobody would choose to suffer from the Irritable Male Syndrome, depression, or bipolar illness, we can recognize the creative daimon that surfaces when we are "crazy but not too crazy." I remember reading the novel *Zorba the Greek,* about a man who is so full of life that he is constantly on the edge of exploding. The gregarious Zorba convinces Basil, a young writer, to invest in a mining venture, which, of course, proves disastrous, financially and otherwise. Along the way, however, young Basil learns more about life, love, and the world of spirit than he could ever have dreamed. However, he still doesn't have the courage to put what he's learned into practice.

I loved that character of Zorba as much as I worried that I would turn into the character of the young man who hungered to let his emotions free but couldn't risk releasing them. After they had parted, Zorba wrote to the young man, expressing the lost potential he saw in him. "You are a pen-pusher, boss, if you'll allow me to say so. You, too, could have seen a beautiful green stone at least once in your life, you poor soul, and you didn't see it."[30]

In remembering Zorba, the young man said, "Spiritual heights, which took us years of painful effort to attain, were attained by Zorba in one bound. And we said: 'Zorba is a great soul!' Or else he leapt beyond those heights, and then we said: 'Zorba is mad!'"[31]

May we all become the great souls we were meant to be and reach high enough to be just a little bit crazy.

EPILOGUE

O ften, people think that authors are very different from themselves. I hope you've found my personal sharing in this book helpful. To get the most up-to-date information on the Irritable Male Syndrome, please visit my Web sites at **www.theirritablemalesyndrome.com** and **www.menalive.com**.

If you'd like to let me know your reactions to this book and how it has affected your life, I'd be pleased to hear from you. The best way to reach me is by e-mail at **jed@theirritablemalesyndrome.com** or **jed@menalive.com**.

I'm working on my next book, which is about male depression. If you'd like to provide information and be part of the research process, please do contact me.

I look forward to hearing from you.

NOTES

CHAPTER 1

1. Miranda Sawyer, "Miranda Sawyer on a New Medical Sensation," *Daily Mirror,* (March 2, 2002).

2. WordNet 1.6. Copyright 1997 by Princeton University.

3. Susan Faludi, *Stiffed: The Betrayal of the American Man* (New York: William Morrow, 1999), dust jacket.

4. Daniel Goleman, *Destructive Emotions: How Can We Overcome Them? A Scientific Dialogue with the Dalai Lama* (New York: Bantam Dell, 2003), 140.

5. Ibid.

6. Kay Redfield Jamison, *An Unquiet Mind* (New York: Random House, 1995), 128.

7. Dan Kindlon and Michael Thompson, *Raising Cain: Protecting the Emotional Life of Boys* (New York: Ballantine Books, 1999), 6.

8. Gerald A. Lincoln, "The Irritable Male Syndrome," *Reproduction, Fertility, and Development* 13 (2001): 567–76.

9. Dictionary.com, accessed April 22, 2003.

10. Ibid.

11. Ibid.

12. Ibid.

13. Duncan C. Gould, Richard Petty, and Howard S. Jacobs, "The Menopause—Does It Exist? For and Against," *British Medical Journal* 320 (March 25, 2000): 858–61.

14. Liz Langley, "Going with the Flow," *Orlando Weekly* (April 4, 2002), http://www.orlandoweekly.com/juice/archive.asp?j=3429 (accessed June 18, 2004).

CHAPTER 2

1. Personal communication with Dr. Larrain Gillespie, January 4, 2004.

2. WHO Global Consultation on Violence and Health, *Violence: A Public Health Priority* (Geneva: World Health Organization, 1996).

3. E. G. Krug, et al., eds., *World Report on Violence and Health* and *World Report on Violence and Health: Summary* (Geneva: World Health Organization, 2002).

4. David D. Gilmore, *Misogyny: The Male Malady* (Philadelphia: University of Pennsylvania Press, 2001), 9.

5. Ibid., 16.

6. Ibid., 224.

7. Ibid.

8. Ibid.

9. William S. Pollack with Todd Shuster, *Real Boys' Voices* (New York: Random House, 2000), xix.

CHAPTER 3

1. John Gottman, *Why Marriages Succeed or Fail . . . And How You Can Make Yours Last* (New York: Simon and Schuster, 1994), 72–97.

2. Ibid., 85.

3. Ibid., 95.

4. Ibid., 147.

5. E. G. Krug, et al., eds., *World Report on Violence and Health: Summary* (Geneva: World Health Organization, 2002), 15.

6. Ibid.

7. W. Fals-Stewart, "The Occurrence of Partner Physical Aggression on Days of Alcohol Consumption: A Longitudinal Diary Study," *Journal of Consulting and Clinical Psychology* 71(1) (2003): 41–52.

8. "Dating Violence," Center for Disease Control, National Center for Injury Prevention Control Fact Sheet, http://www.cdc.gov/ncipc/factsheets/datviol.htm (accessed February 23, 2004).

9. Linda G. Mills, *Insult to Injury: Rethinking Our Responses to Intimate Abuse* (Princeton, NJ: Princeton University Press, 2003), 8.

10. Phil Rees, "Japan: The Missing Million," *BBC News* (October 20, 2002) http://news.bbc.co.uk/1/hi/programmes/correspondent/2334893.stm (accessed November 30, 2002).

CHAPTER 4

1. Broadus Mitchell, *Depression Decade: From New Era through New Deal, 1929–1941* (New York: Rinehart, 1947), vii.

2. Kay Redfield Jamison, *Night Falls Fast: Understanding Suicide* (New York: Vintage Books, 1999), 103.

3. Eric Maisel, *The Van Gogh Blues: The Creative Person's Path through Depression* (Emmaus, PA: Rodale, 2002), 3–4.

4. Kay Redfield Jamison, *Touched with Fire: Manic-Depressive Illness and the Artistic Temperament* (New York: Free Press, 1993), 5.

5. John J. Ratey and Catherine Johnson, *Shadow Syndromes: The Mild Forms of Major Mental Disorders That Sabotage Us* (New York: Bantam, 1998), 12.

6. Ibid.

7. Andrew Solomon, *The Noonday Demon: An Atlas of Depression* (New York: Scribner, 2001), 15.

8. Ibid., 17.

9. Ratey and Johnson, *Shadow Syndromes*, 66.

10. Solomon, *The Noonday Demon*, 16.

11. Ratey and Johnson, *Shadow Syndromes*, 66.

12. Solomon, *The Noonday Demon*, 25.

13. Ibid.

14. Ibid.

15. Ibid.

16. Ibid.

17. Ibid.

18. Ibid.

19. Ibid.

20. Ibid., 26.

21. Ibid., 25.

22. Ibid., 26.

23. *Diagnostic and Statistical Manual of Mental Disorders—Fourth Edition (DSM-IV)* (Washington, DC: American Psychiatric Association, 1994), 327.

24. John Lynch and Christopher Kilmartin, *The Pain behind the Mask: Overcoming Masculine Depression* (New York: The Haworth Press, 1999), 7.

25. Terrence Real, *I Don't Want to Talk about It: Overcoming the Secret Legacy of Male Depression* (New York: Scribner, 1997), 22.

26. Susan Nolen-Hoeksema, *Sex Differences in Depression* (Stanford, CA: Stanford University Press, 1990), 64–76.

27. Lee Robins and Darrel Regier, *Psychiatric Disorders in America* (New York: Free Press, 1990).

28. R. Kessler, K. McGonagle, C. Nelson, M. Mughes, M. Swartz, and D. Blazer, "Sex and Depression in the National Comorbidity Survey. II. Cohort Effects," *Journal of Affective Disorders* 30 (1994): 15–26.

29. Personal communication with Dr. Tom Golden, January 20, 2004.

30. Jed Diamond, *Male Menopause* (Naperville, IL: Sourcebooks, 1998), xxxvii.

31. Kay Redfield Jamison interview by Reid Baer in "Touched with Genius," *A Man Overboard: The Thinking Man's Journal* (August 2003), http://www.amanoverboard.net/August.html (accessed August 2003).

32. Marianne J. Legato, *Eve's Rib: The New Science of Gender-Specific Medicine and How It Can Save Your Life* (New York: Harmony Books, 2002), xi.

33. Ibid., 13.

34. Ibid.

35. Rebecca Voelker, "Depression: A Somber Issue for Women," *Business and Health* (September 2001), 13.

36. Finn Zierau, Anne Bille, Wolfgang Rutz, and Per Bech, "The Gotland Male Depression Scale: A Validity Study in Patients with Alcohol Use Disorder," *Nordic Journal of Psychiatry* 56 (4) (2002): 265–71. See also W. Rutz, et al., "Prevention of Male Suicides: Lessons from Gotland Study," *Lancet,* 345 (1995): 524.

37. Jed Diamond, *Male Menopause* (Naperville, IL: Sourcebooks, 1998), xxxvii. See also F. Zierau, A. Bille, W. Rutz, and P. Bech, "The Gotland Male Depression Scale: A Validity Study in Patients with Alcohol Use Disorder," *Nordic Journal of Psychiatry* 56 (4) (2002): 265–71; William S. Pollack, "Mourning, Melancholia, and Masculinity: Recognizing and Treating Depression in Men" in William S. Pollack and Ronald F. Levant, eds, *New Psychotherapy for Men* (New York: John Wiley & Sons, 1998), 147–66; Sam Cochran and Fredric E. Rabinowitz, *Men and Depression: Clinical and Empirical Perspectives* (San Diego, CA: Academic Press, 2000), 91; Archibald D. Hart, *Unmasking Male Depression* (Nashville, TN: World Publishing, 2001), 54; Philip Kavanaugh, "ADD, Hope for Healing," Los Gatos Therapy Center (Los Gatos, CA); Dietmar Winkler, Edda Pjrek, and Siegfried Kasper, "Male Depression: Clinical Picture, Diagnosis and Treatment," personal correspondence with Siegfried Kasper, November 2002.

38. E. G. Krug, et al., eds., *World Report on Violence and Health* (Geneva: World Health Organization, 2002), 185.

39. Ibid., 186–87.

40. National Center for Health Statistics (Hyattsville, MD: 2002), Table 30.

41. R. Anderson, K. Kochanek, and S. Murphy, "Report of Final Mortality Statistics," *Monthly Vital Statistics Report* 45 (11) (Hyattsville, MD: National Center for Health Statistics, 1997); G. Murphy, "Why Women Are Less Likely Than Men to Commit Suicide," *Comprehensive Psychiatry* 39 (1998): 165–75; Sam V.

Cochran and Fredric E. Rabinowitz, *Men and Depression: Clinical and Empirical Perspectives* (San Diego, CA: Academic Press, 2000), 141.

42. Susan Burks, *Denver Post* (January 3, 2003), www.denverpost.com/Stories/ (accessed January 12, 2003).

43. Centers for Disease Control, "Suicide among Older Persons, United States, 1980–1992," *Morbidity and Mortality Weekly Report,* January 12, 1996.

44. James Gilligan, *Violence: Our Deadly Epidemic and Its Causes* (New York: G. P. Putnam's Sons, 1996), 119.

45. Dan Kindlon and Michael Thompson, *Raising Cain: Protecting the Emotional Life of Boys* (New York: Ballantine Publishing Group, 1999), 3.

46. William S. Pollack with Todd Shuster, *Real Boys' Voices* (New York: Random House, 2000), 148.

CHAPTER 5

1. Siegfried Meryn, "The Future of Men and Their Health: Are Men in Danger of Extinction?" *British Journal of Medicine* 323 (November 3, 2001): 1013–14.

2. Devra Davis, *When Smoke Ran Like Water: Tales of Environmental Deception and the Battle against Pollution* (New York: Basic Books, 2002), 193.

3. Steve Jones, *Y: The Descent of Men* (London: Little, Brown, 2002), 7.

4. Bobbi S. Low, *Why Sex Matters: A Darwinian Look at Human Behavior* (Princeton, NJ: Princeton University Press, 2000), xiii.

5. Matt Ridley, *The Red Queen: Sex and the Evolution of Human Nature* (New York: Macmillan Publishing Company, 1993), 20.

6. Jones, *Y: The Descent of Men,* 5.

7. Terry Burnham and Jay Phelan, *Mean Genes: From Sex to Money to Food— Taming Our Primal Instincts* (New York: Perseus Publishing, 2000), 178.

8. *The World's Women 2000: Trends and Statistics* (New York: United Nations, 2000).

9. D. Hanson, H. Møller, and J. Olsen, "Severe Peri-Conceptional Life Events and the Sex Ratio in Offspring: Follow-Up Study Based on Five National Registers," *British Journal of Medicine* 319 (1999): 548–49.

10. R. Mizuno, "The Male/Female Ratio of Fetal Deaths and Births in Japan," *Lancet* 356 (2000): 738–39.

11. M. E. Lavoie, P. Robaey, J. E. A. Stauder, J. Glorieux, and F. Lefebvre, "Extreme Prematurity in Healthy 5-Year-Old Children: A Re-Analysis of Sex Effects on Event-Related Brain Activity, *Psychophysiology* 35 (1998): 679–89.

12. J. E. Singer, M. Westphal, and K. R. Niswander, "Sex Differences in the Incidence of Neonatal Abnormalities and Abnormal Performance in Early Childhood," *Child Development* 39 (1968): 103–12.

13. D. C. Taylor, "Mechanisms of Sex Differentiation: Evidence from Disease," in J. Ghesquiere, R. D. Martin, and F. Newcombe, eds., *Human Sexual Dimorphism* (London: Taylor & Francis, 1985), 169–89.

14. L. B. Shettles, "Conception and Birth Sex Ratios," *Obstetrics and Gynecology* 18 (1961): 122–30.

15. T. Gualtieri and R. Hicks, "An Immunoreactive Theory of Selective Male Affliction," *Behavioral Brain Science* 8 (1985): 427–41.

16. Ronald F. Levant and William S. Pollock, eds., *A New Psychology of Men* (New York: Basic Books, 1995).

17. Quoted by Natalie Angier, "Why Men Don't Last: Self Destruction as a Way of Life," *New York Times* (February 17, 1999).

18. Ibid.

19. Ibid.

20. Herb Goldberg, *The Hazards of Being Male: Surviving the Myth of Masculine Privilege* (New York: Nash Publishing, 1976), dust jacket.

21. Michael Gurian, *The Wonder of Boys* (New York: G. P. Putnam's Sons, 1996), xvii.

22. Dan Kindlon and Michael Thompson, *Raising Cain: Protecting the Emotional Life of Boys* (New York: Ballantine Books, 1999), vii.

23. Carol Gilligan, Nona Lyons, and Trudy Hanmer, eds., *Making Connections: The Relational Worlds of Adolescent Girls at Emma Willard School* (Cambridge, MA: Harvard University Press, 1990), 4.

24. Mary Pipher, *Reviving Ophelia: Saving the Selves of Adolescent Girls* (New York: G. P. Putnam's Sons, 1994), 9.

25. Christina Hoff Sommers, *The War against Boys: How Misguided Feminism Is Harming Our Young Men* (New York: Simon and Schuster, 2000), 14.

26. I am indebted to Christina Hoff Sommers for gathering a great deal of the data on the educational system and our boys.

27. Carol Dwyer and Linda Johnson, "Grades, Accomplishments, and Correlates," in Warren Willingham and Nancy Cole, eds., *Gender and Fair Assessment* (Mahwah, NJ: Erlbaum, 1997), 127–56.

28. Higher Education Research Institute, *The American Freshman: National Norms for Fall 1998* (Los Angeles: Higher Education Research Institute, University of California, Los Angeles, 1998), 36, 54.

29. Sommers, *The War against Boys,* 24; and U.S. Department of Education National Center for Education Statistics, "The Condition of Education" (Washington, DC: U.S. Department of Education National Center for Education Statistics, 1998), 90.

30. Ibid., 28.

31. Ibid., 29.

32. Higher Education Research Institute, *The American Freshman: National Norms for Fall 1998,* 39, 57.

33. National Center for Education Statistics, *NAEP 1997 Arts Report Card* (Washington, DC: U.S. Department of Education National Center for Education Statistics, 1998).

34. Of students studying abroad, 65 percent are female, 35 percent male; "Study Abroad by U.S. Students, 1996–1997," *Chronicle of Higher Education* (Washington, DC: December 11, 1998), A71.

35. For suspension rates, see U.S. Department of Education, *Conditions of Education* (Washington DC: U.S. Department of Education, 1997), 158. For data on repeating grades, see U.S. Department of Education, *Conditions of Education* (Washington, DC: U.S. Department of Education, 1995), 13. For information on dropouts, see U.S. Department of Education, *Digest of Educational Statistics 1995* (Washington, DC: U.S. Department of Education, 1995), 409.

36. For data on special education, see U.S. Department of Education, *The Condition of Education* (Washington, DC: U.S. Department of Education, 1994), 304. For information on ADD, see American Psychiatric Association, *Diagnostic and Statistical Manual of Mental Disorders* 4 (Washington, DC: American Psychiatric Association, 1994): 82. According to *DSM-IV,* "The disorder is much more frequent in males than in females, with male to female ratio ranging from 4:1 to 9:1, depending on the setting."

37. Helen Fisher, *The First Sex: The Natural Talents of Women and How They Are Changing the World* (New York: Random House, 1999), 83.

38. Horatio Alger Association, *State of Our Nation's Youth 1998–1999,* 4. The survey conducted by NFO Research, Inc., was based on two small but carefully selected samples of students (a cross section of 2,250 fourteen- to eighteen-year olds as well as a computer-generated sample of 1,041 students. The researchers are careful to note that this study is not definitive and provides only a "snapshot in time."

39. National Institute on Drug Abuse, "National Survey Results on Drug Use," *Monitoring the Future Study, 1975–1995,* vol. 1, *Secondary School Students* (Rockville, MD: National Institute on Drug Abuse, 1996): 20; U.S. Department of Education, *The Conditions of Education* (Washington, DC: U.S. Department of Education, 1997), 300, Table 47-3. For crime statistics, U.S. Department of Justice, *Female Offenders in the Juvenile Justice System: Statistics Summary* (Washington, DC: U.S. Department of Justice, 1996), 28–29.

40. The male rate is 47 per 100,000, while the female rate is 8.1 per 100,000. R. Anderson, K. Kochanek, and S. Murphy, "Report of Final Mortality Statistics," *Monthly Vital Statistics Report* 45 (11) (Hyattsville, MD: National Center for Health Statistics, 1997) and from G. Murphy, "Why Women Are Less Likely Than Men to Commit Suicide," *Comprehensive Psychiatry* 39 (1998), 165–75.

41. Fisher, *The First Sex,* 5.

42. Ibid., 31.

43. Ibid., 32.

44. Ibid., 84.

45. Simon Baron-Cohen, *The Essential Difference: The Truth about the Male and Female Brain* (New York: Basic Books, 2003), 1.

46. D. H. Skuse, et al., "Evidence from Turner's Syndrome of an Imprinted X-Linked Locus Affecting Cognitive Function," *Nature* 387 (June 12, 1997): 705–8.

47. Robert S. McElvaine, *Eve's Seed: Biology, the Sexes, and the Course of History* (New York: McGraw-Hill, 2001), 1.

48. Martin E. P. Seligman, *Authentic Happiness: Using the New Positive Psychology to Realize Your Potential for Lasting Fulfillment* (New York: The Free Press, 2002), 30.

49. Gallup Organization, *Gender and Society: Status and Stereotypes: An International Gallup Poll Report* (Princeton, NJ: Gallup Organization, 1996), 6.

50. Fisher, *The First Sex,* 117.

51. Levant and Pollack, *A New Psychology of Men.*

52. Seligman, *Authentic Happiness,* 35.

53. Personal correspondence with Dr. Tom Golden, February 24, 2004.

54. John M. Gottman and Nan Silver, *The Seven Principles for Making Marriage Work* (New York: Crown Publishers, 1999), 34–35.

55. David Gilmore, *Manhood in the Making: Cultural Concepts of Masculinity* (New Haven, CT: Yale University Press, 1990), 17.

56. Norman Mailer, *Armies of the Night* (New York: New American Library, 1968), 25.

57. Gilmore, *Manhood in the Making,* 15.

58. Oscar Lewis, *The Children of Sanchez* (New York: Random House, 1961), 38.

CHAPTER 6

1. Susan Faludi, *Stiffed: The Betrayal of the American Man* (New York: William Morrow and Company, 1999), 16–19.

2. Ibid., 598.

3. Ibid., 29–30.

4. Ibid., 65.

5. Michael Moore, *Dude, Where's My Country?* (New York: Warner Books, 2003), 137–38.

6. Lionel Tiger, *The Decline of Males* (New York: St. Martin's Press, 1999), 2.

7. United Nations Development Programme, *Human Development Indicators: U.S.: 2003,* www.undp.org/hdr2003/indicator/cty_f_USA.html (accessed March 7, 2004).

8. Ibid.

9. Andrew Hacker, *Mismatch: The Growing Gulf between Women and Men* (New York: Scribner, 2003), 6.

10. Ibid., 168.

11. Les Krantz, *The 2002 Jobs Rated Almanac* (New York: St. Martin's Griffin, 2002).

12. Warren Farrell, *The Myth of Male Power* (New York: Simon and Schuster, 1993), 106.

13. Daniel Kadlec, "Where Did My Raise Go?" *Time* (May 26, 2003), 44–54.

14. Jeff Wuorio, "Raising Your Quarter-Million Dollar Baby," Money Central, http://moneycentral.msn.com/content/CollegeandFamily/Raisekids/P37245.asp?Printer (accessed March 7, 2004).

15. Ibid.

16. Hara Estroff Marano, "Coping," *Psychology Today,* May/June (2003), 59.

17. Ibid., 60.

18. Farrell, *The Myth of Male Power,* 292.

19. Ibid., 292–93.

20. Paul Harrington, "On College Campuses, It's a Woman's World," www.nupr.neu.edu/1-03/ri.html (accessed March 7, 2004).

21. Ibid.

22. Ibid.

23. Tiger, *The Decline of Males*, 78.

24. D. T. Kenrick., et al., "Evolution, Traits, and the Stages of Human Courtship: Qualifying the Parental Investment Model," *Journal of Personality* 58 (1990): 97–116.

25. John Townsend, *What Women Want—What Men Want: Why the Sexes Still See Love and Commitment So Differently* (New York: Oxford University Press, 1998), 124.

26. Ibid.

27. Ibid., 125.

28. Edie Weiner, talk given at the World Future Society Conference, San Francisco, July 18–20, 2003.

29. Marvin J. Cetron and Owen Davies, "Vital Signs for National Stability," *The Futurist* (January–February 2002), 8.

30. Paul Wiseman, "China Thrown Off Balance as Boys Outnumber Girls," *USA Today* (June 19, 2002), 1.

31. Ibid., 2A.

32. Ibid.

33. Ibid.

34. Ibid.

35. Ibid.

36. Ibid.

37. Tiger, *The Decline of Males*, 20.

38. Ibid., 7.

39. Ibid.

40. David Blankenhorn, *Fatherless America: Confronting Our Most Urgent Social Problem* (New York: Basic Books, 1995), 1.

41. Judith Bruce, et al., *Families in Focus: New Perspectives on Mothers, Fathers, and Children* (New York: The Population Council, 1995).

42. Alexander Mitscherlich, *Society without the Father* (New York: HarperCollins, 1993), xiii.

43. Ibid.

44. Helen Fisher, *Anatomy of Love: The Mysteries of Mating, Marriage, and Why We Stray* (New York: Fawcett Columbine, 1992), 150.

45. Blankenhorn, *Fatherless America*, 1.

46. Augustine J. Kposowa, "Marital Status and Suicide in the National Longitudinal Mortality Study," *Journal of Epidemiology and Community Health* 54 (April 2000): 254–61.

47. Ibid.

48. Tiger, *The Decline of Males*, 27.

CHAPTER 7

1. Male Depression Questionnaire on *Men's Health* magazine Web site between January 13 and January 21, 2003. Total respondents 3,482. Thirteen percent said they were not at all stressed more easily, 56 percent said that they were sometimes stressed, 27 percent said they were frequently stressed, and 4 percent said they were stressed most of the time.

2. Irritable Male Syndrome Questionnaire on *Men's Health* magazine Web site between February 15 and March 15, 2003. Total respondents 5,971. Eight percent said they were almost never stressed, 45 percent said they were sometimes stressed, 40 percent said they were frequently stressed, and 7 percent said they were almost always stressed.

3. Hans Selye, *The Stress of Life* (New York: McGraw-Hill, 1978), 1.

4. Robert M. Sapolsky, "Taming Stress," *Scientific American* (September 2003), 95.

5. Ibid.

6. S. E. Taylor, L. C. Klein, B. P. Lewis, T. L. Gruenwald, R. A. Gurung, and J. A. Updegraff, "Behavioral Responses to Stress in Females: Tend-and-Befriend, Not Fight-or-Flight," *Psychological Review* 109 (4) (October 2002), 745–50, discussion 751–53.

7. Shelley E. Taylor, *The Tending Instinct: How Nurturing Is Essential to Who We Are and How We Live* (New York: Times Books, 2002), 21.

8. C. Piltch, "Work and Stress," *The Radcliffe Quarterly* 78 (December 1992): 6–7.

9. R. Repetti, "Effects of Daily Workload on Subsequent Behavior during Marital Interactions: The Roles of Social Withdrawal and Spouse Support," *Journal of Personality and Social Psychology* 57 (1989): 652–59. Reported by Taylor, *The Tending Instinct,* 22–3.

10. A. Luckow, A. Reifman, and D. N. McIntosh, *Gender Differences in Coping: A Meta-Analysis,* poster presented to the annual meeting of the American Psychological Association, San Francisco, CA, August 1998. This seems to be true cross-culturally and even among our primate ancestors. See C. P. Edwards, "Behavioral Sex Differences in Children of Diverse Cultures: The Case of Nurturance to Infants," *Juvenile Primates: Life History, Development, and Behavior,* edited by M. E. Pereira and L. A. Fairbanks (New York: Oxford University Press, 1993).

11. Taylor, *The Tending Instinct,* 24.

12. Ibid.

13. Alvin Toffler, *Future Shock* (New York: Bantam, 1970), 2.

14. Ibid., 326.

15. Ibid., 345.

16. Melinda Davis, *The New Culture of Desire: Five Radical New Strategies That Will Change Your Business and Your Life* (New York: The Free Press, 2002), 118.

17. Carlos Iribarren, "High Hostility Level May Predispose Young Adults to Heart Disease," *Journal of the American Medical Association* 283 (2000): 2546–51.

18. X-10 Zone, "Road Rage Takes Its Toll" (July 31, 2001), www.x10.com/news/news/0731_roadrage.htm (accessed May 10, 2003).

19. Davis, *The New Culture of Desire*, 118.

20. X-10 Zone, "Road Rage Takes Its Toll."

21. Ibid.

22. Davis, *The New Culture of Desire*, 15.

23. Jennifer Schneider and Robert Weiss, *Cybersex Exposed: Simple Fantasy or Obsession?* (Center City, MN: Hazelden, 2001), 6.

24. Davis, *The New Culture of Desire*, 76.

25. Richard Restak, *The New Brain: How the Modern Age Is Rewiring Your Mind* (Emmaus, PA: Rodale, 2003), 45.

26. Ibid.

27. Davis, *The New Culture of Desire*, 28.

28. Tom Peters, "No Time Like the Present," *Time* (May 22, 2000), 66.

29. Davis, *The New Culture of Desire*, 119.

30. Ibid., 35.

31. Ibid.

32. Ibid., 34.

33. Schneider and Weiss, *Cybersex Exposed*, 8.

34. John Markoff, "A Newer, Lonelier Crowd Emerges in Internet Study," *New York Times* (February 16, 2000), 1.

35. Schneider and Weiss, *Cybersex Exposed*, 47.

CHAPTER 8

1. Candace B. Pert, *Molecules of Emotion: Why You Feel the Way You Feel* (New York: Scribner, 1997), 9.

2. J. Douglas Bremner, *Does Stress Damage the Brain?* (New York: W. W. Norton & Company, 2002), 5.

3. Nancy C. Andreasen, *Brave New Brain: Conquering Mental Illness in the Era of the Genome* (New York: Oxford University Press, 2001), 35.

4. Robert M. Sapolsky, "Gene Therapy for Psychiatric Disorders," *American Journal of Psychiatry* 160 (February 2003): 208–20.

5. Edward M. Hallowell, *Worry: Controlling It and Using It Wisely* (New York: Pantheon Books, 1997), xiv.

6. Ahmad Hariri and Daniel Weinberger, "Gene May Bias Amygdala Response to Frightful Faces," National Institute of Health press release (July 18, 2002).

7. Dean Hamer and Peter Copeland, *Living with Our Genes: Why They Matter More Than You Think* (New York: Doubleday, 1998), 57.

8. Ibid., 57–58.

9. Ibid.

10. Ernest J. Lovell, ed., *Lady Blessington's Conversations of Lord Byron* (Princeton, NJ: Princeton University Press, 1969), 115.

11. James I. Hudson, et al., *Archives of General Psychiatry,* 60 (2003): 170–77.

12. Hamer and Copeland, *Living with Our Genes,* 67.

13. Ibid., 94.

14. Remi Cadoret, et al., "Adoption Studies Demonstrating Two Genetic Pathways to Drug Abuse," *Archives of General Psychiatry,* 52 (1995): 42–52.

15. Hamer and Copeland, *Living with Our Genes,* 97.

16. Ibid.

17. Simon Baron-Cohen, *The Essential Difference: The Truth about the Male and Female Brain* (New York: Basic Books, 2003), 3.

18. Michael Gurian, *What Could He Be Thinking: How a Man's Mind Really Works* (New York: St. Martin's Press, 2003), 86.

19. Ibid., 94.

20. Richard Restak, *The New Brain: How the Modern Age Is Rewiring Your Mind* (Emmaus, PA: Rodale, 2003), 7–8.

21. Bremner, *Does Stress Damage the Brain?*, 100.

22. Ibid., ix.

23. Ibid.

24. Charles L. Whitfield, *The Truth about Depression: Choices for Healing* (Deerfield Beach, FL: Health Communications, Inc., 2003), 46.

25. Alice Miller, *The Truth Will Set You Free: Overcoming Emotional Blindness and Finding Your True Adult Self* (New York: Basic Books, 2001).

26. Martin Teicher, "Wounds That Time Won't Heal: The Neurobiology of Child Abuse," *Cerebrum* 2, (4) (Fall 2000): 50–67.

27. Ibid.

28. Ibid.

29. Restak, *The New Brain*, 208–9.

30. Reported in Alex Markels, "Woe Is Us: Depression in Men Is an Under-diagnosed Epidemic," *Men's Journal* (November 1998).

31. Pert, *Molecules of Emotion*, 25.

32. Theresa L. Crenshaw, *The Alchemy of Love and Lust* (New York: G. P. Putnam's Sons, 1996), xv–xvi.

33. Ibid., 5–6.

34. James McBride Dabbs with Mary Godwin Dabbs, *Heroes, Rogues, and Lovers: Testosterone and Behavior* (New York: McGraw-Hill, 2000), 16.

35. Crenshaw, *The Alchemy of Love and Lust*, 10.

36. Dr. Winnifred Cutler has published over 35 scientific papers, is co-inventor on five patents and author of six books on hormones and health. In 1986, her co-

discovery of human pheromones received major news coverage in *Time* magazine (12/1/86), *Newsweek* magazine (1/12/87), and a front-page story in the *Washington Post* (11/18/86) because it established the first scientific proof that human pheromones affect the relationship between men and women. Information on her current work is available through The Athena Institute at www. athena@Athena Institute.com.

37. Winnifred B. Cutler, *Love Cycles: The Science of Intimacy* (New York: Villard Books, 1991), 88.

38. Ibid., 89.

39. Ibid., 90.

40. Ibid.

41. John Morley, *Saint Louis University Androgen Deficiency in Aging Men (ADAM) Questionnaire*, Saint Louis University School of Medicine, June 1997.

42. Crenshaw, *The Alchemy of Love and Lust*, 10.

43. Carol Tavris, *The Mismeasure of Women: Why Women Are Not the Better Sex, the Inferior Sex, or the Opposite Sex* (New York: Simon and Schuster, 1992), 148.

44. Ibid.

45. Dabbs with Dabbs, *Heroes, Rogues and Lovers*, 10.

46. Ibid., 45.

47. Ibid., 86.

48. Ibid., 106.

49. Ibid., 109.

50. Ibid., 62.

51. Ibid., 88.

52. Michael Gurian, *The Wonder of Boys: What Parents, Mentors, and Educators Can Do to Shape Boys into Exceptional Men* (New York: G. P. Putnam's Sons, 1996), 10.

53. Jed Diamond, *Male Menopause* (Naperville, IL: Sourcebooks, 1997), xxvi; and *Surviving Male Menopause: A Guide for Women and Men* (Naperville, IL: Sourcebooks, 2000), 69–70. See these two books for a more in-depth description of the hormonal aspects of this life passage.

CHAPTER 10

1. Christiane Northrup, *Women's Bodies, Women's Wisdom: Creating Physical and Emotional Health and Healing* (New York: Bantam Books, 2002), 503.

2. Thomas J. Ritter and George C. Denniston, *Doctors Re-Examine Circumcision* (New York: Third Millennium Publishing Co., 2002).

3. Jean Liedloff, *The Continuum Concept: Allowing Human Nature to Work Successfully* (New York: Addison-Wesley Publishing Company, 1977), 9.

4. Ibid., 36.

5. James W. Prescott, "Body Pleasure and the Origins of Violence," *The Bulletin of the Atomic Scientists* (November 1975), 10–20.

6. Kyle D. Pruett, *Fatherneed: Why Father Care Is as Essential as Mother Care for Your Child* (New York: The Free Press, 2000), 17–34.

7. Kyle D. Pruett, *The Nurturing Father* (New York: Warner Books, 1987), 49.

8. Eleanor E. Maccoby, *The Two Sexes: Growing Up Apart, Coming Together* (Cambridge, MA: Harvard University Press, 1999), 266.

9. David Popenoe, *Life without Father: Compelling New Evidence That Fatherhood and Marriage Are Indispensable for the Good of Children and Society* (New York: The Free Press, 1996), 144.

10. Siegfried Meryn, Markus Metka, and Georg Kindel, *Men's Health and the Hormone Revolution* (Richmond Hill, Ontario, Canada: NDE Publishing, 2000), 142.

11. S. Boyd Eaton, Marjorie Shostak, and Melvin Konner, *The Paleolithic Prescription: A Program of Diet and Exercise and a Design for Living* (New York: Harper and Row, 1988), 45.

12. John Capouya, "Real Men Do Yoga," *Newsweek* (June 16, 2003), 78.

13. Larrian Gillespie, *The Gladiator Diet: How to Preserve Peak Health, Sexual Energy, and a Strong Body at Any Age* (Los Angeles: Healthy Life Publications, 2001), 19–35.

14. Ibid., 95.

15. Ibid.

16. Eugene Shippen and William Fryer, *The Testosterone Syndrome: The Critical Factor for Energy, Health, and Sexuality—Reversing the Male Menopause* (New York: M. Evans and Company, 1998), 51.

17. Ibid., 93–94.

18. Ibid., 48.

19. Gillespie, *The Gladiator Diet*, 94.

20. Shippen and Fryer, *The Testosterone Syndrome*, 51.

21. Meryn, et al., *Men's Health and the Hormone Revolution*, 94–95.

22. C. Hallert, et al., "Psychic Disturbances in Adult Coeliac Disease III," *Scandinavian Journal of Gastroenterology* 17 (1982): 25–28.

23. R. J. Wurtman and J. J. Wurtman, "Brain Serotonin, Carbohydrate-Craving, Obesity, and Depression," *Journal of Obesity Research* 3, Supplement 4 (1995), 477S–80S. Also see Sarah Boseley, "Rival Says Atkins Diet Can Make You Depressed," *The Guardian* (March 2, 2004) accessed www.guardian.co.uk/usa/story/0,12271,1160088,00.html.

24. Michael Castleman, *Blended Medicine: The Best Choices in Healing* (Emmaus, PA: Rodale, 2000), 221–22.

25. Ibid., 222.

26. Ibid.

27. Dharma Singh Khalsa with Cameron Stauth, *Brain Longevity* (New York: Warner Books, 1997), 253.

28. Castleman, *Blended Medicine*, 225.

29. Khalsa with Stauth, *Brain Longevity*, 255.

30. Kay Redfield Jamison, *Night Falls Fast: Understanding Suicide* (New York: Random House, 1999), 250.

31. Hypericum Depression Trial Study Group, "Effect of *Hypericum perforatum* (St. John's Wort) in Major Depressive Disorder: A Randomized, Controlled Trial," *Journal of the American Medical Association* 287 (2002): 1807–14.

32. Gillespie, *The Gladiator Diet*, 91.

33. Ibid.

34. Robert S. Tan, *The Andropause Mystery: Unraveling Truths about Male Menopause* (Houston, TX: AMRED Publishing, 2001), 62–63.

35. James McBride Dabbs with Mary Godwin Dabbs, *Heroes, Rogues, and Lovers: Testosterone and Behavior* (New York: McGraw-Hill, 2000), 163.

36. Ibid.

37. Ibid.

38. Ibid., 143.

39. Ibid., 163.

40. Ibid.

41. Ibid.

42. Shippen and Fryer, *The Testosterone Syndrome*, 53.

43. J. L. Tenover, "Testosterone and the Aging Male," *Journal of Andrology* 18 (1997): 103–6.

44. Malcolm Carruthers, *The Testosterone Revolution* (London: Thorsons, 2001), 68.

45. Press release on testosterone therapy study, November 12, 2003. Report from the National Academy of Sciences, "Testosterone Therapy Studies Should Determine Benefits First, Then Risks; Study Participants Should Be Limited, Carefully Screened." Committee of study, Dan Blazer, M.D., professor of psychiatry and behavioral sciences, Duke University Medical Center, Durham, NC, Institute of Medicine, www.iom.edu/search_results.asp?qs=testosterone (accessed November 14, 2003). See

also Catharyn T. Liverman and Dan G. Blazer, eds., *Testosterone and Aging: Clinical Directions* (Washington, DC: The National Academies Press, 2004).

46. Ibid.

47. Jonathan V. Wright and Lane Lenard, *Maximize Your Vitality and Potency: For Men over 40* (Petaluma, CA: Smart Publications, 1999), 29–30.

CHAPTER 11

1. Martin E. P. Seligman, *Authentic Happiness: Using the New Positive Psychology to Realize Your Potential for Lasting Fulfillment* (New York: The Free Press, 2002), 28.

2. Ibid, 47.

3. Ibid., 48.

4. Ibid.

5. Ibid.

6. For more information, check out The Beck Institute at www.beckinstitute.org/.

7. Albert Ellis Institute, "Rational-Emotive Behavior Therapy," www.rebt.org (accessed March 8, 2004).

8. Dennis Greenberger and Christine A. Padesky, *Mind over Mood: Change How You Feel by Changing the Way You Think* (New York: The Guilford Press, 1995), 15.

9. Ibid.

10. Ibid., 33–45.

11. Richard Davidson, et al., "Alterations in Brain and Immune Function Produced by Mindfulness Meditation," *Psychosomatic Medicine* 65 (July–August 2003): 564–70.

12. Seligman, *Authentic Happiness*, 55.

13. Ibid., 56.

14. Myriam Miedzian, *Boys Will Be Boys: Breaking the Link between Masculinity and Violence* (New York: Doubleday, 1991), 85.

CHAPTER 12

1. James Hillman, *The Soul's Code: In Search of Character and Calling* (New York: Random House, 1996), 9.

2. Ibid., 8.

3. Eric Maisel, *Van Gogh Blues* (Emmaus, PA: Rodale, 2002), 216–17.

4. Hillman, *The Soul's Code*, 8.

5. Vaclav Havel, from http://wikiquote.org/wiki/Hope (accessed March 6, 2004).

6. Po Bronson, *What Should I Do with My Life? The True Story of People Who Answered the Ultimate Question* (New York: Random House, 2002), 47.

7. James V. Gambone, from www.refirement.com (accessed March 8, 2004).

8. Zalman Schachter-Shalomi, "Saging—Not Aging: Are You Saved Yet?" *In Context* magazine (Winter 1994), 17.

9. Zalman Schachter-Shalomi and Ronald S. Miller, *From Age-ing to Sage-ing: A Profound New Vision of Growing Older* (New York: Warner Books, 1995), 11.

10. Rainer Maria Rilke, *Letters to a Young Poet* (Novato, CA: New World Library, 1992), 35.

11. Information about Marshall Rosenberg and his work can be gotten from the Center for Nonviolent Communication Web site www.cnvc.org/ and by reading Marshall B. Rosenberg, *Nonviolent Communication: A Language of Compassion* (Encinitas, CA: Puddle Dancer Press, 2000).

12. Marshall Rosenberg, "CNVC Founder Marshall Rosenberg's Response to the Events of September 11," *The Center for Nonviolent Communication,* posted September 27, 2001, at www.cnvc.org/responmr.htm.

13. Ibid.

14. Ibid.

15. Malidoma Patrice Somé, *Of Water and the Spirit: Ritual, Magic, and Initiation in the Life of an African Shaman* (New York: G. P. Putnam's Sons, 1994), 23.

16. Ibid., 310.

17. Personal communication with Mitch DeArmon, February 6, 2004.

18. Personal correspondence with Dr. Mark Schillinger, June 21, 2003.

19. Ibid.

20. DeArmon, February 6, 2004.

21. Robert Bly, *The Sibling Society* (Reading, MA: Addison-Wesley Publishing Company, 1996), viii.

22. Quoted by Michael Lynberg, *The Path with Heart* (New York: Warner Books, 1995), 20.

23. Ibid., 17.

24. David Gutmann, *Reclaimed Powers: Toward a New Psychology of Men and Women in Later Life* (New York: Basic Books, 1987), 203.

25. Ibid.

26. Scott Russell Sanders, *Staying Put: Making a Home in a Restless World* (Boston: Beacon Press, 1993), xvi.

27. Ibid., 13.

28. William James, *The Varieties of Religious Experience* (New York: Random House, 1902: Random House, 1999), 81.

29. Quoted in *McMan's Depression and Bipolar Web*, "Kay Jamison Interview," www.mcmanweb.com/article-247.htm (accessed June 22, 2004).

30. Nikos Kazantzakis, *Zorba the Greek* (New York: Simon and Schuster, 1952), 340.

31. Ibid., 341.

INDEX

Underscored page references indicate tables.

OTHER RODALE BOOKS
AVAILABLE FROM PAN MACMILLAN

1-4050-6718-7	Healing Without Freud or Prozac	Dr David Servan-Schreiber	£12.99
1-4050-3340-1	When Your Body Gets the Blues	Marie-Annette Brown & Jo Robinson	£10.99
1-4050-2097-0	Six Questions That Can Change Your Life	Joseph Nowinski	£8.99
1-4050-4191-9	Healing the Hurt Restoring the Hope	Suzy Marta	£12.99
1-4050-0665-X	Get a Real Food Life	Janine Whiteson	£12.99
1-4050-4182-X	The Doctors' Book of Home Remedies	A Prevention Health Book	£20.00

All Pan Macmillan titles can be ordered from our website, *www.panmacmillan.com,* or from your local bookshop and are also available by post from:

Bookpost, PO Box 29, Douglas, Isle of Man IM99 1BQ
Tel: 01624 677237; fax: 01624 670923; e-mail: *bookshop@enterprise.net*;
or visit: *www.bookpost.co.uk.* Credit cards accepted. Free postage and packing in the United Kingdom

Prices shown above were correct at time of going to press.
Pan Macmillan reserve the right to show new retail prices on covers which may differ from those previously advertised in the text or elsewhere.

For information about buying *Rodale* titles in **Australia**, contact Pan Macmillan Australia.
Tel: 1300 135 113; fax: 1300 135 103; e-mail: *customer.service@macmillan.com.au*;
or visit: *www.panmacmillan.com.au*

For information about buying *Rodale* titles in **New Zealand**, contact Macmillan Publishers
New Zealand Limited. Tel: (09) 414 0356; fax: (09) 414 0352;
e-mail: *lyn@macmillan.co.nz*;
or visit: *www.macmillan.co.nz*

For information about buying *Rodale* titles in **South Africa**, contact Pan Macmillan
South Africa. Tel: (011) 325 5220; fax: (011) 325 5225;
e-mail: *roshni@panmacmillan.co.za*